This is the book about human trafficking I have been looking for. By sharing his story, Raleigh Sadler helps to demystif⟨ issue, and provides us with keys on how we can play our pa⟨ ⟩g about solution. *Vulnerable: Rethinking Human T*⟨ ⟩lenge and inspire you to truly love your ne⟨ ⟩f. A timely book for this hour.

Christin⟨ ⟨ampaign

C. S. Lewis once described Cl⟨ ⟩. fighting religion." Those who are serious about follc⟨ ⟩rist into the world will also be serious about fighting against what is *wrong* in the world, especially where injustice and abuse are the norm. As the father of two girls, I am especially appreciative of Raleigh's efforts in *Vulnerable*, which is a sort of roadmap for fighting for the hearts of, and fighting against the oppression of, girls and women who are potential or real victims of the sex trade. Much of the content and stories in this book are unsettling . . . and purposefully so. For when our hearts are unsettled, we are moved to action. I pray that *Vulnerable* will impact you and your community in this way.

Scott Sauls, senior pastor of Christ Presbyterian Church in Nashville, Tennessee, and author of *Befriend* and *Irresistible Faith*

God has called Christians to come alongside and advocate for the most marginalized in our society. Today as we speak, there are thousands in our communities who have been trafficked against their will, whose lives are not viewed as valuable, but as property for the powerful. To engage in this important work of justice, Christians must be biblical in their thinking. This book helps unpack what it means to both fight for the vulnerable and realize our own vulnerability, how in our weakness, we find the strength to step into the mission of God. I urge you to thoroughly read this book, to let it shape your approach to activism, and then pass it on to a brother or sister in Christ.

Dan Darling, vice president of Communications for the Ethics and Religious Liberty Commission and author of *The Dignity Revolution*

I've had the immense privilege of seeing Raleigh grow from an interested bystander to a real leader in helping people understand the gravity of the global problem of human trafficking and what the average person can do to make a difference. We can feel paralyzed in the face of this immense challenge. *Vulnerable: Rethinking Human Trafficking* can help all of us find our place in helping vulnerable people find freedom, peace, and justice. I'm so encouraged to see Jesus followers helping lead the way in combatting human trafficking. Come join God in his work of entering into the broken places with the light and love of Christ.

Kevin Palau, president of the Luis Palau Association and author of *Unlikely: Setting Our Differences Aside to Live Out the Gospel*

The church is at its best, and is living out the redemptive realities of the gospel most fully, when it is running toward the vulnerable and broken with truth, hope, and grace, rather than remaining in safety and comfort. In *Vulnerable*, Raleigh Sadler describes with vivid clarity one of the hardest arenas of our modern world. But, like the sound guide he is, Raleigh points to where and how the church can bring the light and life of Christ.

John Stonestreet, president of the Chuck Colson Center for Christian Worldview and coauthor of *A Practical Guide to Culture*

Human trafficking has risen into public consciousness over the past few years even thought this type of exploitation has been a global phenomenon for centuries. Trafficking is modern day slavery and is the fastest growing criminal industry in the world. The stories and statistics can be overwhelming. The Bible does not hesitate to depict the harsh reality of violence and oppression, and it clearly calls us to fight for justice and mercy for all people as God intended. But what can an ordinary person do to respond? In *Vulnerable*, Raleigh offers wisdom and hope as well as tangible responses to fight trafficking.

Justin S. Holcomb, Episcopal priest, seminary professor, and author

This book is both a passionate call for help and a handhold for where to start. Before reading *Vulnerable* the gap between my everyday life and those who are being exploited seemed, if I'm honest, almost insurmountable. But Raleigh's stories invited me to walk right up to the hurting and look into their eyes—not as a hero, but as a follower of Jesus. I identified with them, I got a new grasp on trafficking—and I got a conviction that I can't look away.

Grace Thornton, author of *I Don't Wait Anymore*

Raleigh brings a message that all churches need to hear. Through stories and lived experience, *Vulnerable* breaks myths and focuses on what trafficking victims truly need—equipping all of us to make real a difference.

Rebecca Bender, survivor leader, author, and CEO

Raleigh Sadler is an extraordinarily important voice for the voiceless trapped inside of sex trafficking.

Mac Pier, founder and CEO of Movement.org and author of *A Disruptive Gospel*

Raleigh Sadler strips away our myopic view of human trafficking as an evil "out there," far removed from our day-to-day lives. It's hidden in plain sight, anywhere there's an "exploitation of vulnerability for commercial gain." Through candid interviews, personal stories, and examples of vulnerability, Sadler makes us aware of how humans are trafficked, and how we can help to stop it. The book is eye-opening, practical, and gospel-focused. It's radically changed my understanding of this pervasive evil, and what I can do to bring about change.

Chad Bird, author and speaker

Raleigh Sadler's work speaks to a new generation of Christians and carries a vital message: blessed are the vulnerable, for they will be strong.

E. Benjamin Skinner, author of *A Crime So Monstrous: Face-to-Face With Modern-Day Slavery*

This is a necessary book. At once searing, revealing, and, yes, vulnerable, it's an antidote to the paralysis that most people feel when they learn about human trafficking. Drawing lessons from the experts and from the Scriptures, Raleigh Sadler answers the perennial question, "How can I help?" with a lucid and practical call to arms, especially for the Christian Church. The problem is not too big for us to tackle. We don't need a police badge or training in cyber crime. We can fight human trafficking right where we live by training our eyes to see vulnerability, by educating our minds to understand its causes and consequences, by opening our hearts to care about the people suffering under its weight, and by summoning the courage to engage.

Corban Addison, international bestselling author
of *A Walk Across the Sun* and *A Harvest of Thorns*

One of the greatest myths of our present age is that slavery is a thing of the past. In vivid and sometimes uncomfortable detail, Raleigh Sadler busts this myth to unveil the truth about a travesty occurring right under our noses. If you care about justice, human dignity, and the good news of Jesus Christ, then read this book post-haste. *Vulnerable* is a rousing call to confront one of the biggest human rights epidemics of the modern era that can be ignored no longer.

Jonathan Merritt, author of *Learning to Speak God from Scratch* and contributing writer for *The Atlantic*

This book achieves something rare and important: it opens our eyes, keeps the reader engaged, and empowers all of us to make a difference in our world. And Sadler does this while resisting the urge to nag or motivate people to act through guilt. By seeking Christ-like eyes, he helps us all detect invisible chains that enslave so many in our day. Instead, he centers his message on the way in which the good news of Jesus is able to open up new possibilities for ethical life in the world. I urge everyone who cares about vulnerable people among us to read this book and spread its insights.

Jeff Mallinson, DPhil, professor of Theology and Philosophy at Concordia University Irvine and author of *Sexy: The Quest for Erotic Virtue in Perplexing Times*

In this important and much needed book, Raleigh offers a helpful framework for understanding vulnerability—in others and in ourselves—and how this can help us see the dark reality of so many that is often hidden in plain sight, help us to push past fear of feeling like we can't do enough, and shape our response to the difficult, overwhelming injustice that is human trafficking. As Christians, it's empowering to remember that God isn't dependent on us, but he has invited us to participate in the work he is already doing, and can use us not just in spite of but through our own vulnerability.

Jamie D. Aten, PhD, founder and executive director
of the Humanitarian Disaster Institute at Wheaton College
and author of *A Walking Disaster: What Katrina and
Cancer Taught Me About Faith and Resilience*

Every day, Raleigh Sadler is helping churches move from awareness to advocacy to action in today's fight against human trafficking. In his book, *Vulnerable: Rethinking Human Trafficking*, Raleigh shares captivating stories, insightful interviews, and practical resources to help equip the church to lead in that fight. *Vulnerable* is a wake-up call to the church that slaves might be living next door or even sitting in our pews. *Vulnerable* is also a thoughtful, gospel-saturated answer to how we can demonstrate love to those most vulnerable in our communities.

Nathan Creitz, pastor of City Life Church, New York City

Packed with practical wisdom that flows not from human demand but from the grace of God, *Vulnerable* gives us a powerful account of how personal experience, expert knowledge, and scriptural focus shape a deep concern for justice. An urgent and highly recommended read!

David Zahl, founder and director of Mockingbird Ministries

Raleigh Sadler has written a book that is passionate, thoughtful, and very practical. Be ready for some deep insights and some challenges to our previous common perceptions. Read it and you will never think of vulnerability in the same way.

Taylor Field, pastor and director of Graffiti
Community Ministries, Send Relief Missionary,
New York City, and author of *Upside Down Leadership*

"God doesn't need your good works," says Martin Luther "but your neighbor does." This oft-quoted saying brings to mind a radical notion—that In Christ, We are free from our own frenzied preoccupation with saving ourselves and instead are set free to love our neighbors. In his book, *Vulnerable: Rethinking Human Trafficking*, Raleigh Sadler explains that human traffickers often prey upon those most vulnerable. The practical insights offered in this book will guide you as you discover how to respond to the injustice around you while the focus on the gospel will remind you why you want to do it in the first place.

Elyse Fitzpatrick, author of *Finding the Love of Jesus from Genesis to Revelation*

RALEIGH SADLER

VULNERABLE

RETHINKING
HUMAN TRAFFICKING

PUBLISHING GROUP

NASHVILLE, TENNESSEE

Published by B&H Publishing Group
Nashville, Tennessee

Dewey Decimal Classification: 306.77
Subject Heading: HUMAN TRAFFICKING \ SEX CRIMES

Cover photos © Nik Merkulov and meinzahn / 123rf

Unless otherwise noted, Scriptures are taken from the English Standard Version. ESV® Text Edition: 2016. Copyright © 2001 by Crossway Bibles, a publishing ministry of Good News Publishers.

Also used: New International Version®, NIV® Copyright ©1973, 1978, 1984, 2011 by Biblica, Inc.® Used by permission. All rights reserved worldwide.

Some names in this book have been changed to protect the identities of those in the stories.

The web addresses referenced in this book were live and correct at the time of the book's publication but may be subject to change.

1 2 3 4 5 6 7 • 22 21 20 19

This book is dedicated to the memories of Davin Henrickson and Debra Connery Smith, who taught me more about vulnerability through their journey with cancer than I would have ever learned in a book. Without Davin, I would have never taken the step of faith to move to NYC. Without Debra, I would have never taken the steps necessary to launch Let My People Go. This book is for both of you!

ACKNOWLEDGMENTS

I would like to thank my mom and dad, Raleigh and Lissa Sadler. Thank you so much for modeling for me how to process vulnerability, even at an early age. You always taught me that each person matters regardless of their station in life.

I would also like to thank Liz Lockwood for always listening and helping me to process the Lord's leading over the last couple of years.

A special thanks goes out to the Let My People Go team. First, I'd like to thank my board of directors: Seth Polk, Courtney Celestino, Josh Branum, and Dan Darling for your time and encouragement. Thanks also to the LMPG Board of Advisors past and present: Larry Christensen, Kevin Palau, Shandra Woworuntu, Dr. Jarvis Williams, Corban Addison, Ben Skinner, Dr. Gerry Breshears, Kristin Keen, Rev. Jacob Smith, Iryna Makaruk, Taylor Field, Darryl Williamson, and Chris Lim.

I am thankful for Dr. Melissa Jane Kronfield, Jonathan Walton, Que English, all those at the New York State Anti-Trafficking Coalition, Thomas Estler, Rabbi Diana Gerson, and Zac Martin for all that you do to lead faith communities to end oppression in the city of New York. Thanks also to my friends at the Metropolitan New York Baptist Association (MNYBA) who allowed me the space to experiment and start Let My People Go in 2013. Thanks to Mike Bartel for being a true friend in the fight.

Thanks to everyone mentioned or interviewed in this book. You were part of this journey and mentioned by name on purpose. Oh, the stories that we could tell.

To all of my friends who are survivors and overcomers, you have left an indelible impression on me, as well as this book.

Thanks also to Hannah Grundmann, who came as a research assistant in faith helping me work toward this goal. Thanks to Amanda Ozaki-Laughon, who worked so diligently on research and footnotes. Thanks to Hilary Boerger for helping with my research as well.

Thanks to Lewie Clark, Elyse Fitzpatrick, Jonathan Merritt, Ben Skinner, Jeff Mallinson, Boz Tchividjian, Dan Price, Chad Bird, Erick Sorenson, Jeremiah Simmons, and Grace Thornton, who possibly without knowing it encouraged me to start, endure, and finish the writing process.

I thank my phone, without which, as you will discover in this book, none of this would have been possible.

Thanks to Taylor Combs, for pacing with me from start to finish.

Finally, God, thank you for showing me that in light of your divine providence nothing that we experience in life is wasted. Through brokenness, we are made whole.

CONTENTS

Section One:
When Vulnerability Is Exploited

Section Two:
Recognizing Vulnerability in Scripture

Section Three:
Recognizing the Vulnerability Around Us

Section Four:
Recognizing Your Own Vulnerability

Section Five:
Recognizing Your Vulnerable Mission

Section Six:
Responding to the Vulnerability of Others

FOREWORD

R aleigh Sadler's vulnerable." Those words jolted me to alarm.
The author of this book, who had been my student years ago in seminary, had sent me a prepublication copy for review, through my office. A colleague at work sent me an electronic version of the manuscript, so I could refer to it as I travelled. The email, though, was in the midst of many other messages, and when I opened up my account on my phone waiting to disembark a plane, all I could see were the subject lines. This one was "Raleigh Sadler's vulnerable."

Anyone watching me would have seen my shoulders hunch and my left palm extend skyward, as I muttered to myself, "He's vulnerable to *what*? What does that *mean*?" It only took a second or so to realize that the subject line was about a book, Raleigh Sadler's *Vulnerable*. The plane-landing micro-emergency was over.

Many things, though, went through my mind when I read those words. After all, I have had former students serve in very austere and dangerous contexts on the mission field. The subject line easily could have meant something along the lines of, "Raleigh Sadler's vulnerable to the Ebola virus, and he is hospitalized somewhere in a remote camp" or "Raleigh Sadler's vulnerable to severe harm from malaria he picked up in a distant jungle." I've also had too many loved ones to count wreck their lives through addictions or sexual immorality and so forth. The subject line could have meant, "Raleigh Sadler's vulnerable to a recently-revealed dependence on

methamphetamines," or "Raleigh Sadler's vulnerable to temptation, having been caught smuggling cocaine and pornography." Or,
maybe, it could have just meant what I've seen many times before,
a statement about psychological health. "Raleigh Sadler's vulnerable
right now; facing burnout in ministry and questioning his future."

Thankfully, none of those things were true. As soon as I could
see the rest of the subject line, I was relieved. "Ah, this is Raleigh's
new book. This is what I've been waiting for: a needed ministry calling Christians and others to care for those trafficked now includes
a written resource, calling our consciences to serve. Raleigh Sadler
has written *Vulnerable*; Raleigh Sadler is not himself vulnerable!"

It didn't take long reading this book before I realized how
wrong my sense of relief was. Raleigh Sadler is vulnerable, indeed.
No, not to any of the scenarios I sketched with my imagination
above. But he is indeed vulnerable—to harm, to discouragement, to
sin, to the devil, and, ultimately, to death. And so am I. And so are
you. That's precisely why we need the message of this book.

Right now, as you read this, girls and boys, men and women,
are being treated as property, bought and sold for slave labor, for
sexual violation. Right now, as you read this, there are people, made
in the image of God, who believe that their futures are hopeless,
that nothing waits for them but further objectification, further violation, further violence. The situation is so horrific in its enormity
that many wonder whether anything can be done at all. Many then
turn, like the walkers on the road in Jesus' parable of the Good
Samaritan, shielding their eyes or consciences from those being rav-
aged. After all, to involve oneself is scary, because it means opening
oneself up to risk—the risk of failure, the risk of harm to oneself, the
risk even of being hurt by loving those who are imperiled.

But what seems to be the problem is also the solution. That's
the message of this book. Those in harm's way do not need mythic
superheroes. The vulnerable need to be heard by the vulnerable. We
bear one another's burdens (Gal. 6:2). That doesn't mean that some
of us don't have burdens, and that they are the ones called to love.
We all have burdens, areas of vulnerability. We shore one another

up where we are strong, and they, in turn, help us where we are weak. The oppressed and the trafficked are in need of awakened consciences and concentrated work for justice for them. They need that from real people—people who sometimes don't know exactly what to do, people who will sometimes fail, from vulnerable people.

In the struggle for justice, vulnerability does not impede us from helping the marginalized and hurting; vulnerability is necessary. The people of God in biblical Israel, after all, could love the sojourners in their land, the oppressed in the fields, precisely because they were once enslaved in the land of Egypt (Lev. 19:34). When we see ourselves as invulnerable, as self-creating gods, that's when we start to believe, wrongly, that prosperity and strength is a sign of value, and that weakness should be ignored. As Christians, our signs are not those of "power," as the world defines power.

A fish, one of the earliest emblems of Christianity, reminds us that we are bodily creatures, in need of food lest we die. And, of course, the cross points us to the fact that we are, all of us, no matter how seemingly strong, rooted in our identity in the most vulnerable circumstance possible—a crucifixion by the Roman Empire outside the gates of Jerusalem. Therein we find the wisdom of God, and the power of God, that turns upside down the "wisdom" and "power" of what the world around us celebrates and craves (1 Cor. 1:18–2:8). From that standpoint, we find the supernatural power to sacrifice ourselves for the hurting and the imperiled.

Raleigh Sadler's vulnerable. Thanks be to God. That's why he can write this book. You are vulnerable. That's why you, with the energy of God, can stand up for those who are in harm's way. This book will show you why, and prompt you to think about how.

Russell Moore, president, Ethics and Religious
Liberty Commission and author of *Onward:
Engaging the Culture without Losing the Gospel* and
The Storm-Tossed Family: How the Cross Reshapes the Home

BEFORE YOU READ
VULNERABLE: RETHINKING HUMAN TRAFFICKING

Some of the stories included will give intimate details of the experience of vulnerability as well as the experience of human trafficking survivors. In some cases, certain chapters will describe instances of violence and sexual assault. While these details may be difficult to read, they give an accurate depiction of the realities of human trafficking. Please take this into account as you begin reading this book.

V IS FOR VULNERABLE: AN INTRODUCTION

"You need to teach me how to fight!"

Those were my exact words after the unthinkable happened. I had just finished sharing about how we can fight human trafficking at a church near the Bowery in Lower Manhattan. It was Super Bowl Sunday. In my line of work, that day is generally always booked. Many believe that the Super Bowl is the largest human trafficking event of the year.[1] Needless to say, the pastor felt that it was a good idea to have someone speak on the issue.

Have you ever had one of those days where everything seemed to work in your favor? That was the case for me that evening. The message went off without a hitch and several people in the congregation genuinely wanted to learn more. It was a resounding success. As I left the church, I remember walking with my head held high until I saw someone who could barely keep her head up.

As I descended the steps into the subway, I saw a young woman sitting on a bench waiting for her train. I immediately noticed two things about her: 1) she was in her mid-twenties and dressed as if she had been at a nightclub; 2) she was completely inebriated. She could barely keep her head up as she waited. It was all that she could do to keep herself from falling over. I looked as if to try to hide the fact that I was actually looking at her. *What is wrong with her?* I wondered. *She must be high.* To be honest, seeing someone intoxicated on New York City public transit is not exactly rare. But still, something was different about this woman.

Within a minute or two, the train came. As the doors opened, without warning, a young, well-dressed man in his late twenties came out of nowhere and grabbed her. It was apparent that they knew each other at some level. He yanked her arm violently, causing her to lurch forward and drop something. Out of the corner of my eye, I could tell that it was a passport. He then proceeded to violently push her onto the train, grabbing the passport as the doors closed.

And I did nothing. As the train pulled away, my senses came to me and I began realizing what had happened. This woman may have very likely been drugged. She was being taken away to "God knows where" to have "God knows what" done to her. Instantly, I was broken. I had failed. I was seen as an authority on human trafficking, and when the chips were down, I failed to respond. This overwhelming sense of grief overflowed into shame and regret. Not only had I failed to know how to respond in the moment, but I couldn't shake the reality that I was supposed to know exactly what to do.

But the situation gets worse. This did not happen in the middle of the night on an isolated subway platform. It was 8:00 p.m. on a Sunday night. There were people everywhere . . . and no one else seemed to notice.

In what took less than three seconds, my life changed forever. I can't be certain that it was human trafficking; however, I am certain that this woman was vulnerable and the man with her was abusing her. (Even if it was human trafficking, you'll discover in the pages that follow that this is not what it always looks like.)

You never forget a moment like that. It's in those moments that we have a choice to make: we can either beat ourselves up for the foreseeable future or we can make a conscious decision to never allow that to happen again on our watch.

Later that night, I called a friend who works in federal law enforcement. "You need to teach me how to fight!" Sensing the frustration in my voice, he said, "Okay, we can do that. I know a guy. But," he said inquisitively, "is that the best thing that you could have done in that moment?"

"Well, no. But at least it would have been something."

If you picked up this book, chances are that you may feel just like me. You have heard about human trafficking and you want to do something about it, but you are clueless as to where to start. Others of you may feel that you have nothing to offer, so you decide to do nothing in hopes that someone else will do something. You are looking at your life right now and thinking, *What can I do? I'm not exactly a superhero.* Fearing the alternative, still others of you are doing the first thing that pops into your mind. You are just like I was when I asked my friend to teach me how to fight—you'd rather risk doing the wrong thing than doing nothing. I understand. But what my friend was so graciously trying to teach me that night was that reacting without knowing the facts would not only have put myself in danger but also the girl that I was trying to help. So the question remains, how can ordinary people like you and me fight a global injustice like human trafficking?

Human Trafficking 101

According to the Global Slavery Index, there are as many as 40.3 million people held in what amounts to modern-day slavery.[2] Cases have been reported in every country,[3] as well as every state in the United States.[4] Whether they are trafficked into the commercial sex industry, the agricultural sector, or the hospitality and service industries, each person has one thing in common: vulnerability. Someone who has power, influence, and status is exploiting someone who doesn't.

Simply put, *human trafficking is the exploitation of vulnerability for commercial gain.* For this reason, human trafficking can happen anywhere because there are vulnerable people everywhere.

Often when it comes to vulnerability, we attempt to compartmentalize "causes." One evening I had a conversation with an ethics professor at a Christian liberal arts school. I was excited to pick his brain about several social issues, which he was more than willing to oblige, until we came to human trafficking. As soon as he discovered that I had founded an organization focused on this particular issue, his countenance changed. He became visibly frustrated. "I don't teach my students about human trafficking!" "Why?" I asked in bewilderment. "Because I feel like these students would rather focus on sex trafficking than other issues." He went on to explain that he could show me girls in the city who were being forced to terminate their pregnancies, but I couldn't show him people who were being trafficked. I paused for a moment. "They are the same people."

As we see this global injustice through the lens of its basic common denominator, we realize that it is not a "one issue" kind of problem. Every type of complex vulnerability can feed into human trafficking. Regardless of whether someone is homeless, undocumented, LGBTQ, in the foster care system, or in the penal system, they are vulnerable to exploitation. With that said, human trafficking is a "catch-all" injustice. When you find yourself intentionally loving people, who are at the end of their rope, you will find yourself doing the work of prevention, intervention, and aftercare all at once. Truth be told, the very vulnerable person with whom you are spending time could be trafficked, may be trafficked, or has been trafficked. The only way for us to discover their story is for our story to intersect with theirs.

A Vulnerable Definition

At this point, you have already read the word *vulnerable* or a derivative thereof several times. You are probably beginning to pick up what I'm laying down. Vulnerability at some level plays a role in the development of the exploiter and the development of those most often exploited. It's an integral part of all that drives this commercial exploitation. Like a shark sensing blood in the water, traffickers intentionally look for those without the protection and support that a healthy family or close community can provide. These traffickers are preying on people—like the girl I saw on the subway—who are trapped in situations beyond their control. At the core of both the problem and the solution of human trafficking is vulnerability.

For us to understand the problem of human trafficking, we not only need to focus on vulnerability, we need to understand what it means. If you were asked to define the word, what would you say? Chances are you would arrive at one of two definitions immediately. First, vulnerability can be defined as experiencing an unmet need.[5] This need can be material, emotional, psychological, and/or financial. Therefore, if you see someone experiencing homelessness, this particular person is vulnerable to exploitation because he or she does not have access to adequate safe housing. I think that we could all agree that someone facing this predicament would be vulnerable to a myriad of different risks.

Another common way of explaining vulnerability is to use words like *transparency* or *authenticity*. We do this naturally when we open ourselves up to those around us. Each of us has had moments when we have taken a risk and shared something painful with a close friend. You know you have because you can't shake the feeling. It's like your skin is being ripped from your bones. You know that you have opened up to someone else when you wake up with a "vulnerability hangover."[6] As you think back to what you said, your mind is flooded with questions: "Did I say too much? Does this person think that I'm crazy? Why didn't I just keep my mouth shut?" In reality, you were being courageous and you risked rejection to be open and transparent with another person.

For the purposes of this book, we are going to examine the underlying root of both of these popular definitions. *Merriam-Webster* defines vulnerability as being "capable of being physically or emotionally wounded; being open to attack or damage." In other words, this definition assumes that both of the definitions above are true and accurate.

You might be thinking, *But aren't we all vulnerable?* The answer is yes. There are times when each of us faces an unmet need and we are vulnerable to some form of exploitation. But for the purposes of this book, allow me to make something perfectly clear: due to a variety of factors, some people are more vulnerable than others.

Take Chris and Melissa, for example. Chris is an exhausted yet hopeful twelve-year-old boy who has been bounced from foster home to foster home in search of a forever family. Melissa has been married for three years to a loving husband with two adorable yet "busy" kids. Her husband is currently out of work, so Melissa has taken on two jobs to keep food on the table. For Melissa, the challenge of being the breadwinner and a "good mother" feels next to impossible. Both Chris and Melissa have distinct vulnerabilities, yet Chris more so given his unique situation. Knowing the difference, traffickers are intentionally looking for those who are living in the margins without protection or status. They are looking for those who are hidden in plain sight.

As you think about this, who would be those most vulnerable in your community? Would it be the person working in your favorite local restaurant, whose documentation papers are not exactly legal? Maybe it's the young man who was recently kicked out by his parents after "coming out." Maybe it's the woman who has been in and out of prison and has found it impossible to find a job that pays a living wage so that she can better provide for herself and her family.

A New Perspective

Because of the multifaceted nature of human trafficking, it is difficult if not impossible to write an exhaustive treatment. For this reason, you will find that many books have already been written addressing human trafficking from multiple vantage points. One author may address it from a sociological point of view, while another chooses to address the political challenges, and still others through psychological, legal, philosophical, or financial lenses. This is as it should be. Each book is written from a different angle and will offer you fresh new ways of viewing the problem. As you read books written from different authors, this will not only give you, the reader, a more enlightened understanding of the subject matter, but will also keep you from becoming sluggish in your search for the truth about human trafficking and the most helpful way to respond.

This being the case, in *Vulnerable: Rethinking Human Trafficking*, you will be challenged to view human trafficking and vulnerability from a new, gospel-centric perspective. As I noted earlier, not only does vulnerability play a vital role in the problem of human trafficking, but it is also a vital part of the solution. This paradigm of vulnerability will be fleshed out throughout the rest of this book.

As we examine the Bible, we find that God's solution to fighting human trafficking includes enlisting his church. Yes, that church, the one that is filled to the brim with those who are simultaneously sinful and justified. Those who in Christ are both broken and whole. God isn't looking for the "perfect person" to stand against injustice. The perfect person has already addressed our injustice and is now calling us to join him.

Jesus Christ motivates vulnerable people, like you and me, to love other vulnerable people by becoming vulnerable for us, to the point of death. This is the overarching point of this book. So no matter who you are, what you have done or what has been done to you, you have a voice. Through his vulnerability, Christ has met you in the middle of your vulnerability and has set you free to walk with others. Like my experience in the subway, your story of vulnerability doesn't exist to simply bring you shame and to remind you of your inadequacies. On the contrary, it is the very thing that qualifies and empowers you to enter into the vulnerable stories of others.

Each of us has a story and, collectively, we are on a journey to justice. None of us have it all figured out. Thankfully, God continues to grow and shape us through the experience of our own vulnerabilities. But he doesn't stop there. By God's design, as we experience the vulnerabilities of others, we find ourselves growing exponentially. Likewise, the more we resist both our own vulnerability and that of others, the more stagnant and insular our Christian lives will become. For this reason, each of the stories and interviews that you find in this book will reflect how our experiences of vulnerability and the vulnerability of others have shaped each one of us.

Vulnerable: Rethinking Human Trafficking is divided into six sections:

1. *When Vulnerability Is Exploited.* In the first section, you will discover the nature of human trafficking and how it is manifested in your community and around the world.

2. *Recognizing Vulnerability in Scripture.* Here, we will see how the thread of vulnerability is woven throughout the Bible. Regardless of where you find yourself in the Bible, you will find that God has a habit of picking the "worst" candidates to carry out his mission. So, relax. You are among friends.

3. *Recognizing the Vulnerability Around Us.* As you ponder this theme of vulnerability, you will learn how to identify those around you who traffickers may target.

4. *Recognizing Your Own Vulnerability.* There is no way to address the brokenness of your community without experiencing pain and hardship. There will always be some kind of "blow back" as you are engaging with broken people. What many of you may not be prepared for is that *as* you begin to recognize the vulnerabilities of others, you will find that your own vulnerabilities may be triggered. In this section, we will learn about how we can discover and harness the power of our own perceived weaknesses and vulnerabilities.

5. *Recognizing Your Vulnerable Mission.* God has a plan to care for those whose voices are not heard, and guess what—you are part of it. This can be frightening, as many of us feel that we can't help anyone else, because we have too many issues of our own. However, that's exactly was God is calling us to do. Though it feels counterintuitive, God challenges each of us to move forward, even though we may feel unqualified for the task ahead of us.

6. *Responding to the Vulnerability of Others.* Using what you have learned throughout the book, you will be equipped with practical tools to use as you address the needs around you.

This journey may lead you right into the middle of what you may fear the most: vulnerability. I hope you'll come along anyway, and I promise that God will meet you as you step out in faith.

The Girl on the Train

Remember my phone call from earlier? After listening for a few moments, my friend asked me a question: "Do you know what I would have done in your situation? I would followed them at a close distance. Not too close, but close enough to have an idea of where they were going. Once they arrived somewhere, I would call 911 or 311, describe what I saw, and ask the police for a welfare check." He gave me the tools that I need to actually do something. Since that day, I have received frantic calls from friends around the country. Each time, I reassure them, encourage them, and show them that they can do something to care for that vulnerable person in front of them. Because someone was able to do the same for me.

This book has been written to help you know how you can fight human trafficking by loving those most vulnerable. Spoiler alert: You don't have to change your major or your career, you don't have to learn Krav Maga, and you don't even have to join the police academy. You can actually do something to engage human trafficking by simply being who you were created to be.

My hope is that as you read, you will be better equipped to see the problem, to see your part in the problem, and to see how you—yes, you—can be part of the solution. Whether you are a stay-at-home parent, an account executive, a doctor, a musician, or a trauma survivor, you have a role to play. You are part of God's plan to bring freedom to those trapped in slavery. No matter where you find yourself, God is calling you to do something about it, and he has been preparing you for this your entire life.

WHEN VULNERABILITY IS
EXPLOITED

While human trafficking spans all demographics, there are some circumstances or vulnerabilities that lead to a higher susceptibility to victimization and human trafficking.

—National Human Trafficking Hotline[1]

CHAPTER 1

A WAKE-UP CALL

On January 3, 2012, I heard a speech that would ultimately change the trajectory of my life.

"Together we can end human trafficking."

This six-word challenge was given to a crowd of more than 46,000 college students gathered at the Passion conference in downtown Atlanta. As I heard this charge, I found myself not only sitting in the nosebleed section of the Philips Arena, but also sitting in disbelief. On one hand, I felt a strong desire to "fight human trafficking," but on the other hand, I was completely at a loss as to how to even begin to engage this issue.

It might help if I gave you a little background about myself. I was a college pastor and that's all I ever saw myself being. I had no desire to be a senior pastor or hold any position of leadership within my denomination. I just wanted to work with college students.

This sense of calling began when I was a student at the University of Central Florida. God made it clear that he was calling me into this type of work. Working with students was basically the "end game" for me. Since God changed my life in college, I wanted to give back. I guess you could say that I was doing what I had always dreamed of doing.

That's why I was so confused. As I prayed and wrestled with those six words, I looked down the aisle at the students that I had brought with me. I was shaken. All of a sudden, everything seemed to be in flux. It was as if my eyes had been opened to something that I had been blind to my entire life. God was breaking my heart over the exploitation of people that I had never met, people whose names I may never know. In that moment, I knew deep down that God was calling me to action, but I didn't know how to respond. Or, maybe I did know how I should respond, but I feared the consequences.

Have you ever had one of those moments when you find yourself literally arguing with yourself? There was no one around, but there was still an argument. I knew in that moment that I was supposed to immediately jump on board. But I had questions, even doubts. I remember thinking, *How am I going to fight sex trafficking? I wear cardigans; I'm not going to kick down the door of a brothel.*

Because of this inner conflict, I was frustrated for the rest of my time in Atlanta. As the conference came to a close, I felt defeated. *Am I supposed to change my career? Do I need to go back to school and start over?* Let's call a spade a spade—as knowledgeable as my seminary professors were, they could not prepare me for this moment. I knew how to preach a sermon and do baptisms, but it's not like they offered any training on responding to modern-day slavery. I had no idea of what to do.

As I continued to ponder these questions over and over, I decided that even though I was scared, I still needed to do something. I needed to make a decision and move forward. So I did. I decided to will myself to stop thinking about it. I chose to suppress this calling and the questions that came with it and went about my normal life. *Chances are,* I thought, *this has nothing to do with God and it's just something I ate. Maybe this is all in my head.* I guess I figured that if God was really calling me to fight human trafficking, he would make it *painfully* clear.

And that he did. *Painfully* clear.

Shortly after returning to West Virginia, where I was living at the time, my life began to unravel. Now, you are probably thinking, *Well, that's a little dramatic, isn't it?* I understand. I would have been right there with you had I not been experiencing it myself. Within the span of six months, I would come face-to-face with not one, but two, life-changing wake-up calls.

A Reality Check Times Two

The first wake-up call happened on a Saturday. I looked down at my phone to see that I had missed a phone call from my boss. Since we didn't exactly talk on a daily basis, I figured that it had to be important. I told my friends, "I think that I may be losing my job." Why else would he be calling me on a Saturday?

So, I quickly excused myself and stepped outside to call him back. The phone rang for what felt like an eternity. As he answered the call, he got to his point quickly. My "dream job" was being defunded. Due to a strategic focus shift, my employer would no longer be able to fund those working in collegiate ministry. This was the job for which I had been preparing for the majority of my adult life, and it was coming to an end. As a kid, I remember what my mother would say when we faced what felt like impossible situations: "Welp. Thems the breaks." For me, I did not like these "breaks." I was absolutely powerless to do or say anything to change my situation. Needless to say, I was facing a minor identity crisis. What would I do now? Who was I without this job?

So without a clear sense of direction, I began traveling, praying, and looking for something new. I went to churches and universities all over the country to find a place where I could land and start afresh. The process tended to go this way: emails would lead to phone calls. Phone calls to vision trips. Vision trips to interviews. I feel like I literally spoke to every employer in the continental United States. But no matter how many calls I made or trips I took, nothing seemed to materialize. I was not passionate about any of the opportunities in front of me. It was like I was worse off than when I started.

I vividly remember coming home from one of these trips. As I rode back from a meeting with my friend Jim Drake, then a church planting catalyst in West Virginia, I checked my email. I knew immediately that something was wrong. It was in that moment that I came face-to-face with another life-altering event. As I read the following words from my friend Davin's wife, Lauren, I was paralyzed:

> We received the results of Davin's CT scan yesterday, and the cancer has spread throughout his abdomen. Any future treatments (chemo, radiation, etc.) are more likely to cause discomfort than to help, so now our treatment focus is on pain management. We are meeting with some staff from Hosparus (http://www.hosparus.org) tonight, to help Davin decide if he wants to try to remain at home for this time of waiting or if the hospital would be better. The doc said he isn't in the business of guessing, so we don't really have a guess as to how soon God will take Davin to be with Him. For now, we wait. It is bittersweet, but we can rejoice that Davin will be free from suffering soon. Praise God for the perfect healing to come! "For to me to live is Christ, and to die is gain." —Philippians 1:21[1]

I was undone. The pain you feel when you lose a loved one is unbearable. The only way I can describe it is that you feel this confluence of every type of pain imaginable. You are simultaneously processing your pain mentally, spiritually, and emotionally. But it's not just your pain that you're processing. You are actually feeling pain at the thought that your friend or loved one is experiencing pain. This mingled with the fact that you and all of those close to you are about to face a sudden loss, whether you like it or not. Life as you know it is about to change forever.

In that moment, I realized that Davin, one of my best friends in the world, was dying, and I didn't know what to do. When confronted with his vulnerability, mine became evident to me.

Davin was one of the first people I met when I arrived at the Southern Baptist Theological Seminary in 2003. It didn't take long for us to become friends and then roommates. Davin and I consistently challenged each other to grow closer to Christ. He was just that kind of guy. He never gave off the "holier than thou" impression; as a matter of fact, he knew he didn't have it all together. He wore that fact like a badge. He was authentic, and I respected that.

But there was more to him. Davin was a Renaissance man of sorts. The guy could do anything he put his mind to. He was the kind of guy that could fix what was wrong with his car after watching a YouTube video. One particular instance stands out in my mind. During my thirtieth birthday party, as we began to grill hamburgers, I realized "we" had forgotten the spatula. By "we," I really mean "I." Regardless, here we are at the park—raw hamburger meat, a grill, and people, but no spatula. I paced around for about ten minutes and then returned to find Davin holding a spatula. But this was no ordinary kitchen utensil. No, Davin had built it out of a few twigs and a Red Bull can! That was Davin.

I remember one evening, as he and I were talking through a struggle that I was going through, "Blessed Be Your Name" by Matt Redman came on the radio. As the song played, he focused intently on the lyrics. "Blessed be Your name on the road marked with suffering. Though there's pain in the offering, blessed be Your name." Davin stopped and looked at me and said, "This is what it's about." Even in that moment, he understood that our vulnerability and suffering pushes us to depend more on the gospel and less on ourselves. That was my friend, "MacGyver the theologian."

Following our graduation from seminary, he and I took different directions, but that didn't keep us from staying in touch. We still celebrated the big events in each other's lives. I came in for his wedding, and he came to West Virginia for my ordination. I'll never forget that night, when Davin left the T.G.I. Friday's in Cross Lanes, West Virginia, to make his way back home. We stopped for a second. As we talked, it felt like we were never going to see each other again. I guess we both realized that we were growing up—that we were beginning to find our way. He told me that he was finally going to Idaho to serve a church. He was pursuing his dream and his calling. I remember as his car pulled out of the parking lot that things were going to be different, but that we would remain friends no matter what.

A week later, Davin called me. I could tell by the tone of his voice that this wasn't going to be one of our usual hilarious catch-up sessions. He told me that during his trip to Idaho, he had felt a mass in his abdomen. He was going to the doctor to have it checked out. I remember practically commanding him to let me know what the doctor said as soon as he knew. The news wasn't good. The doctor confirmed that it was beta cell lymphoma.

As one does when faced with cancer, he and his wife opted to begin the chemotherapy regimen immediately. Davin's dream of being a pastor had been put on hold. At this point, we all figured that this belonged to the category of "momentary afflictions." Sure, it was horrible. But this was Davin. You couldn't keep this guy down. I *knew* that God had led Davin into this season of life so that God could be glorified through his healing. I remember telling him that several times. It just made sense; he would be healed. But days turned to weeks and weeks to months with no marked improvement in his condition.

The treatments began to take their toll on his body. As he began to waste away, I noticed that the mood of our conversations began to shift. They were no longer light and jovial, but heavy and poignant. He was now talking less about "getting better" and more about "dying well." As you probably have guessed by now, this didn't sit well with me.

I'll never forget one day that I came to Louisville to spend the day with him and catch up. As we were headed to lunch, Davin looked at me with a face marked by solemn bewilderment and simply stated, "If God decides to heal me for his glory . . . I understand that. But what if his plan is for me to die? I don't understand that."

I tried to respond with a deep theological answer that would satisfy his question and put him at ease. But I struggled to find the words. All I could do was point to the cross of Christ. But even as I did, there was a part of me that didn't feel this was fair. I found my own "theology of glory" tested as I was confronted with a "theology of the cross."[2]

A Vulnerable Journey

After reading Lauren's email, I was speechless. I pulled off the road and into a truck stop to gather my thoughts. Evidently, this was something I couldn't suppress. It's in moments like these when we are forced to square with the reality that we are not invincible. Death has a way of backing you into a corner and refusing to let you escape. I could not fix what was wrong with myself or what was wrong with my friend. In that moment, I truly felt helpless. I couldn't change anything. No amount of positive thinking or encouragement was going to change this outcome. The only thing I could do was move forward and experience it. So, since I really didn't have a choice, I decided to run headfirst into it.

I tried to pull myself together enough to drive home so that I could make plans to visit Davin one last time. However, before I could head to Louisville, I had one more thing that I needed to do. I needed to speak at a local campus ministry. At this point, I still had a job. Believe it or not, the text that I was supposed to preach on that evening was Philippians 4:13. As I pulled myself together, I read the text: "I can do all things through [Christ] who strengthens me."

It's almost comical as I think about it now. For me, in that moment, this verse went from being a pithy saying that you would see on a Christian T-shirt to being a promise that I needed. This was a promise that Davin needed as well.

As I spoke to the students, I was reminded that Christ is not hindered by our fears, limitations, vulnerabilities or the precarious situations in which we may find ourselves. Rather, the brokenness that we experience on a daily basis is the catalyst that drives us back to the only source of strength that will never fail.

Reflecting on this truth gave me the courage to walk into the house and face my friend. It's funny how sometimes we want to give people advice for how to process and handle grief, but when it comes to us, we always seem to be at a loss for words. Sure, we have Scripture memorized, but when it comes to applying the truth of God's Word, well, that's a different story altogether.

I had spent the entire drive to Louisville alternating between sporadic prayer and trying to think of how I was going to start the conversation with my friend. Now, the moment had arrived. As I walked into the house through the garage, I saw Davin sitting down in the living room. I sat down on the couch next to him and immediately said the first thing that came into my mind. "So how are you feeling?" *Ugh.* I thought to myself, *You idiot. Why would you say that?* But Davin being Davin just looked at me and said, "What do you mean? How am I feeling about dying?" I said, "Umm. Yeah." "Eh," he shrugged his shoulders.

The ice had been broken. Now, we were able to really start talking. For a moment, it was as if we weren't both overwhelmed by the fact that his life was coming to an end. I was actually shocked when he started to ask me about my job situation. It's amazing that though he was suffering, he thought to ask me about what was going on in my life. He was genuinely concerned. Generally, when we go through difficult life events, we become unbelievably self-focused. But he seemed to be as frustrated about my life as I was. It's almost as if the pain he was experiencing gave him more empathy for the pain of others.

The more that we talked, the more that we reflected on how God was working through what we were both experiencing. As we talked, I began reading Philippians 3:8–11:

Indeed, I count everything as loss because of the surpassing worth of knowing Christ Jesus my Lord. For his sake I have suffered the loss of all things and count them as rubbish, in order that I may gain Christ and be found in him, not having a righteousness of my own that comes from the law, but that which comes through faith in Christ, the righteousness from God that depends on faith— that I may know him and the power of his resurrection, and may share his sufferings, becoming like him in his death, that by any means possible I may attain the resurrection from the dead.

The apostle Paul counted everything as loss. Unlike me in that moment, his identity was not grounded in anything that could be taken away from him. Instead, he considered his achievements as "rubbish." *Rubbish*. If you don't know what this word meant in the original Greek language, I encourage you to look it up. It's a fun, if not slightly awkward, word study. Paul used this specific word to express that his worth did not reside in the sum of all his accomplishments. Paul's life goal was to identify with Christ and his righteousness. The gospel not only saved him, it motivated him to live differently.

As we talked, I looked over at my friend, who was sitting across from me at the kitchen table, and said, "Davin, I don't know what's coming around the corner, but this is the time when you can glorify God." I'm not really sure I actually knew the gravity of what I was saying in that moment, but Davin seemed to agree. Not only had his empathy been heightened, but his desire to glorify God had only grown. I would find out at Davin's funeral that after he learned he would die, he, in a sense, welcomed death. He knew he would cease striving with sin, which now broke his heart more than ever before, because he had a newfound understanding of the price that Christ paid for it.

Over the next five days, Davin's family and I laughed together. We cried together. We sang together. We suffered together. We drew upon each other for support.

As I saw Davin embrace the reality of his death, I began to wrestle with my own sense of mortality. In an attempt to process what I was experiencing, I began reading *The Last Enemy* by Michael Wittmer. I immediately regretted this decision as I read the opening chapter:

> You are going to die. Take a moment to let that sink in. You are going to die. One morning the sun will rise and you won't see it. Birds will greet the dawn and you won't hear them. Friends and family will gather to celebrate your life, and after you're buried they'll return to the church for ham and scalloped potatoes. Soon your job and favorite chair and spot on the team will be filled by someone else. The rest of the world may pause to remember—it will give you a moment of silence if you were rich or well known—but then it will carry on as it did before you arrived. "There is no remembrance of men of old," observed Solomon, "and even those who are yet to come will not be remembered by those who follow" (Eccl. 1:11). You are going to die. What a crushing, desperate thought. But unless you swallow hard and embrace it, you are not prepared to live.[3]

William Cowper, the eighteenth-century English hymn writer, penned these words in the hymn "God Moves in a Mysterious Way:"[4]

> Behind a frowning providence, He hides a smiling face.

Somewhere in all of this confusion and sadness, I could see God smiling. Let's be honest, generally, people read *Chicken Soup for the Soul* or something faintly uplifting when they get down in the dumps. They read something that is designed at some level to make them feel better about the situation in which they find themselves. Not me. Nope, I go straight for the "death book." But oddly enough, that paragraph opened my eyes to what God was doing in my life. The harsh truth was exactly what I needed. I had to realize that, like Davin, my days were numbered as well.

Without knowing it, I had been scared to move forward. I was stuck in a type of paralysis. I wanted to be in control of my life, but I was painfully aware that I wasn't in control of anything. At some level, I was intrigued by the thought of doing something to engage the human trafficking conversation, but I was enslaved to my own fear.

My fear manifested itself in a few clear ways. On one hand, I was afraid to die. My friend's impending death had sent a shudder down my spine. As long as I knew, I had been afraid to die, but I chose to avoid thinking about it. On most days, I could distract myself, but Davin's death put thoughts of my own death front and center.

I was also afraid to live. As I thought about it, I realized that the majority of my "faith journey" had consisted of me drifting from one comfortable job to the next. I was allergic to discomfort. Now don't misunderstand me, I suffered. Yes, like everyone else, I can look back over my life and see moments of great pain. As a matter of fact, these moments have shaped me. But beneath the veneer of my Christian life, I had become a master at avoiding pain if it was at all possible. If it were up to me, I would do everything in my power to mitigate any potential suffering.

But that night, I was powerless. As I lay in bed reading *The Last Enemy*, I realized a few things about myself. I was afraid to be vulnerable. I was afraid to take risks. Honestly, I realized that up to that point, I hadn't really been walking by faith. Sure, I thought I was, but something else entirely had taken place. I had become an expert in risk management, always taking the safest option available.

That's when the light came on. Finally, it made sense. Davin was about to die, without ever fulfilling his dream of vocational ministry.[5] I still had a choice. How would I respond?

I remember what happened next like it happened yesterday. Lying on a fold-out bed in Davin's in-laws' basement, I prayed, "God, forgive me. I have been afraid to follow you. I have no idea what I am supposed to do, but I know you are in control. Show me what you want me to do. I'll follow you wherever you lead." As soon as I said, "Amen," I knew that this was a dangerous prayer. But honestly, I was exhausted. I knew in that moment I could no longer run from my calling to fight human trafficking. Yes, it was uncertain. But in the midst of the uncertainty was the God in whom I believed, calling me to follow him. I had no idea what God would do, but I was determined to stake my future plans on him.

Realizing that I had an expiration date, I chose to trust God even if the next step forced me to confront all of my fears. Two days later, Davin died.

I think that we have conditioned ourselves to avoid the inevitable reality of our own temporality. We avoid any talk whatsoever of our own limitations. Here's the truth: we are vulnerable. We will suffer and we will die. You probably won't find those words on a Hallmark greeting card, but they are, nonetheless, true.

I had come to embrace that certainty. I no longer had the strength to run from pain or fear. As my journey with Davin came to a close, I noticed that God had worked in my life through both my experience of my own weakness and Davin's battle with cancer. Little did I know it, but Davin had been modeling vulnerability the entire time. He had nothing to prove to anyone. He had no backup plan. He just lived until he died.

Moving Ahead

Earlier I said that *vulnerability is not only part of the problem, but it's part of the solution.* This solution demands that we love those who are susceptible to exploitation because in some way all of us, no matter how guarded, are in the same boat. Davin's experience of vulnerability exposed my vulnerability. Now that my eyes were opened, I began to see how vulnerability played a role in human trafficking.

My remaining time in West Virginia went by in the blink of an eye. I had meant what I said to God. I was finally willing to follow him, even if that meant following him into an uncertain life path. So I began right where God had me.

I learned that West Virginia was one of the last remaining states in the United States without state-wide human trafficking legislation, so I did the only thing I knew to do. I went to a friend with whom I had been teaching Sunday school and asked him a bunch of questions. My friend, Jeff, happened to work as legal counsel to the state's governor.

"How can this happen? How can we be so slow to the game?"

"Raleigh, you may need to write legislation."

"Umm. Sure. Whatever. We just need to do something."

Two weeks later, he sent me a proposed bill. It was well-thought-out and similar to what had been passed in other states. "Great! This is perfect," I said. But Jeff slowed down my celebration. "For this to pass, we need people at the capitol to show support." So I began reaching out to college students around the state. And it passed! Through this experience, God gave me a passion to mobilize people to love the vulnerable and, in a way, made my uncertain calling just a little more clear. In the months to follow, reflecting on the gospel, I became increasingly aware that *Christ motivates vulnerable people to love other vulnerable people by becoming vulnerable for us.*

So, I sold everything I had and moved to New York City without any guarantee of success. This was, how do you say, a new approach for me. It's true that any time you attempt to break a lifelong pattern, you are going to experience anxiety. But I didn't just experience my own—I had to deal with the anxiety of others as well. I remember as I began the process of moving to New York, several of my pastor friends expressed their concern. "This is irresponsible, how can you do this?" "You're crazy." "Do you really think that God is calling you to do this?"

Though in the past couple of years many of my friends have called me personally to apologize, it still makes me laugh when I think about it. In a sense, they were right.

Whether we know it or not, each of us has been conditioned to protect ourselves at all costs. We do everything we can to guard our sense of status and identity. We are deathly afraid of "losing," so we build our own fortifications and "biblical" defenses for why we are refusing to live radical, unhindered lives. Baptizing our desire for control, we use the Proverbs as proof-texts, and the Gospels and the Pauline epistles as support for our preference of always choosing the safest and most comfortable option. But at the heart of all our theological posturing lies the bitter truth that we are scared. We don't want to suffer. We don't want to be vulnerable.

To be frank, we are positively mortified at the thought that our standard of life lacks the permanency we crave. Essentially, we fear risking who we are and what we have. Our senses of identity depend on our being in control of our destinies. In that context, I guess that you can say that I was taking a risk. Like Davin's vulnerability exposed my own, my journey into vulnerability was actively exposing the fears and limitations of many around me.

As a matter of fact, this move was one of the biggest risks that I had ever taken. There was no safety net or backup plan. But as I laid it all on the line and stepped out in faith, I realized that I was exactly where God wanted me to be. The moment that I hailed my first cab at the JFK Airport as a New York City resident, I knew that there would be no turning back.

I now know that God calls each of us to be a voice for those whose voice is not heard, as well as to empower those who have been disempowered to raise their own voices. But part of his calling requires us to face our fears and trust God with the results. Even as I write this, I am cringing ever so slightly. We don't want to lose control, but for us to follow Christ, we have to give up control. I would have never known the blessing of vulnerability had I not been forced to confront my worst-case scenario. Through the painful process of acknowledging my own fears and limitations, God opened my eyes to care to see those who are vulnerable around me.

CHAPTER 2

EXPOSING THE MYTHS

As I think back to the day I decided to suppress my calling, I realize that my problem was not just that I didn't know what to do, it was that I honestly didn't know what human trafficking was. As far as I was concerned, I was being challenged to start a safe home or to investigate sex trafficking rings. If that was the case, I felt woefully unqualified. I'm not nor have I ever been a lawyer, police officer, licensed counselor, or sex trafficking survivor.

What I didn't know at the time was that I had a flawed understanding of the nature of human trafficking. It's true that we can all do something, but first we have to separate facts from fiction. You and I will never be able to recognize and respond to sex and labor trafficking appropriately if we do not have an accurate picture of what it is. In my case, the majority of what I knew about it came from the sensationalized depictions on television and in movies that I had seen and unconsciously accepted as truth. Without really thinking about it, I guess I just assumed that every case was like the movies. Now, we understand that the rest of life doesn't work that way, but for some reason, when we watch movies on human trafficking, we tend to think that every real-life incident must look just like the movie *Taken*. I had accepted this idea as truth at some level, and that's why I felt ill-equipped.

Whether someone is trafficked into prostitution, forced labor, or domestic service, they all have one thing in common. Each of them is hidden in plain sight. We walk by those who have been victimized on a daily basis and have no idea. Maybe it's the short-order cook at your favorite restaurant, or the young woman that you see every time that you go to the nail salon, or possibly it could be the day laborer that's doing the remodel on a house on your street.

What makes matters worse is that those who are trafficked are ultimately hidden right behind our assumptions. Though this hurts to admit, our lack of awareness of their vulnerability allows this to go on unchecked. Don't get me wrong, you may have heard about human trafficking on the news and maybe you have even read a book, but awareness is more than knowing something exists. It's more than putting a red "X" on your hand once a year.[1] We become aware as we learn how to recognize and respond to the trafficking in our communities and around the world.

Our assumptions inform how we respond to everything, including exploitation. In other words, we will act based on what we believe to be true. Therefore, we need to re-examine our assumptions.

However, before we begin this process, we have to recognize what we believe right now, in this moment. Over the next several pages, you will learn how to deconstruct the fallacies to which you are unknowingly clinging. The more that you know, the more equipped you will be to fact-check the misinformation that is bombarding you each time you turn on the television or open your laptop. In the words of my favorite eighties cartoon series *G. I. Joe: The Real American Hero*, "knowing is half the battle." In a similar way, before you can understand what modern-day slavery is, you have to learn what it isn't. Here are some of the most commonly believed trafficking myths, as well as the truth about what's really happening.

Myth-Busting 101

Myth #1: Trafficking usually happens when victims are kidnapped, drugged, and chained to a radiator.

Since I have already mentioned it, it might be a good idea to ask if you have ever actually seen *Taken*. Liam Neeson plays an ex-CIA operative, Bryan Mills, with "a very particular set of skills." His daughter, played by Maggie Grace, goes to Paris for the week with her best friend. At first everything seems to be going swimmingly. Shortly after they arrive in France, they meet a charming young man at the airport and decide to split a cab with him. Little do they know that he is not as innocent as he seems. In actuality, he is a recruiter for an Albanian sex-trafficking ring. Within no time at all, the traffickers break into the flat where the girls are staying and kidnap them both. Bryan Mills now has four days (or to be even more dramatic, he has 96 hours) to rescue his daughter, who has been abducted and drugged, and is about to be sold to Middle Eastern businessmen.[2]

Now say it with me: "*Taken* is a movie. It's not real life." I actually don't think you really said it out loud. Seriously, I'm not kidding. Stop reading for a moment and say it to yourself: "*Taken* is a movie, and Bryan Mills is a fictional character."

They say "confession is good for the soul." I hope so, because almost every time I speak at a church or a university campus, someone asks me a variation of the following question: *"Everyone is kidnapped, right?"*

The danger in holding to this assumption, or any unchecked assumption for that matter, is that you are very likely to miss what is right in front of you. In reality, someone does not need to be "taken," physically beaten, or chained to be trafficked. Though this can and does happen, it is considered rare.[3]

You may be reading this and thinking to yourself, *If that's true, then why don't people just leave?* Before we get to the answer, promise me you'll never say that out loud. If by some fluke you actually do say it within the hearing of others, please make every effort to not

say it to someone who has experienced trafficking or intimate partner abuse. Your well-meaning curiosity could be the very thing that
triggers someone's retraumatization.

RECOGNIZING THE CHAINS

Make no mistake, the chains exist, but they are often in a different form than many of us expect. In many cases, the chains bind-
ing a victim to his or her exploiter are psychological and emotional.
Exploiters will use means of power and control in their "relationship," such as threats, fraud, or other fear tactics to ensure compliance. Some victims even have perceived "freedom" and can get
permission to leave to go to the doctor's office, work, or even their
local church.[4] This has become known as traumatic bonding—you
may know it as Stockholm syndrome.

On August 23, 1973, four people were taken hostage in a bank
robbery in Sweden by Jan-Erik Olsson, a thirty-two-year-old career
criminal, and an accomplice. Fearing for their lives, the hostages
had no other choice but to ask permission before they could eat or
use the bathroom. They began to depend on their captors for these
basic human needs. The captors would respond by giving them
small graces. "You can stand up and walk around the bank." "You
can use the bathroom." Over time, the hostages began to become
sympathetic to Olsson's cause, to the extent that they no longer saw
their captors as enemies, but as friends. One of the hostages went to
the extent of saying, "I fully trust Clark and the robber. I am not
desperate. They haven't done a thing to us. On the contrary, they
have been very nice. But you know . . . what I'm scared of is that
the police will attack and cause us to die." Six days later when the
standoff ended, it became evident that the victims had formed some
kind of positive relationship with their captors.[5]

This type of bond can be seen in those who have experienced
trauma at the hands of an abuser or a trafficker. For example, one
of my friends, who was trafficked by a so-called boyfriend, shared
with me that when a person has experienced repeated cycles of traumatic abuse at the hands of their trafficker, they find themselves in

a position where they would rather risk death than disobedience. In her own words, "One would rather jump off the Brooklyn Bridge than risk disobeying their pimp." A belief develops that at some basic level, the person who is hurting them actually cares for them, while others, like law enforcement and family members, do not have their best interests at heart.

Taking this in account, to correct previous standards that only considered physical harm and kidnapping, the Trafficking Victims Protection Act (TVPA) of 2000, addressed the more subtle forms of coercion. I will talk about the TVPA in more detail in the next chapter.[6]

Another important aspect to note is that people can be trafficked without being kidnapped by movie-style villains. Several years ago, I asked a group of college students to describe a profile of a trafficker. The students gave the answers that we would most likely predict. "It's that shady guy who has been in and out of prison or the homeless guy that nobody is watching." Little did they know that not only were they failing to give an accurate description of most traffickers, but they were also potentially describing those upon whom traffickers often prey.[7]

The Victimizers

So who are the traffickers? How would you have answered the question in the last paragraph? What do you think they look like?

Easy, they look like you and me. They often conduct themselves as ordinary people. They live in nice apartments or the suburbs. They have neighbors. They mow their lawns. They eat at the restaurants in your neighborhood. They may even go to your church. Believe it or not, they often come across as being friendly or charismatic. But there is a side to them that we do not see—a side that they have hidden from the watching world.

In an attempt to cast light on this reality, one study found that 68 percent of the perpetrators were male, while 32 percent were female. After reviewing 116 cases involving 382 traffickers, it was

discovered that 93 percent of the victims were trafficked by someone within their own community.[8]

It happens in our own backyards! This truth blows many of the
minor myths to which we hold completely out of the water. This
isn't just happening because the victims live near a border or a major
highway system. It's not something that only happens to foreign
nationals or refugees. Human trafficking happens anywhere there is
vulnerability. It can happen anywhere because there are vulnerable
people everywhere. Where you find vulnerable populations, you
will find someone willing to exploit them. This continues to happen in our communities because those with power often willingly
choose to exploit those with considerably less power.

Needless to say, it's not always a "stranger danger" situation. It's
most likely someone you already know. A Chicago study found that
68 percent of victims surveyed were recruited for sex trafficking.
The study interviewed 100 women under twenty-five who were still
under the control of their trafficker. Regardless of their individual
situations, their recruiters typically fell into one of three categories:
family members, friends, and/or professional traffickers. Of those
interviewed, 23 percent considered their trafficker their boyfriend,
19 percent were enlisted by friends or close acquaintances, and 10
percent were recruited by a family member. Another 12 percent
were recruited by a previously unknown trafficker.[9]

These findings are not limited to large cities, however. A study
in Ohio interviewed 115 individuals who were under the age of
eighteen when they were trafficked. Of those surveyed, 59 percent
were recruited by a female friend already involved in prostitution;
another 23 percent were forced by a female that first acted as if she
were a friend. While 10 percent of those interviewed were trafficked
by a male member of a foster family, 18 percent were trafficked by
a male friend.[10]

The point is, our belief that only the mafia and street gangs
traffic people in foreign countries does a huge disservice to those
who actually have been victimized. Given the data, people are more
likely to be trafficked by someone that they know. But this "Taken"

myth is not a stand-alone myth; it overflows into the next myth we're going to examine together.

Myth #2: The Super Bowl Myth

Chances are you have heard that there is a connection between human trafficking and major sporting events like the Super Bowl. All you have to do is a simple Google search of "human trafficking and the Super Bowl" to render approximately 733,000 hits.

In light of this fact, each year as we prepare to watch the big game, we are inundated with news stories of how human trafficking is at fever pitch. This connection began in 2011, when the Attorney General of Texas pronounced that the Super Bowl is the "single largest human trafficking incident" in the United States.

In the article entitled "Is the Super Bowl Really the U.S.'s Biggest Sex Trafficking Magnet?," journalist Sebastien Malo interviews Bradley Myles, the chief executive of the Polaris Project, a nonprofit working to combat and prevent modern-day slavery. "All this is, is a one-day snapshot into what otherwise is a 365-day problem," he told the Thomson Reuters Foundation. "The same traffickers that are committing trafficking . . . during the Super Bowl, they're going to wake up in the morning on Monday and do the same thing."[11]

Human trafficking is an industry that profits from the exploitation of vulnerability. It operates according to the law of supply and demand. As a whole, human trafficking is a $150-billon dollar industry, with $99 billion coming from commercial sexual exploitation and the remaining $51 billion coming from forced labor exploitation.[12]

Regardless of whether an industry is legitimate or illegitimate, one thing is for certain: the law of supply and demand is at play. In human trafficking, the demand to purchase sex or cheap labor lies in the hearts and minds of the consumers. Tori Utley says it this way: "Put simply, without demand there would be no supply—there would be no customers for traffickers, thus no need to victimize men, women, and children."[13]

According to the Polaris Project, "It is found during the Super Bowl, but it is also found at motorcycle rallies in South Dakota, in the fields of Florida, in gangs in California, and in brothels in Washington, D.C." The National Human Trafficking Resource Center hotline, powered by Polaris, has received reports of human trafficking in all fifty states.[14] Ergo, it would be a huge misstep to believe that the problem of sex trafficking is like a perverted Christmas, only happening once a year.

In reality, there appears to be no massive influx of trafficked women into the city where the Super Bowl is being held. Statistics show that there is, at most, a slight uptick, but ultimately not a dramatic increase in sex trafficking during major sporting events.[15] Though we may be hyperfocused during the Super Bowl, we must remember that trafficking happens every day and it always involves those most vulnerable. When we only focus on major sporting events, it limits our vigilance to only one day a year.

Myth #3: Only social outcasts buy sex.

Surveying 4,851 men in a representative sample of American households from 2001–2010, the General Social Survey (GSS) asked interviewees two questions. First, each person was asked if they had ever purchased sex within their lifetime. If the answer was "yes," then they were asked if they had purchased sex within the last year. Approximately 13.9 percent of men between the ages of eighteen and seventy-five reported that they had purchased sex in their lifetime, while 1 percent reported buying sex within the last year.[16] Let's pause for a moment. Even if we assume that all of those interviewed were being honest, though 1 percent seems relatively small, this percentage represents 48 of those interviewed in the study. This is a lot of people who have admitted to buying sex. This is not something that we can brush under the rug.

In May 2016, agents of the Tennessee Bureau of Investigation posed online as underage girls, leading investigators to the arrest of thirty-two people, two of whom were ministers. The pastor and the "pastor in training" responded to an ad placed on a website by what they thought was a fifteen-year-old girl.[17]

Operation "Someone Like Me" took its name from the words of an eighteen-year-old who had been trafficked three years prior. In the *New York Times* article, "Two Tennessee Ministers Are Among 30 Arrested in Prostitution Sting," Christine Hauser explains how law enforcement took their cues from this survivor.[18] "For an hour we talked with her in minute detail; how they end up agreeing to meet, the slang," Agent Quin said. At the end of the training conference call, the agents thanked her. After a silence, according to the agent, she said: "No, thank you. You don't know what it means to someone like me that the T.B.I. is willing to go out and rescue these girls."[19] As a result of the sting, the two men were arrested on felony trafficking charges.

This just goes to show that just as anyone can be a trafficker, anyone can be a sex buyer. This is not restricted to a certain ethnic or religious background. Sex buyers can include those with social status and financial means as well as those without.

Normally, in order prove in a federal court of law that a case is sex trafficking, one would have to show that either force, fraud, or coercion were used to make the person complicit in the act. But if someone is under the age of eighteen and sold for sex, they are automatically considered victims of human trafficking.[20] Basically, anytime someone who is underage is being prostituted, whether it is online or on the street, that person is trafficked. With that said, there is no such thing as a "child prostitute." So you can go ahead and wipe that from your vocabulary.[21]

For many of us, it's easy to focus on sex traffickers and those in prostitution, but if we were honest with ourselves, we'd have to admit that there is a part of us that wants to avoid thinking about the sex buyer. We don't think that anyone that we know would ever think to buy sex, but I have found that it's far more common than you know.

But there are other contributors to human trafficking in addition to the sellers and buyers. You may not be buying sex, but as you will see in the next section, you don't have to buy sex to create demand for human trafficking.

Myth #4: Human trafficking is only sex trafficking.

Generally, the conversation goes something like this: "Human trafficking is just horrible. I can't believe that people would actually do that! I can't believe that all those girls are trafficked for sex."

It's true, people are trafficked for sex. Though the majority are women and girls, victims of sex trafficking can include boys and men as well.[22] In 2016, it was estimated that 4.8 million people were victims of forced sexual exploitation.[23]

When we think "sex trafficking," our knee-jerk reaction is to think of forced street prostitution. It just makes sense, because that's what we see the most in movies and on the news. However, sex trafficking is often more nuanced than that. Victims who are being commercially exploited for sex can be forced into prostitution, but they can also be forced into pornography, stripping, live-sex shows, mail-order "marriages," military prostitution, and sex tourism. Needless to say, sex trafficking is multifaceted and is always evolving.[24]

IS PROSTITUTION SEX TRAFFICKING?

Now this raises another question: Is all prostitution sex trafficking? If you want to start a heated debate in a flash, just ask this question and watch what transpires. For example, many in the anti-trafficking movement, while not conflating every act of prostitution with sex trafficking, will say that prostitution at its very core is demoralizing, manipulative, and exploitative to those involved, while there are many in the empowered sex worker camp that would argue that prostitution is a bona fide vocation and that the anti-trafficking movement is interfering with their right to make an honest living.

For us to make any kind of assessment, we must examine what is involved in "choosing this life." In an article entitled "The Commercial Sexual Exploitation of Women and Girls: A Survivor

Service Provider's Perspective" in the *Yale Journal of Law and Feminism,* a survivor echoes the same sentiment as mine as she thinks about her own story:

> Tragically, my story reflects that of thousands of child victims of sexual exploitation in the United States. For most, the exploitation does not begin the first time they are prostituted; 75–95 percent of prostituted individuals were sexually abused as children. Although involvement in prostitution is correlated to childhood sexual abuse, the connection is generally ignored. In a pilot study of 130 individuals prostituted on the streets of San Francisco, 57 percent of those studied reported that they had been sexually abused as children, 32 percent reported that rape was their first sexual experience, 16 percent reported that their first sexual experience was with an adult friend of the family, 26 percent reported that their first sexual experience was with a relative, and 27 percent stated that their first sexual experience was with a person five or more years their senior.[25]

To put it another way, though they may have appeared to have made a choice, in reality, the choice had already been made for them. So though one may actually be working in prostitution without having been trafficked, it's clear that they are in a situation where exploitation and demoralization are seen as the norm. For this reason, throughout this book, you will not find me using the word *prostitute*, but rather referring to someone as being "prostituted."

In addition to street prostitution and massage parlors, brothels can be found in spas, strip clubs, and even residential homes. Often, we walk by these places without knowing what is really going on behind closed doors.

With that said, we recognize that sex trafficking does happen and we have seen a few examples of what it can look like. But we must also realize that there is more to human trafficking than just sex trafficking. This pervasive myth blinds us to our neighbors who have been forced to provide the services that we require on a daily basis.

FORCED LABOR

In 2012, the International Labor Organization (ILO) released a shocking report that estimated that of those enslaved around the world, approximately 22 percent are in forced sexual exploitation and 68 percent have been trafficked into forced labor exploitation.[26] According to the ILO, the overwhelming majority of human trafficking is for forced labor.

Forced labor exploitation can take place in agricultural settings, construction crews, domestic work, begging, door-to-door sales, hospitality and service industries, child labor, and manufacturing factories. Men, women, boys, and girls can be forced to work on farms, building projects, fishing boats, and in garment factories. In addition, they can be coerced into domestic servitude as well, working as a household servant or a nanny. Like sex trafficking, cases have been reported in every country in the world.[27]

It was my first week in New York City. I had been asked to take a group of college students sightseeing around the city. This was especially hilarious since I knew about as much about the city as anyone in the group, but, fake it 'til you make it, right? So the group and I began to take the city, one borough at a time. At the end of a very long day, we decided to head into Manhattan. It seemed odd to me that every student was dying to go to Chinatown. Don't get me wrong, I really love the cultural aspects of this particular neighborhood, but for some reason, I had never expected that every one of the students shared my appreciation. Why were they so dead-set on going to lower Manhattan?

As I listened to them talk amongst themselves at a subway stop in the Bronx, it all became clear. Apparently, several of them had been saving up their spending money to buy "knockoff" purses. As we waited for the train, I implored their college pastor to encourage his students to rethink this. My reasoning was simple: it was a basic exercise in the law of supply and demand.

It's a fact that counterfeit purses are very inexpensive. Since that's true, we have to ask ourselves how much money actually went into the production of the bag. In other words, how could the cost be that low if those who had made them were being paid fair wages?

At some point, we have to recognize that in ways like this, we are contributing to the funding of organized criminal organizations. Even though we are doing so at a basic level, we are actually giving money to people who are exploiting other people. To be honest, traffickers traffic—that's what they do, whether they are selling drugs, guns, people, or purses. As we purchase black market goods, we are investing in the economic engine driving a culture of exploitation.

The point for us to remember is that people are trafficked to provide all the goods that you and I need to live the lifestyle of our choosing. Whether it's a purse, a bag of rice, a T-shirt, or even a fish sandwich, slavery touches far more of the things we love to buy and wear than any of us would guess.[28]

In order for us to have a better understanding of labor exploitation, lets review two actual federal court cases. First, let's take a look at the *United States v. Kil Soo Lee*. From 1998 to 2000, Lee, a Korean businessman, recruited approximately 270 women from China and Vietnam to work in his garment factory in American Samoa. Ensuring that he would make the highest profits possible from his American consumers, Kil Soo Lee used financial penalties to keep the workers from leaving the Daewoosa factory.[29] This act of creating a financial debt is known as debt bondage.[30] According to the International Labor Organization, debt bondage impacts 50 percent of victims of forced labor.[31] Essentially, traffickers, like Lee, will require their workers to pay off a large debt before they can leave the sweatshop. However, the traffickers take pains to make sure that the debt continues to accrue, making payment a near-impossible task.[32]

Lee employed another technique used by both sex and labor traffickers. To ensure that he didn't lose workers, he locked them in the compound. In other words, he restricted their freedom of movement. Often, the fact that someone cannot leave their place of employment or that they cannot leave without a chaperone is a clear indicator of trafficking.

He additionally coerced them with threats of arrests, deportation, physical assault, and food deprivation. In February 2003 Kil Soo Lee was convicted of criminal charges of involuntary servitude, extortion, and money laundering. Lee was sentenced to forty years in prison.[33]

To think that people are just trafficked to make the clothes we wear would be yet another false assumption. They are also forced to plant, pick, and produce the foods we eat on a daily basis.

With that in mind, let's examine the case of the *United States v. Flores*. Miguel Flores and Sebastian Gomez employed more than 400 male and female workers in both Florida and South Carolina. The crew, comprised of undocumented immigrants from Mexico and Guatemala,[34] was forced to work twelve-hour days, six days a week. Many of the workers were paid as little as $20 a week for their work picking tomatoes and citrus.

As the Coalition of Immokalee Workers looked into the case, they discovered that those who attempted to leave the site were threatened, and one was even pistol-whipped.[35] Taking the name from a former epicenter of forced labor exploitation, Immokalee, Florida, the Coalition of Immokalee Workers (CIW) is a nonprofit organization focused on improving the wages and working conditions of migrant workers. In an interview with the CNN Freedom Project, Lauren Germino, the cofounder of CIW, talked about the Flores case, which was the first human trafficking case that they had worked. "In that one, we found out that workers were being held by armed guards, prevented from leaving, pistol-whipped, some sexually assaulted."[36] Flores and Gomez were sentenced to fifteen years in prison and forced to pay $39,615 in restitution.[37]

As we have seen so far, human trafficking is not solely sex trafficking. It's important that we know the distinction so as to be able to respond appropriately.

For this reason, the United Nations chose to enact the Palermo Protocols on December 12, 2000. The purpose of the protocols is to clearly explain the UN's position on the smuggling of migrants, the trafficking of firearms, and trafficking in persons. According to the protocol, "trafficking in persons" is defined as:

> the recruitment, transportation, transfer, harboring or receipt of persons, by means of the threat or use of force or other forms of coercion, of abduction, of fraud, of deception, of the abuse of power or of a position of vulnerability or of the giving or receiving of payments or benefits to achieve the consent of a person having control over another person, for the purpose of exploitation. Exploitation shall include, at a minimum, the exploitation of the prostitution of others or other forms of sexual exploitation, forced labour or services, slavery or practices similar to slavery, servitude or the removal of organs. . . . The consent of a victim of trafficking in persons to the intended exploitation set forth shall be irrelevant where any of the means set forth have been used.[38]

In this definition, we find the act, means, and purpose of human trafficking. The act: the recruitment, transportation, transfer, harboring, or receipt of people. The means: force, fraud, and coercion. The purpose: people are trafficked for *"prostitution . . . or other forms of sexual exploitation, forced labour or services, slavery or practices similar to slavery, servitude or the removal of organs."*

The point is simple: human trafficking is much more than sex trafficking. Though sex trafficking is a part of the problem, it's not everything. Our limited understanding will keep us from seeing those who are enslaved around us, and we need to know how to identify those who are potentially being trafficked.

Myth #5: Victims will always self-identify.

Rafael Cadena-Sosa, a forty-six-year-old Mexican national, pled guilty to conspiracy and to holding a person in a condition of involuntary servitude in January 2015. During his plea, Cadena-Sosa admitted that he, along with several of his family members, deliberately approached young women and girls under false pretenses. With the promise of legitimate jobs in the service and hospitality industries in the United States, he lured them into commercial sexual exploitation.[39] Cadena-Sosa, like most traffickers, focused on those most vulnerable around him. In a recent study, it has been reported that women and girls account for more than 99 percent of all victims, with children compromising more than one fifth of the total.[40]

In the months spanning from August 1996 to February 1998, the Cadena family brought as many as forty women and girls to both Florida and South Carolina. Rather than working as waitresses and hotel workers like they had been promised, these unsuspecting victims were forcibly prostituted to service primarily Mexican migrant workers.[41]

To keep the girls compliant, Cadena-Sosa used a variety of coercive methods. First, he held them in debt bondage, by forcing them to pay off their ever-increasing smuggling debt. To further induce submission, he would employ a cocktail of violence, sexual assault, and threats to both the victims and their families. The girls were forced to "work" twelve hours a day, six days a week. Adding insult to injury, the money they received was to be given immediately to their trafficker to pay down their "debt." Anyone who attempted to run or escape would be tracked down, beaten, and raped upon capture.

After being sentenced to fifteen years, Cadena-Sosa was forced to pay $1,261,563 in restitution to sixteen different victims.[42]

As we can tell by the Cadena case, these women were coerced to do what they normally would have never chosen to do. They were made to relinquish all freedom and agency to their captors. Using fear, Cadena-Sosa virtually guaranteed that his victims would not run.

Unbeknownst to many of us, those who have been trafficked often do not seek help or self-identify as victims. There are a myriad of reasons, ranging from general distrust to trauma to violence and threats of violence.

For some, they are constrained by a traumatic bond. They just couldn't imagine that they are being exploited. In their minds, they are just in the middle of a "difficult" situation. But as we see in the case above, each of these girls was being conditioned to stay. Regardless of how much they wanted to extricate themselves from the hell they were experiencing, they were made to feel helpless. Fearing brutal violence, rape, debt bondage, and threats to their families, the victims were left with few to no options. This is how a trafficker operates. They want to make their victim either fearful of them or entirely dependent upon them.

Mellissa Withers, writing for *Psychology Today*, says that "traffickers are experts in psychological manipulation. Common tactics involve convincing victims that they're in a loving relationship with their traffickers, making sure victims feel that they're fully dependent on the trafficker for all of their basic needs, and making sure that victims know (or believe) that they're under constant surveillance."[43]

Some common threats could include:

> "If you tell anyone, I'll tell your family and friends what you've done."

> "Who you going to run to? The police? We'll call the police and have you arrested."

> "If you tell anyone, we'll call immigration and get you deported."

> "If you stop, we'll just do this to your little sister. You can't run from us."

As I mentioned earlier, the worst thing that you could say is "Why didn't you just leave? Why didn't you just get help?" This is incredibly disempowering to these survivors who have experienced trauma. We must be careful with our questions, because we have no idea what each person has been through.

Where Do We Go from Here?

As we love vulnerable people, we are loving those who are often in the crosshairs of would-be exploiters. As we get involved in the lives of others, there is always a risk. We will always stand to lose something. But in all this thinking about losing, we never seem to focus on all that we will gain.

If we want to love others, we have to leave the comfort of self-protection strategies. As we leave our own comfort zones and experience our own vulnerability, we will begin to see those living in discomfort more clearly. It's only when we stop "protecting" ourselves from the people that we are called to help that we will be positioned to act to help our neighbors. As we open our eyes to see those most often marginalized in our community, will we begin to finally acknowledge that human trafficking can happen in our own backyard.

But here's the kicker—you and I will not begin to grow until we see a need for it. As we think about how our assumptions can lead us to inaction, how will we respond? Now that we recognize what we should not believe, what should we believe about human trafficking?

CHAPTER 3

A MUCH-NEEDED CONVERSATION

H ello Jessica, this is Raleigh," I said in a markedly defeated tone. "What's up?" Jessica asked.

Jessica Minhas and I had known each other for about seven years. Though we had the same major at the University of Central Florida and mutual friends, we didn't meet until we found ourselves hanging out with the same people at Wick's Pizza in Louisville, Kentucky.[1]

Jessica had moved to NYC several years prior to find her calling. She was now leading in the New York City anti-trafficking space. For this reason, she had been encouraging me to follow my calling from the moment I started running from it. I guess that she could see potential where I couldn't. But on this day as we talked on the phone, I was feeling embarrassed.

I had recently applied for a job with a particular anti-trafficking organization. It seemed like a perfect fit. The organization was offering the role of a collegiate mobilizer. Given that the nonprofit was basically operating from a Christian worldview and they were in need of someone with my particular skill set, I just knew that this was my dream job 2.0. If there ever was a sign from God, this was it. So I rapidly filled out the application and submitted it. And so began the waiting game.

However, I didn't have to wait too long, as it only took them two days to respond with an answer. Pro tip: when an organization only needs two days to decide if you are a worthy candidate, it's generally either a definite "yes" or an absolute "no"; there's no middle ground. The email read as follows: "Thank you for submitting an application, but we are going in another direction."

Are you kidding me? I thought. *There's no way. This doesn't make sense.* I was crushed.

So as Jessica and I talked on the phone, I explained that though "I thought I was called to fight human trafficking, I guess I'm not supposed to anymore. I'm glad we cleared that up."

Jessica paused for a moment. It was one of those pregnant pauses that builds anticipation for what is about to happen next. "That's stupid. It just means that you aren't supposed to work for them. You just need to move to New York and figure it out."

"Move to New York and figure it out." Not bad advice, in retrospect. Now that I think about it, she made a really good point. Her candor was jarring enough to shake me out of my self-imposed funk and to open my eyes to what God may have in front of me. I laughed, and to be honest, I still laugh when I think about it. She was exactly right. Maybe God was calling me to do something that was entirely new to me.

As you are considering how God may be calling you to engage people in the margins, you need to be aware that he may be calling you away from what you think you should do and to a ministry custom-built for you. God has given you specific gifts and passions to be used as you love him and love your neighbors. As God shapes us, he is shaping us to serve those hurting around us.

However, none of us will ever follow God's call to love those most vulnerable in isolation, if not for the simple fact that this work is beyond any one of us. We can't do it alone. We may start alone, but in time, the sheer magnitude of the problem will come crashing down on our heads.

It's in those moments that we have a choice to make: 1) Burnout and quit or 2) Walk with others who have the same passion. But one thing is certain: We can't do this work on our own.

If we are to identify and respond to the vulnerabilities of others, we need others to walk with us in our vulnerability. More than that, by ourselves, it is nearly impossible to identify our own issues, much less the issues of others, without other people being involved in the deliberation process. Left to ourselves, we will continuously fall into the trap of choosing only what comes natural to us. When given the choice, we will always hedge our bets and go with the safest option. This is why we need others to help us process where God is leading us.

Community is the most underrated tool needed to discover how God is calling us to love our neighbor. When we are walking with others, the idea of being the reluctant solitary hero goes right out the window. Because quite frankly, due to our own human frailty, we are not enough on our own to meet the needs of those most broken. Acknowledging that you are not the hero is the first step in allowing Christ to have his rightful place in the process.

Following my phone call with Jessica, I moved to New York to "figure it out." Not one week later, as I sat down with a friend to have lunch, I received a call from another friend of mine who worked with InterVarsity Christian Fellowship. "We are about to do a major anti-trafficking event in New York City," he said with excitement. "It's called the Price of Life. The actual event is in a year, but we are going to spend the year preparing for it. Would you volunteer to mobilize churches?"

"I mean, yes, but I work with college students."

"I know but this is what we need."

Following the call, I looked at my friend and said, "You're not going to believe what just happened."

She smiled. "It looks like you are exactly where God wants you."

After the transition that I had experienced, these words gave much-needed relief to my soul. I was finally engaging human trafficking.

For the next six months, I racked my brain to think about how many different ways I could connect with churches in New York. Given that I was brand-new to the city, I had to think fast. So I began to speak at any pastoral gatherings I could find. I looked up and emailed any pastor whose contact information I could find. I also asked several friends to connect me with their pastor friends. All of this was in the effort to create a team of pastors who were passionate about ending human trafficking. But I think the most pivotal decision of this period was the decision to host a small panel discussion specifically geared toward the needs of clergy and church leaders.

Almost six months to the day that I began volunteering, we held a panel discussion. Featuring leaders from the New York Anti-Trafficking space, the event was called "Let My People Go." It was my hope that the pastors and church leaders who were in attendance would pick up the prophetic mantle of Moses as he called out to Pharaoh saying, "Thus says the LORD, the God of the Hebrews, 'Let my people go, that they may serve me'" (Exod. 9:13). Like Moses, I figured that we, as pastors, could point those who are both physically and spiritually enslaved to the redemption that awaits them.

Throughout this book, you'll read lots of conversations. Like my conversation with Jessica, each conversation in this book is with someone who is considered an expert in their particular field of study. This person will serve as a guide for us as we continue to follow where God is leading us. The goal of each conversation is to help us to take one more step toward learning how Christ motivates vulnerable people, like you and me, to love other vulnerable people by becoming vulnerable to the point of death for us.

We can't do it on our own.

My First Trip to the World Trade Center

"What do you mean you can't find the address?" I muttered to the cab driver. "It's the World Trade Center!" By this point, I was irate. My girlfriend and I took a deep breath and calmly asked the driver to stop the car and to drop us off right where we were. Like it or not, we were going to be late.

As we finally found the building, made our way into the packed room, and began looking for open seats toward the back, the preliminary speaker was just finishing his introduction: "It is our pleasure to introduce Ambassador Luis deBaca, the Ambassador-at-Large to Monitor and Combat Trafficking in Persons."

As the Ambassador took the podium, the room, filled with a veritable "who's who" of New York City lawyers and Not-for-Profit leaders (and us), grew quiet. Every person seemed transfixed on the podium. The reason soon became evident.

Prior to being appointed to his then-current position by the Obama Administration, Ambassador deBaca had become known as one of the most decorated Federal prosecutors in the history of the United States. Beginning as a prosecutor in the Civil Rights Division of the Justice Department (DOJ), deBaca would be named the DOJ's Involuntary Servitude and Slavery Coordinator, leading to his becoming the nation's first Chief Counsel of the U.S. Human Trafficking Prosecutions Unit. During this time, he worked to develop and pioneer the "victim-centered" approach to investigating human trafficking cases. With his history of prosecuting federal human trafficking cases, he became instrumental in the drafting of the Trafficking Victims Protection Act of 2000. DeBaca's three-pronged strategy of prevention, prosecution, and protection has become the standard for those working in this field. From the time that he began working at the DOJ in 1993, deBaca worked to convict more than 100 traffickers and has helped rescue and rehabilitate more than 600 people trapped in modern-day slavery.[2]

As you might guess, this was more than a job for Louis deBaca. It is said that for each case he prosecuted, he would handwrite the Emancipation Proclamation on the outside of the folder; never forgetting the reason he became a prosecutor.

His passion for a slave-free world began during his childhood. E. Benjamin Skinner remarks that "as a Mexican-American child growing up in Iowa, deBaca described Edward R. Murrow's 1960 exposé of migrant labor exploitation, *Harvest Of Shame*, as 'our lunch counter,' a galvanizing moment akin to the early northern epiphanies about southern injustice during the Jim Crow era."[3]

As deBaca began to speak, he shared about one of his previous cases in New York City. The "Deaf Mexican case," as it has been called, was a landmark case with regard to opening the eyes of both New Yorkers and people around the country to the hidden nature of commercial exploitation.

Anthony DePalma, of the *New York Times*, describes it this way. "For most deaf Mexicans, there are no teletype telephone services, like those common in the United States. No doorbells have lights attached, no smoke alarms emit flashes and no television programs have closed captions. If they can find work, the deaf do the most menial of jobs, cleaning floors or sanding wood. The legal minimum wage is about $3 a day, but the deaf often find their employers paying them less than other workers. For many, begging on the subway or selling cards printed with the sign language alphabet is the way to survive here."[4]

It is not shocking for anyone who has been to New York City to see people selling trinkets. What is shocking, however, is the realization that not everyone begging and selling knickknacks is there by choice. Thousands of deaf Mexican workers were forced to sell these trinkets. If they were not able to sell a certain amount each day they would be beaten by their traffickers.[5] This went on unchecked because no one thought anything was wrong.

Deborah Sontag explains that "using written notes and sign language, the immigrants told the police that they had been forced by a man who had smuggled them into the United States to work 18-hour days as trinket vendors, selling $1 key chains on subways and airports. Some of the women made allegations of sexual assault, the police said; one had a black eye."[6]

As deBaca shared about this case, I was struck by how the traffickers preyed upon their vulnerability. Given the fact that these immigrants were undocumented and unable to communicate with those around them, they were easy prey. They were truly vulnerable.

As I thought about what he was saying, I couldn't shake the feeling that I had walked by those who were potentially trafficked and had no idea.

I have never forgotten that presentation. The manner in which deBaca addressed justice issues as well as vulnerability made an impact on me. For this reason, I could think of no one better to talk with me about human trafficking than Ambassador deBaca.

A Capitol Conversation

It was a cold Saturday morning as I looked out of my hotel window in Washington, D.C. I peered past the hunter green curtains and caught a glimpse of the Washington Monument in the distance. This setting was quite fitting since I was about to have a conversation with a United States diplomat. As I picked up my phone, something occurred to me—I had virtually no idea what to expect. Would he get behind the purpose of the book? Would he agree with the approach? I had no idea. The only thing that I knew at the moment was that the phone was ringing.

"Hello! It's Lou deBaca."

"Ambassador! How are you?"

"Raleigh, I'm doing well. So tell me a little bit about the project and what I can do to help."

After pausing a moment to gather my thoughts, I explained the reason for our phone call. "My goal so far in the book is to showcase that at its simplest form, human trafficking can be described as the exploitation of vulnerability for commercial gain. And for those of us who are people of faith, I believe that God is calling us to fight human trafficking by loving those most vulnerable."

I explained to the Ambassador that as we focus on these vulnerable populations, we are, in essence, targeting the very people that the traffickers target. I figured that since traffickers are looking for vulnerable people, it only stands to reason that the church should be looking for them as well.

"That's really the picture I want to paint throughout this book because I don't think that we need more people coming out of churches raiding massage parlors or trying to kick down doors of brothels and rescue people from a standpoint of superiority and 'having it all together.' I've actually heard people say this, Lou: 'Look at this sad and pitiful person who was trafficked. I need to help them.' I want each person that reads this book to realize that in our own ways, we're sad and pitiful too.

"Really, the primary theme we'll revisit throughout this book is that God motivates vulnerable people like you and me to love other vulnerable people by his own vulnerability for us."

"It's not an 'us and them' situation, regardless of our station in life; it's just kind of all of us. We are all broken. So, how can we walk alongside people instead of seeing them as problems to be fixed? I want to show that it is possible to actually be present and to really 'do life' with vulnerable people in a way that's not only biblically consistent, but also appropriate and dignifying."

"Excellent," said deBaca, "I think that there is a lot of good stuff in there to actually pull from. I mean, what's so interesting is the radical notion, and I have to warn you that I am very much colored by Catholicism."

Now, I had heard rumors that the Ambassador was a man of faith, but I had no idea that he was going to lead from his faith tradition. Seizing upon the idea of the book, deBaca began to articulate an approach for us as we seek to respond to the human trafficking in our communities.

DeBaca explained that we often try to play God by fixing everyone, but in doing so, we adopt a paternalistic approach—one that is actually inconsistent with the God of the Bible. "It's kind of at odds with the entire point of view that the most powerful entity in existence humbles [himself] by being born into an occupied people as a refugee to a poor family who has to eke out a very tenuous existence and then allows himself to be tortured and murdered for the redemption of all.

"Up until then," he continued, "everything had always been that there was this great big, huge, powerful thing that would smite those who needed smiting." But the gospel of Jesus "[turned] it on its head and [said], 'I too am vulnerable.' In fact, the vulnerability of God [in Christ] is what . . . makes it worthy of being a world religion.

"Just so you know who you're talking to, that is how I start as far as why I have faith and why I believe."

As Ambassador deBaca shared, I could tell that the vulnerability of God, as manifested through the life, death, and resurrection of Jesus, was the bedrock not only of his theology, but also of his methodology. For the Ambassador, our being rooted in a clear understanding of God's vulnerability in Christ is essential if we are to act accordingly. In other words, our theology actually matters as we begin to enter the arena of social engagement.

He went on to make this point: "You see that what flows out of that within the New Testament is not Jesus kicking down doors and yanking out people. I mean, there's obviously some tables that get knocked over at the temple, but there's quite a bit of 'leave that to the professionals.' Just leave that to the centurions. To the degree that the centurion has any play in Catholic tradition, it's very much that he's under civic authority, and that civic authority and God's authority are not the same thing."

His point is that our actions flow from what we believe. Whether we like it or not, what we believe about God will come out as we interact with those most vulnerable. Will we attempt to fulfill the "hero" archetype or will we present ourselves as a fellow sufferer in need of redemption? Are we going to act as the "centurion" or will we take on the divine mantle of vulnerability?

Ironically, the more that he talked from his Catholic perspective, the more that I began to reflect from my perspective as a Protestant. The idea of Christian vigilantism, or as he describes it, a "paternalistic rescue model," takes me to Martin Luther's teaching on the "theology of glory" and the "theology of the cross." Gene Edward Veith differentiates between the two theologies in this way:

A theology of glory expects total success, finding all the answers, winning all the battles, and living happily ever after. The theology of glory is all about my strength, my power, and my works. A theologian of glory expects his church to be perfect and always to grow. If a theologian of glory gets sick, he expects God to heal him.

And if he experiences failure and weakness, if his church has problems and if he is not healed, then he is often utterly confused, questioning the sufficiency of his faith and sometimes questioning the very existence of God.

But, Luther pointed out, when God chose to save us, He did not follow the way of glory. He did not come as a great hero-king, defeating his enemies and establishing a mighty kingdom on earth. Rather, He came as a baby laid in an animal trough, a man of sorrows with no place to lay His head. And He saved us by the weakness and shame of dying on a cross. Those who follow Him will have crosses of their own: "If anyone would come after me, let him deny himself and take up his cross and follow me" (Matt. 16:24).[7]

Essentially, our response to human trafficking will illustrate to which theology we ascribe. If we immediately jump on board saying, "We need to save the girls! Let's go beat down the doors of brothels," it's a safe bet that we are operating from a hidden theology of glory. Our inner "centurion" is begging to be let out so that he can conquer all the evil in our world.

Don't get me wrong—it isn't bad to want to rescue people; that's actually a very normal, human desire. But a theology of glory will place a premium on our role in the immediate "event" of rescue, while the theology of the cross directs our focus to see the idea of rescue as more of a process than a defining moment. In each of us is the desire to be a savior. We'd be lying if we said that there was never a time when we had salvific impulses. It's in our DNA.

The theology of the cross takes a slower, often more messy approach. It correctly points others to the cross of Jesus, our true Savior, who died the death reserved for a Roman criminal to bring us freedom. As we take the way of the cross, we acknowledge that Christ is our true emancipator and that we are called to follow him as we serve hurting people for the long haul.

Continuing to flesh out his foundation of faith, the Ambassador shared that "the idea of Christian raids have always struck me as people who want to help out. People who don't feel that they have the tools to help out with service provision or things like that, and yet it's very much assuming a role that Christ did not assume himself and did not impress upon all of us that we should assume."

"Rather," he explained, "there's the entire idea of—it's very funny to me, both with the prostituted woman and with the Samaritans, and for that matter much of the moving parts of the New Testament—Jesus allowing himself to be helped by outcasts or people who were thought of [as outcasts]. It's not necessarily him giving water to someone or him washing somebody else's feet. It's the idea that he kind of subordinates himself."

As I thought about it, I was reminded anew of the radical nature of Christ's earthly ministry. Christ not only served the poor, he allowed them to serve him as well. He could see his divine dignity in the spotted face of the leper. He could see the worth of the prostituted woman as she anointed his feet with oil. This is why he empowered the broken by allowing them to grow from a place of being passive recipients of grace to being active participants. This idea of empowerment is what is left out for many of us as we ponder Christian social action. In all of our well-intentioned rhetoric of "being a voice for the voiceless," we forget that these people already have a voice—we are just talking so loudly that no one can hear them.

Clarifying this point, the Ambassador added that "the interactions that Christ had with outcasts or with people we think of as vulnerable . . . may very well have been trafficking victims. Yet that is him humbling himself to be literally on their level, both physically and socially. Again, he was talking enough to everybody that was around him that had not yet conceptualized the fact that they were dealing with God in their midst . . . It was shocking that he would put himself on their level. What's mind-blowing . . . once you realize that he's not just a man, [is] that he's putting himself on their level as opposed to going over to the Romans or the folks who were ruling as puppet governments under the Romans. He wasn't going over and being like, 'Oh, I'm an equal of Herod.' He's going over and saying, 'I'm the equal of this Samaritan who you've been shoving.' That, to me, has to necessarily lead us to not only a much more service-oriented response to human trafficking, but frankly, it demands that we end up having survivor-led advocacy and that we listen to them and move to a position of them being colleagues as opposed to them being acted-upon rescues who are so lucky that we came and rescued them."

A Vulnerable Focus

This approach may not exactly get you headlines, but as you will see, it will yield lasting results. Having explained how his faith serves as a foundation, deBaca went on to articulate how a vulnerable approach should be our primary focus and concern.

"A perfect example of that is the Coalition of Immokalee Workers and the Fair Food Standards Council in Florida, where you've got people who had been enslaved. You've got other people who haven't been enslaved but had plenty of horrible things happen to them out in the fields who've come together and have put together an extremely effective model of worker-led advocacy that's actually making a difference.

"That's not because Greg Asbed, who just got the 2017 MacArthur Genius Grant, and Laura Germino were the kind of educated-white-folk American citizens who went out to help start the coalition (CIW). It's not because Greg and Laura came and rescued all these vulnerable people. It's because Greg and Laura saw the people that they were working with as colleagues and they, with those people, came together and made the Coalition of Immokalee Workers. . . . I think that's exactly the spirit that this needs to unfold and, frankly, those are the programs that end up being around for twenty years and making a huge impact on an entire sector.

"It's not a 'rescue and run' or even worse, a 'rescue and videotape and go raise money' kind of approach. I get that that's hard, and that's why the people who do it are special and unique, because it is hard, but I never read anything in the Bible or otherwise that said that living your faith was going to be the easy route.

"Anyway," he paused, "I'm sorry, and I apologize. That's probably not directly responsive to anything that you were planning to ask me."

"Are you kidding me?" I retorted. "I feel like that hit the nail on the head for the tone of this book. With that said, I want to tell you a little bit about my story."

After recounting the origin point of my journey with human trafficking, I shared how I became passionate about mobilizing churches to action while in West Virginia. "Shortly after that," I continued, "I ended up selling everything, moving to New York City to fight human trafficking, really not knowing what that meant. . . . Not too long after I got to New York City, I was invited to the World Trade Center to hear an ambassador speak by the name of Luis deBaca. From the moment you started talking, I was like, *this person is a person of faith.* I don't think you said anything explicitly, but I could tell."

As I finished talking, Lou waited a couple of moments before responding, "Well, we did a lot to get Passion off the ground and to support Louie Giglio and everything else, so I may have been even farther in the background than you know."

I had no idea. But deBaca wasn't done, he continued to share how he was intricately involved in the passing of the state legislation in West Virginia. I began to recognize that in each stage of my personal story, without knowing it, I had been impacted by the work of Louis deBaca.

Commenting on my journey, he added, "Your journey is the way that a sustainable journey ends up happening . . . I go around and speak all the time about how people need to take whatever they do for a living and apply it to human trafficking. I feel very strongly about that, that if you are a Certified Public Accountant, you should not then say, 'Well, I'm going to go raid brothels.' If you're a CPA, you shouldn't say, 'I'm going to build houses for a trafficking shelter.' It's like, if you're a CPA, you need to go down and help in financial literacy and budgeting classes for people who are trying to put their life together, or maybe you end up volunteering on the finance committee at an NGO (non-governmental organization). *Use the thing that you've been given and use the thing that you're good at.*"

It can be so easy to be tempted to believe that we are not qualified to engage modern-day slavery. But as I heard what Lou was saying, I was reminded that God has been shaping each of us through our own vulnerability for such a time as this. Each of us has gifts and abilities that we can use. I promise you that as we grow where we are planted, we will be able to do much more than if we tried to serve in a way that is not a fit with who we are.

The Victim-Centered Approach

I later asked Lou, "As you were named to that position of Ambassador-at-Large to Monitor and Combat Trafficking in Persons, you would employ a victim-centered approach. Could you share a little bit about that?"

He happily obliged. "One of the things about the victim-centered approach is that it very much looks to put oneself first and foremost into the shoes of the person who's gone through this and think about how you then do a respectful investigation. I think that's one of the things that people need to really focus on. When we first started talking about it, in a lot of ways it was basically trying to convince prosecutors and, to some degree, federal agents that they actually had the ability to make decisions in their cases that broke in favor of what the victim needed, as opposed to the interests of the state being paramount. Let me break that down for you. The notion of a trafficking victim as being primarily a witness to a crime who then ends up being controlled by the prosecution and the state so that it can get what it needs for its prosecution is basically the way especially sex trafficking victims had been treated for the previous 100 years. . . . If somebody wouldn't testify against their pimp or seemed to be reluctant to testify against their pimp, they'd get thrown in jail or they'd get held, charged with criminal contempt for refusing to talk to the grand jury, or they'd be held in a material witness ward because through that lens, that person is only of interest to the government as to the information that they could give.

"Now, everybody has a duty when they're subpoenaed to answer the government's questions. Clearly, I was a federal prosecutor for so long, I believe very strongly in that. But trafficking victims' ability to actually meet that, step up to that duty, has to be seen through the lens of the trauma that they went through and the specific psychological profile. . . . Their ability to comply with legal orders isn't always as well-formed as . . . if we assume that we're dealing with the member of a drug gang who's lying just because he wants to cover up his involvement."

"A lot of the victim-centered approach was simply a way to basically . . . put down those coercive tools and to start instead figuring out, *Well, what does this person need? Why does this person need it? How can I actually help provide it?*"

How did deBaca and others come to embrace this approach? He reflected, "We were gradually coming to the realization that the most important thing in this was restoring these folks and vindicating the violation of their rights as opposed to simply waiting."

The Trafficking Victims Protection Act of 2000

"Wow," I said. "What my readers would probably not know is that these cases that you worked—the Flores, the Deaf Mexican case, the Cadena case, and the Kil Soo Lee case—as you were doing this, you were crafting the TVPA. One of our mutual friends, Ben Skinner, he told me your cases and your influence were very critical to the TVPA. Is that accurate?"

"Yeah," he said in agreement. "I remember one day having to basically push back a meeting on legislative drafting up in Attorney General Reno's office because I couldn't get from the jail in Florida to the airport in Miami . . . we were like, 'Okay. Rat out your friends a little faster because I have to get to the airport.' Which, clearly, you don't say. I just remember changing the flight in the car, running south and dumping the car in Fort Lauderdale so that we could get back to D.C. Literally things that happened that morning in a local jail where we had a guard who was starting to [crack] in Florida were then directly incorporated by the Attorney General Janet Reno that afternoon in what we should do as far as the criminal permissions were concerned."[8]

That's when the Attorney General was officially tasked with finding a solution.

That solution was the TVPA 2000. The Trafficking Victims Protection Act (TVPA) of 2000, along with its subsequent reauthorizations, is the first comprehensive federal law enacted to address trafficking in persons.

The law provides a three-pronged approach of prosecution, protection, and prevention (the Three P's).

Prosecution

This involves passing laws that criminalize sex and labor trafficking. As these laws are enforced, the goal is to see the abusers face punitive measures, like time in prison and paying financial damages to the victims.

Protection

This involves recognizing and responding to victims. In essence, providing them with much-needed medical care and housing. In certain cases, they are placed in witness protection.

Prevention

This involves raising awareness of the problem of human trafficking both nationally and locally. As people become aware of the problem, they are freed to think differently and promote an approach that identifies as well as impacts the causal aspects of this injustice.[9]

In addition to the Three P's, much like the UN's Palermo protocols, the TVPA gives us clear definitions regarding the act, the means, and the purpose of human trafficking. It defines *sex trafficking* as the recruitment, harboring, transportation, provision, obtaining, patronizing, or soliciting of a person (ACT) for the purposes of a commercial sex act (PURPOSE), in which the commercial sex act is induced by force, fraud, or coercion, or in which the person induced to perform such an act has not attained eighteen years of age (MEANS).

Whereas *labor trafficking* is the recruitment, harboring, transportation, provision, or obtaining of a person for labor or services, through the use of force, fraud, or coercion for the purposes of subjection to involuntary servitude, peonage, debt bondage, or slavery.[10]

One important feature of the TVPA is that physical transportation from one location to another is not a requirement. Like I have said already, you don't have to be kidnapped and brought into another country or state to be trafficked. Trafficking simply doesn't imply movement. People can be trafficked without ever leaving their hometowns or their homes for that matter.

Though trafficking may not involve physical transport, it does always involve manipulation. Another feature the TVPA addresses is the subtle coercive tactics used by traffickers to manipulate victims, which for our purposes we will summarize as force, fraud, and coercion.[11]

Up to this point in the book, I have mentioned these three means of human trafficking, but allow me to explain in more detail:

Force

Force could include physical abuse, compelled substance abuse, emotional abuse, rape, and/or sleep deprivation. This is probably the most common means individuals think of when it comes to trafficking, but it is not the most frequently employed tactic for recruiting would-be victims.[12]

Fraud

In many cases, traffickers use fraud as a recruiting tool. Examples of fraud include but are not limited to promising a certain job overseas (only to charge exorbitant amounts of money to the victim and then traffic them into a brothel), a dangerous industrial job, a restaurant, a construction crew, door-to-door sales, a begging or peddling ring, and so on. Fraud is used as means of trafficking domestically as well. In many cases, those trafficked into the commercial sex industry have been tricked into doing a favor for an intimate partner, who is intentionally grooming them for prostitution.

Coercion

When a trafficker coerces a victim, he or she might withhold the victim's documents, threaten violence to loved ones, threaten to blackmail the victim by sending photographs of the victim to his or her family and friends, withhold drugs from the victim, threaten to call the authorities and have the victim deported, and so on.

The above means are used to carry out the exploitative practices of commercial sexual exploitation, labor exploitation, domestic servitude, and organ trafficking. In other words, people can be exploited for sex through prostitution or online pornography; exploited for labor through construction crews and in the service industry; exploited as domestic servants by being a nanny or forced to work in the hospitality industry; exploited through organ trafficking, where they are used primarily for their organs which are then sold on the black market.

As I have mentioned earlier, traffickers are intentionally looking for those with less power and influence. Using this power differential to their advantage, they exploit the weaknesses of their victims. As force, fraud, and coercion are used, we see the detrimental impact of the exploitative use of power and control. To give us more of an understanding of these methods, I have included the power and control wheel.[13]

The Rights Approach

Describing the strength of the TVPA 2000, Lou explained that "this is a rights approach. I think a lot of people end up seeing it as a morals crime, a vice crime, or even a transnational organized crime. All of those areas of criminal law flow from a societal control and protection law enforcement approach, whereas the 13th Amendment approach of the Civil Rights Division starts out from the notion that somebody has violated the human rights of someone else as guaranteed by the U.S. Constitution and that the federal government has a role to play in vindicating those rights.

"At the end of the day you can't get to the victim-centered approach on human trafficking if the seeds had not been planted in a rights-based approach . . . If you're doing the cases to maintain social order, then you end up treating the victims as pests who need to be deported or need to be put in jail. If you do this starting from [the position that] somebody's human rights were violated and that the state is the guarantor of those rights, then you necessarily have to address their restoration, their full participation, their human dignity. . . . We can continue to have the trafficking movement flow out of this rights language and this concept of core human rights. I think at that point, we continue to win."

Adding one closing note, the ambassador said, "This probably is going to sound strange for somebody who has spent twenty-five years using, of course, the power of the state to address this, [but] the only way that you end up fighting evil is with love and you have to be able to figure out how to do that with everything you have, which includes using federal money to support groups around the world, coming up with new ways to have it so that this is not matching hate with hate and it's not matching violence with violence. It also means bringing people to justice who need to be brought to justice. Mercy for the guilty can be cruelty to the innocent, but at the same time, *if you start from the notion that . . . every one of us is broken . . . that puts things in such a different place.*"

RECOGNIZING VULNERABILITY IN SCRIPTURE

There is nothing more ugly than a Christian Orthodoxy without understanding or compassion.

—Francis Schaeffer, *The God Who Is There*[1]

CHAPTER 4

FIG LEAVES, JUSTICE, AND A COUPLE OF MASKS

Anyone who prioritizes justice and mercy has lost sight of the gospel."

That's *exactly* what I thought. As an eager seminary student devouring what I read of the Bible, I could see two things very clearly: man's great need and God's great salvation.

Now, there were other things that I could not see so clearly. Unbeknownst to me, I had no concept for how God was calling us to love our vulnerable neighbors. I was blind to certain Scriptures—as if I had become an accidental Pharisee. No matter how many verse-by-verse studies I worked through, I was reading right past the texts that addressed vulnerability, justice, and mercy.

I don't think I am alone here. This can happen to any of us. The reason that this is so likely is because each of us tends to cling to certain Scriptures at the expense of others. We enjoy reading, memorizing, and studying the verses that are most germane to our needs in a given moment. Often the texts that are the most meaningful to us are the texts that hit home in the reality in which we live.

After I graduated seminary, the reality I lived began to crumble. The comfort that theological education afforded me gave way to a job market in the middle of an economic downturn. The year was 2007.

As I sent out résumés, I was greeted by silence. If I did receive an answer, it was something to the effect of, "We are not hiring right now. Good luck and God speed." My seminary hubris was now morphing into more of a sad bitterness. "I did all the right things, God, I checked all the boxes. Why can I not get a job? God, where are you?" In the months to come, God would show me that he was right down the street, in the place I least suspected.

That's when a friend from church reached out to me and told me about an orphanage in Louisville that was hiring. I had no previous orphanage experience, but figured that if there was a steady paycheck involved, I could figure it out. So I filled out the application and, much to my surprise, within a couple of weeks, I was hired.

Now, rather than having theological discussions over coffee, I was learning how to talk to children who had grown up in the foster care system. Each of these kids had experienced things that most of us could not imagine. Rather than receiving love and care from their parent or guardian, many were abused emotionally, psychologically, physically, and sexually.

With each shift that I worked, I began to see more clearly. I remember waking up one cold Christmas Day and realizing that all my friends and loved ones were in other states. And there I was, stuck in Louisville, because I was scheduled to work. I guess someone had to hold down the fort.

Feeling down in the dumps with literally no place to go for the ceremonial Christmas meal, I made my way to my neighborhood Chinese restaurant and had a quick bite before my shift. Side note: If you want to find vulnerable people, go to a Chinese restaurant on Christmas Day. We are all there.

After I finished my lo mein, I headed to the children's home. What I saw next absolutely blew my mind: children ripping open presents. Laughter and wrapping paper filled the halls. The joy they were experiencing was written on their faces. As I experienced God's joy in the faces of these children, I realized that God was right where he has always been—in the midst of those most vulnerable. *God was in the orphanage.*

I pondered how to address the needs of this new reality, so I began to search the Scriptures. I initially began looking for key verses that could help me better care for those who were in my charge. As God's love for vulnerable people became clearer to me, I started seeing things in the Scriptures that, for me, had previously lay undiscovered.

This reminds me of a story that Jim Wallis, a *New York Times* bestselling author, public theologian, and the founder of Sojourners, shares from time to time. Apparently, when he was in seminary, a classmate took an old Bible and cut out "every single reference to the poor." By the time they were done, the Bible was literally in shreds. Remembering that old Bible, Wallis says, "It was falling apart in my hands. It was a Bible full of holes. I would take it out to preach and say, 'Brothers and sisters, this is our American Bible.'"[1] For many of us, our Holy Bible is a Bible full of holes. Though we aim to understand the whole counsel of God, we often miss certain key themes revealed therein. Sadly, the fact remains that our lives cannot be impacted by a truth that we don't understand.

You may be like me. I believed (and still believe) beyond a shadow of a doubt that the gospel must be proclaimed to every living person on the planet. But in all of my passion for the proclamation of the gospel, I somehow missed God's divine directives for the demonstration of the gospel—for justice, mercy, and love of my vulnerable neighbors. In attempting to see souls saved, I lost sight of the beauty and holistic nature of the good news of Jesus Christ.

The Moment I Realized I Was a Hypocrite

Fast-forward to 2015. Though I began to see the themes of justice and mercy throughout the Scriptures, my thoughts on these matters were still in process. This fact became clear to me as I crossed the street at the corner of 71st and Broadway on the Upper West Side. I was on my way to an anti-trafficking coalition meeting in Manhattan, only to realize that I was missing the point. For some reason, it seemed the more I focused on human trafficking, the less I was focusing on vulnerable people.

But I wasn't alone. No matter where I went, I would meet people who had been called to "end slavery," but not called to help orphans, the widows, or the refugees. That's when my cynical nature began to rear its ugly head. "Do we have the same passion for those experiencing homelessness? Do we have this same passion for those trapped in the foster care system? How can we focus on human trafficking at the expense of all the vulnerabilities that feed into it?"

To make matters worse, I remember literally having to step over my homeless neighbor who was laying in the middle of the street so that I could get to meeting where we were addressing sex trafficking. I did not do this consciously, but I was in such a rush to "fight human trafficking" that I walked right past him. I missed the vulnerable person right in front of me. When the realization of this hit me, I recognized that there was a disconnect. I felt like a total hypocrite. I immediately stopped walking to the meeting and began praying, "God, how do you want your church to fight human trafficking? Help me understand."

In the months to come, God would show me his answer in the pages of my Bible. It was like no matter where I looked I found Scriptures pointing to those without power, status, and financial means—those who could be easily exploited. With each text I read I began to notice verses describing the "widow, orphan, and sojourner," and the "least of these." Now that the holes in my Bible were being filled, I was able to see God's passion for redemption in a new light. In other words, fighting human trafficking and other injustices from a standpoint of addressing vulnerability is nothing new. It's actually a biblical paradigm.

The Beginning of Vulnerability

In the opening chapters of Genesis, we find God creating everything out of nothing. With each act of creation, perfection is achieved and God declares what he creates to be "good." On the sixth day, God creates mankind. As the jewel of his creation, Adam was unlike the rest of the created order. Being created in God's own image, humanity stood apart.

It's here in the opening chapters of the Bible that we are confronted by our own inherent vulnerability. As Adam tends to the garden, he is dependent on God. From this posture of total reliance, he must trust God for the food that he eats, as well as the air that he breathes. It's clear that he can't exist without God.

Shortly after Adam is introduced, we discover that "it is not good that the man should be alone" (Gen. 2:18). Adam's vulnerability is further seen in his dependence on God to create a helpmate who's perfectly suited for him. The genius of God's design is that Adam, by virtue of his creation, can do some things without a partner, but ultimately cannot flourish in isolation.

Adam was hardwired for community. Look at the intimate communal language he uses to describe Eve: "This at last is bone of my bones and flesh of my flesh; she shall be called Woman, because she was taken out of Man" (Gen. 2:23). Adam is overjoyed. Finally there is someone with whom he can share his life. As we can tell from the language used, the lives of both Adam and Eve were created for intimate community with God and with each other.

Human beings were *created to be vulnerable.* Our vulnerability is not a plan B. It's not a result of the curse. As you can plainly see, we, as seen in our first earthly representatives, were made to be vulnerable long before Eve was tempted by the serpentine voice of the enemy. In other words, our perceived weakness and need for dependence on God and others is by divine design; it's a good thing.

God has created each of us with needs and limitations. For example, there is a reason that you cannot fly or breathe under water. God has designed you to perfectly fit his purpose for you—to represent him as you cultivate the creation in which he has put you. We may choose to believe that these limitations are inadequacies, but that's simply not true. The Creator's knowledge of his creation far surpasses our attempts to know ourselves. God knows exactly what we need to function in accordance with our design. God made Adam and Eve exactly as they were so that they could flourish in peace and harmony (*shalom*) in their Edenic paradise. Each perceived limitation is a reminder that, like Adam, we can call upon God to meet us at our point of need.

In the garden, we find the first man and woman were "both naked and were not ashamed" (Gen. 2:25). This is significant for us as we seek to understand vulnerability from a scriptural perspective. The fact that they were "naked" points to their need to trust someone other than themselves for their protection. They were free to be exposed because God walked among them.

In addition to being "naked," they also were "not ashamed." The Bible is one of the few places in the world where we can find these two phrases together. Often, when we think about the concept of nakedness, we are flooded with feelings of shame and inferiority, but in the garden, nakedness and weakness were not shameful at all. It was the way that things were supposed to be. Though they were physically exposed, they were covered by God's sovereign love and care, and they were fully accepted by one another.

Sin Warps Our Understanding of Vulnerability

But then Genesis 3 happened. Adam and Eve did the one thing they were commanded not to do. Eating from the tree of life was not a mistake as much as it was open rebellion. As a result, they recognized their nakedness. Experiencing shame and fear for the first time in human history, they quickly sowed fig leaves together to serve as ad hoc loincloths. Rather than experiencing joy in God's presence, they hid from him.

Because of their sinful disobedience, they were expelled from the paradise to which they had grown accustomed. Sin effectively inverted their natural desire to love God and each other. Now, rather than living with God and others in community, Adam and Eve were compelled to leave the only home they ever knew. Their vibrant relationship with God and each other was severed. Thus, relational brokenness became the new normal.

With the introduction of sin, our vulnerability was exacerbated. Sin, having effectively broken the world, impacts humans both individually and corporately. The disobedience witnessed in the fall had not only personal ramifications, but systemic ramifications as well.

What do I mean by "systemic ramifications"? The corporate effects of the fall are systemic or structural in nature. So, we use terms like "systemic injustice" to describe these effects. Tim Keller explains this well when he writes, "A system of economics or politics or justice can be selfish and oppressive, with many of the supporters of the system fairly unconscious of its effects."[2] In other words, individuals take part in cultural systems, each person bringing their brokenness with them. Ergo, institutions and even cultural mindsets can be unjust, just as we can individually think and act unjustly.

It is important to address this because individuals who are benefitting from systemic injustice are usually unaware that it is even taking place. To paraphrase what David Foster Wallace, author of *Infinite Jest*, said in a commencement speech: "If you ask a fish 'how's the water,' the fish will probably respond with, 'what in the world is water?'"[3]

For this reason, the world as we know it is haunted by "isms." Classism, racism, ethnocentrism, sexism, and ageism find their beginning in a tainted paradise. Every other "ism" feeds on our unchecked biases and prejudices that flow from our need for reconciliation with God.

Rather than running *to* God in our fragile moments, we, like our first parents, run *from* him. Rather than living in light of our natural weakness and dependence, we find ourselves sowing our own fig leaves. Sin has made each of us hyper-vulnerable while at the same time putting us in a combative place of independence, self-justification, and denial.

Our situation becomes more clear as we watch the de-evolution of humanity's first family. As we continue to read throughout Genesis, we find that Adam's household has become the epitome of a "dysfunctional" family. With each successive generation, we discover more and more drama. Having been separated from the intimate protection found in the presence of God, they chose to protect themselves at all costs, even if it resulted in the exploitation of others.

Life Outside of the Garden

From the outset, Adam and Eve begin to have domestic squabbles. As the curse dictates, Eve's desire shall be contrary to her husband, but he will rule over her (see Gen. 3:16). They no longer get along like they used to, and the thrill is gone. But their issues don't stop there. Their son Cain kills his brother, Abel, to cover the shame he felt when God accepted Abel's sacrifice over his.

Their descendants do not fare any better. After experiencing a flood destroying all of humanity because of their rampant disobedience, Noah, probably reeling from the trauma that he had experienced, gets drunk and falls asleep naked. His son Ham thinks this is hilarious. He laughs at his father's nakedness, while Shem and Japheth, Noah's other sons, do everything that they can do to honor their father by covering him without looking upon him (see Gen. 9). A mere seven chapters after Adam and Eve in the garden, there is no more "naked and not ashamed."

Then you have Babel. To cover their feelings of inferiority, "all the inhabitants of earth" gathered together at Babel to build a tower. "Come, let us build ourselves a city and a tower with its top in the heavens, and let us make a name for ourselves, lest we be dispersed over the face of the whole earth" (Gen. 11:4). They came together to protect themselves and to find their significance in their self-made superiority. If you think that this city and tower were built without exploiting others, you have another thing coming.

This list would be incomplete without mentioning Tamar, a two-time widow without children. In her culture, she would be rendered destitute if she remained in her current state. Given that her father-in-law failed to give her in marriage to his youngest son, she took matters into her own hands. She covered herself with a veil to disguise herself as a prostituted woman. She then presented herself to her father-in-law and got pregnant—all to reclaim her dignity. You can't make this stuff up.

In every episode that we see post-fall, we find people running from their weakness and vulnerability, all the while seeking "saviors" that only lead them away from the one who can actually save them. Though it looks different in every case, most of our sin involves us running from "nakedness" in search of something to cover it up.

We have a track record for doing anything we can to cover up our vulnerability—even if it means taking advantage of those more vulnerable than us to do it—and we humans are still in the business of wearing fig leaves and masks.

In our sin, we do everything we can do to live a meaningful and self-protected life. But, whether we know it or not, we leave a wake behind us that ultimately impacts those less fortunate. Whether we park in the handicap spot just for a few minutes so we can "get a few things" at the store or we move out of our neighborhoods because the community is changing, we are affecting our most vulnerable neighbors while trying to address our immediate "needs."

The Bible, unlike other ancient texts, does not shy away from vulnerability. Rather than solely celebrating power, we find God revealing that he loves those mired in vulnerability to the extent that he brings justice to those in need.

Justice and the God Who Loves It

According to Bethany Hoang, author of *Deepening the Soul for Justice*, "fighting injustice can be excruciatingly hard work. It can be exhausting. It is relentless. But Jesus offers to make our burdens light, even the burden of fighting injustice. . . . Seeking justice begins with seeking God: our God who longs to bring justice; our God who longs to use us." In other words, "seeking justice doesn't begin at the door of a brothel. Seeking justice begins with seeking the God of justice."[4]

The word *justice* is found more than two hundred times in the Bible. Its Hebrew form, *mishpat*,[5] can be defined several different ways, including "to treat people equitably," or "to give them what they are due."[6] The Greek form, *dikaiosyne*, is most commonly translated as "righteousness" or "the state of someone as he ought to be."[7]

Author and theologian Nicholas Wolterstorff bases his definition of justice on *rights*. For example, if one is given what he or she deserves based upon the rights inherent to being human, then justice is shown.[8] Therefore, when rights essential to being human, created in the image of God, are denied, injustice occurs.[9] In his book *Generous Justice*, Tim Keller offers an even simpler definition: "justice is care for the vulnerable."[10] Basically, this is intentionally loving the vulnerable person in front of you, treating them as they deserve to be treated.

As I have hinted earlier, injustice happens when those with power and status exploit those without power and status. Justice, on the other hand, is the right use of power. At its root, it means that those with power use their time, treasure, talents, and privilege to promote the flourishing of those who lack power.[11] We see this explicitly in Psalm 82:2–4: "How long will you judge unjustly and show partiality to the wicked? Give justice to the weak and the fatherless; maintain the right of the afflicted and the destitute. Rescue the weak and the needy; deliver them from the hand of the wicked."

We also see the prophet Micah calling us to the same action: "He has told you, O man, what is good; and what does the LORD require of you but to do justice, and to love kindness [mercy], and to walk humbly with your God?" (Micah 6:8). God is calling those who follow him to give to others what they are due. To love justice and mercy as we walk with him. To meet the needs in front of us (mercy) as well as address the causes of those needs (justice). He calls us to join him in justice and mercy because he loves justice.

But justice is not merely something that God loves; it's inherent in his character. God is a God of justice. Justice, being an attribute of God, characterizes and colors everything God says or does. He is infinitely just. Realize, then, how significant it is that the biblical writers introduce God as "a father of the fatherless and protector of widows" (Ps. 68:5). This is who God is: he identifies with the powerless. He takes up their cause.[12]

In his seminal work, *Experiencing God*, author Henry Blackaby explains that for the Christian, the key to discovering the will of God for one's life is to "find where God is at work and to join him there."[13] The Scriptures testify that if we desire to find where God is at work, we need only to identify those who are most vulnerable to exploitation. Who are the "widows, orphans, and sojourners" in our community? Who are the "least of these" among us? In essence, the believer does not have to bring the God of justice to those who are hurting because he has already arrived and is inviting us to participate.

God identifies those most vulnerable.

Though God shows no partiality and is just in all his dealings with mankind, we can see throughout the Scriptures that he loves those most vulnerable. God's eyes are opened to the plight of the poor. He sees what others fail to see. The psalmist writes, "Why does the wicked renounce God and say in his heart, 'You will not call to account'? But *you do see, for you note mischief and vexation, that you may take it into your hands; to you the helpless commits himself; you have been the helper of the fatherless*" (Ps. 10:13–14, emphasis mine).

In the Exodus narrative, God's greatest picture of redemption in the Old Testament, God speaks to Moses at the burning bush, saying, "*I have surely seen the affliction of my people who are in Egypt and have heard their cry because of their taskmasters. I know their sufferings,* and I have come down to deliver them out of the hand of the

Egyptians" (Exod. 3:7–8, emphasis mine). The psalmist reminds us of this truth: "For he delivers the needy when he calls, the poor and him who has no helper. He has pity on the weak and the needy, and saves the lives of the needy. From oppression and violence he redeems their life, and precious is their blood in his sight" (Ps. 72:12–14). Echoing this scriptural refrain, James, the brother of Jesus, encourages the Jerusalem church, "Listen, my beloved brothers, has not God chosen those who are poor in the world to be rich in faith and heirs of the kingdom, which he has promised to those who love him?" (James 2:5). God sees and identifies with those who are often unseen.

God identifies with those most vulnerable.

Throughout the Old Testament, God is actively not only identifying vulnerable people, but identifying *with* them. We see this clearly in the book of Proverbs. "Whoever oppresses a poor man insults his Maker, but he who is generous to the needy honors him" (Prov. 14:31). "Whoever is generous to the poor lends to the LORD, and he will repay him for his deed" (Prov. 19:17). "The rich and the poor meet together; the LORD is the Maker of them all" (Prov. 22:2).

But this is not a concept found solely in the Proverbs or the Old Testament; God also identifies with the vulnerable through the incarnation of Christ. In what theologians call the *condescension*, Christ makes himself vulnerable to the point of becoming like those he came to save. "Foxes have holes, and birds of the air have nests," Jesus said, "but the Son of Man has nowhere to lay his head" (Matt. 8:20). The second person of the Trinity was functionally homeless.

Jesus drives this point of identification home further in what has become known as the parable of the sheep and the goats. Jesus adds:

> "'For I was *hungry* and you gave me food, I was
> *thirsty* and you gave me drink, I was a *stranger* and
> you welcomed me, I was *naked* and you clothed me,

I was *sick* and you visited me, I was in *prison* and you came to me.' Then the righteous will answer him, saying, 'Lord, when did we see you hungry and feed you, or thirsty and give you drink? And when did we see you a stranger and welcome you, or naked and clothe you? And when did we see you sick or in prison and visit you?' And the King will answer them, 'Truly, I say to you, as you did it to one of the least of these my brothers, you did it to me.'" (Matt. 25:35–40, emphasis mine)

Christ, who from eternity past was not vulnerable, took on vulnerability to the point that he could identify with all of those who are vulnerable. The six vulnerabilities listed appear to summarize all of the vulnerabilities of those with whom he identifies.

Paul, picking up on this idea, reminds the Corinthian church "that though [Jesus] was rich, yet for your sake he became poor, so that you by his poverty might become rich" (2 Cor. 8:9). God identifies with those that could be exploited and he invites his followers to participate.

God challenges his people to join him.

"You shall not mistreat any widow or fatherless child. If you do mistreat them, and they cry out to me, I will surely hear their cry, and my wrath will burn, and I will kill you with the sword, and your wives shall become widows and your children fatherless." (Exod. 22:22–24)

A righteous man knows the rights of the poor; a wicked man does not understand such knowledge. (Prov. 29:7)

Open your mouth for the mute, for the rights of all who are destitute. (Prov. 31:8)

Learn to do good; seek justice, correct oppression; bring justice to the fatherless, plead the widow's cause. (Isa. 1:17)

"If you pour yourself out for the hungry and satisfy the desire of the afflicted, then shall your light rise in the darkness and your gloom be as the noon-day." (Isa. 58:10)

Let the thief no longer steal, but rather let him labor, doing honest work with his own hands, so that he may have something to share with anyone in need. (Eph. 4:28)

"Fear not, little flock, for it is your Father's good pleasure to give you the kingdom. Sell your possessions, and give to the needy. Provide yourselves with moneybags that do not grow old, with a treasure in the heavens that does not fail, where no thief approaches and no moth destroys. For where your treasure is, there will your heart be also." (Luke 12:32–34)

Religion that is pure and undefiled before God the Father is this: to visit orphans and widows in their affliction, and to keep oneself unstained from the world. (James 1:27)

If anyone has the world's goods and sees his brother in need, yet closes his heart against him, how does God's love abide in him? (1 John 3:17)

As you can tell from the verses listed above, God, who identifies with those most vulnerable, commands his followers to do the same. He does so throughout the entire scope of redemptive history in his Word. As a matter of fact, God meets the needs of the oppressed *through* his people. Through the tangible love and care of the church, God answers the cries of the oppressed. Those who have truly "gotten the point" of their religion will naturally find themselves loving their neighbors. This is why Jesus appears to be so indignant with the Pharisees and the religious teachers of his day.

In Matthew 23, Jesus pronounces judgment on the scribes and Pharisees: "Woe to you, scribes and Pharisees, hypocrites!" (v. 23). Notice the wording here. Jesus calls them hypocrites. In the original Greek, we find a peculiar word picture here. It's of someone wearing a mask to cover his true identity. The Pharisees were found guilty of covering themselves to the point that they exposed their neighbors. Jesus further strips them of their fig leaves as he explains, "For you tithe mint and dill and cumin, and have neglected the weightier matters of the law: justice and mercy and faithfulness. These you ought to have done, without neglecting the others. You blind guides, straining out a gnat and swallowing a camel!" (vv. 23–24). Though they looked the part externally, they neglected what really mattered—the weightier matters of God's law. Though they had all the external trappings of religion, the Pharisees were dead on the inside—whitewashed tombs.

Christ's rebukes of the Pharisees show us just how close justice is to God's heart! If the Pharisees had truly loved God, they would have loved justice, because God is just. However, their disregard for the poor, the sick, the widow, the sojourner, and the unclean is evidenced in that in all of their reading and studying, they failed to grasp and obey the heart of God's law.[14]

Additionally, in the early church, justice was not a suggestion as much as an expectation. The commands to love God, to love others, and to do justice are found in the law of God. These imperatives fall on each of us, yet we fail to keep them. Christ kept the law in its totality, perfectly, and suffered punishment on our behalf. This good news did for us what study and meditation cannot do. It realigns our focus to love God and others before ourselves.

But What Happens When We Don't See Justice?

In this chapter, we see that God has a passion for justice and mercy; however, we also see the ever-present brokenness around us. How can we reconcile the goodness and justice of God with suffering that we see happening on a global scale through human trafficking? Gary Haugen, president of the International Justice Mission, offers a unique perspective on this frequently asked question in his book, *Terrify No More*:

> For many of us, the ugliness of abuse and oppression in our world leads us, quite understandably, to ask: Where is God in the midst of such suffering? Even if we have drifted to a place in life where we rarely address God, there is something about the rank cruelty of exploitation and the naked brutality of human violence that seems to lift our objection almost involuntarily to something larger and beyond ourselves . . .
>
> But over time, having seen the suffering of the innocent and the crushing of the weak all around the world, my plea has changed. More and more I find myself asking not, Where is God? but, Where are God's people?
>
> Given all the power and resources that God has placed in the hands of humankind, I have yet to see any injustice of humankind that could not also be stopped by humankind. I find myself sympathizing with a God who, speaking through the ancient prophet, told his people, "You have wearied the LORD with your words . . . by saying, . . . 'Where is the God of justice?'" (Mal. 2:17 NIV). *Increasingly, I feel quite sure of the whereabouts of God. My tradition tells of a Father in heaven who*

*refused to love an unjust world from a safe distance,
but took his dwelling among us to endure the humility of false arrests, vicious torture, and execution.*

This is the God who could be found as *"a man
of sorrows, and familiar with suffering"* (Isa. 53:3
NIV). The more I have come to know him, the
harder it has become for me to ask such a God to
explain where he has been. In fact, surprisingly, I
don't generally hear the victims of abuse doubting
the presence of God either. Much more often I
hear them asking me, "Where have *you* been?"[15]
(emphasis mine)

Wrestling with his own vulnerability, Christ called out to the
Father in the Garden of Gethsemane. As he prayed, he knew his purpose: to right the wrongs that began in another garden. To reconcile
sinful humans, like you and me, to God and each other. For this
reconciliation to take place, Christ would be betrayed and sold out
to the Roman authorities. To cover our sin, he was stripped, beaten,
and crucified. God's answer to injustice was to pour out his wrath
on Christ, who though sinless became our substitute. At the cross,
God's desire for justice was satisfied. Again, we see that vulnerable
people are now free to love other vulnerable people because Christ
was made vulnerable for them. In light of this theme, as people of
the cross, we find ourselves journeying toward a just kingdom.

CHAPTER 5

JOURNEYING TOWARD A JUST KINGDOM

Jesus, preparing to give his first public address in his hometown of Nazareth, unrolled the scroll of Isaiah, finding his text. From the outset, Jesus wanted his hearers to be clear on his mission. "The Spirit of the Lord is upon me," he read aloud, "because he has anointed me to proclaim good news to the poor. He has sent me to proclaim liberty to the captives and recovering of sight to the blind, to set at liberty those who are oppressed, to proclaim the year of the Lord's favor" (Luke 4:18–19).

Effectively announcing his kingdom mission statement, "he rolled up the scroll and gave it back to the attendant and sat down. And the eyes of all in the synagogue were fixed on him. And he began to say to them, 'Today this Scripture has been fulfilled in your hearing'" (vv. 20–21). In front of those who had known him all of his life, Jesus declares that he is the King, the Messiah they were expecting. At this point, Jesus dropped the proverbial mic and sat down.

In his first public sermon, Christ points those in the synagogue to the plight of those most vulnerable, and his plan for their redemption. Using designations like "poor, captives, the blind, and the oppressed," Christ explains that for these people, bad news is not simply a possibility, it's a reality. And it's into this reality that he has entered, bringing "good news."

When those in his hometown heard what Jesus had just said, they were amazed. Don't gloss over this part. Those attending the synagogue that Saturday were taken off guard, and for good reason.

It's easier to understand their reaction if we look at the historical and cultural context. Ever since 586 BC, Israel had been under foreign occupation. Assyria, Babylon, and now Rome had ruthlessly oppressed the people of Israel. As you would imagine, political tensions were at fever pitch. The people of Israel wanted freedom and were waiting for a messiah, a militaristic king, who would ultimately deliver them from Rome and re-establish their nation.

It's in this context that Jesus announces that he is the King that they are expecting. But he has come in a way that they didn't expect. He came bringing the kingdom of God in two stages. On one hand, the kingdom is already here, because the King came to earth; but on the other hand, we still experience suffering and oppression, so we know that the kingdom is not yet here in its fullness. Theologians call this paradox, inaugurated Eschatology, or the "already/not yet."

Quoting Isaiah 61, Jesus explains the good news: he is bringing a just kingdom into an unjust world. Taking a prophecy describing Israel's long-expected messiah, he applies it to himself. "The Spirit of the Lord is upon *me*, because he has *anointed* me" (emphasis mine).

The concept of anointing carried with it a commission. In ancient Israel, prophets and kings were anointed with oil and commissioned to carry out a certain task: for some it was to be God's mouthpiece to speak to God's people; for others it was to lead politically. Here, Jesus is set apart to do both. Jesus is essentially saying that he is the King who will fix the broken world by bringing a kingdom that is characterized by justice, a place where no one is taken advantage of and all people are treated with equity.

As we discovered in chapter 4, justice can be best defined as rendering to others what they are due. Picking up on this idea, Dr. Cornel West, an author, philosopher, and Ivy League professor, is famously quoted as saying, "Justice is what love looks like in public." This notion of "love made public" is made manifest as the kingdom of God is revealed. Christ has come to bring a kingdom community where love, fairness, and justice are normative behavior; where these "ideals" are lived out daily.[1] This kingdom is a place where God's people live in right relationship to him and to each other. In this new eschatological community, no one is marginalized, because all are equal. No one is vulnerable, because everyone has each other's best interests at heart.

Good News for the Poor

Reflecting on the concept of poverty in the Old Testament, the word "poor" in many cases refers to those who are materially poor. Without money, food, and access to proper medical care, they were unable to meet their own needs and were thus susceptible to a slew of exploitative tactics, like forced prostitution or forced labor. In their condition, their only hope was God. For this reason, we find God repeatedly calling the Israelites to meet the needs of the "widow, orphan, and sojourner."

But in the New Testament, especially Luke and Acts, the Greek word for the "poor" also refers to those trapped in spiritual poverty. As Jesus quotes Isaiah 61, he refers to these two separate contexts simultaneously. With that said, this "good news" is that Jesus is bringing a salvation that is holistic. He desires to save us from material poverty as well as spiritual poverty. Christ didn't come to earth and become poor like us to only redeem a part of us. He wants to save us in our entirety. In other words, he cares about our physical needs as well. The arrival of the present/future kingdom of God is proof.

Under his reign, there will also be liberty for the captives, sight to the blind, and liberty to the oppressed, and the year of the Lord's favor will be proclaimed. For anyone who was listening to Jesus that Saturday, the "year of the Lord's favor" would have rung a bell. This was a time written of in the Mosaic Law when anyone serving as a slave in Israel to pay off family debt would be freed to return to their families. Jesus is telling us that where we are headed, slavery is just a memory; as a matter of fact, this will be the only dominion in history not built on the backs of slaves. Those of us trusting in Christ can rest assured that our physical and spiritual debts will be cancelled. Here again, Christ is inviting us to experience true freedom.

This desire for freedom was what each of those to whom Jesus ministered directly earnestly hoped for. As you think about those to whom Jesus ministered during his earthly ministry, the following will all come to mind:

- The unclean—lepers, prostituted women, those forbidden from entering the temple, demon-possessed
- The poor
- Widows
- Children
- The sick—paralytics, lepers, dying, dead, the woman with the bleeding disorder
- The social outcasts—tax collectors, sinners, Gentiles, Samaritans, Roman occupiers[2]

Though Christ healed many during his time on earth, there were many that he didn't heal. The point of these miracles was not to eradicate poverty or sickness; if that were the case, then Jesus' ministry was a failure. Jesus knew that the presenting issues of those listed were not always their prevailing issues. In fact, they were just preludes to a deeper brokenness, the kind that could not be healed superficially. Instead, the purpose of these miraculous acts was to attest to his divinity and kingship. Each act of healing was essentially a billboard displaying what could be expected out of this "already/not yet" kingdom.

Life in the Already

Christ came to address physical captivity and oppression as well as our slavery to sin. As we submit to the kingly reign of Jesus Christ, we find ourselves not only being forgiven of our sin and rebellion, but reborn as citizens of this new divine nation. As the righteousness of Christ becomes our banner, we are made alive spiritually, given the Holy Spirit as a reminder that the kingdom is near and that we have not been forgotten.

When the kingdom comes one day in its fullness, injustice will be done away with completely and sin will be no more. Ultimate justice, ultimate *shalom* (a state of peace and flourishing, of all things being as they should be socially, economically, and spiritually) will be experienced in the physical presence of Christ.

Finishing his sermon, Jesus appears to have prematurely stopped quoting Isaiah. If you continue to read Isaiah's prophecy, the very next phrase is that the messiah will bring "the day of vengeance of our God; to comfort all who mourn" (Isa. 61:2).

Why on earth would Jesus leave out this important and expected piece? I mean, this was his closer. The crowd would have erupted with joy at the thought that he was to bring an abrupt end to their subjugation.

As I read this text, I think that Jesus leaves the wrath of God out of his first sermon for two reasons. First, the "day of vengeance" will come, but it will not come until the kingdom comes in its fullness. This "day of vengeance" is reserved for the "not yet."

The second and less apparent reason is that Christ would experience the "day of vengeance" in our place on the cross. Though sinless, Christ took the punishment that we as sinners deserved. Christ died for all who were astray—the liars, the cheaters, the pornographers, the idolaters—all of us. The only person to ever truly live a just life died for the unjust. This is the good news of the kingdom—Christ crucified for us. But it's only good news for you if you receive it; we receive it through repentance and faith. "From that time Jesus began to preach, saying, 'Repent, for the kingdom of heaven is at hand'" (Matt. 4:17). Both repentance and faith are two sides of the same coin. Repentance literally means to turn from sin, and faith means to turn to God. Repentance is turning from the "kings" or functional saviors in which you have trusted and faith is turning to the risen King, Lord, and Savior. In faith, we are believing that though we have rebelled against God, Christ died for us to make us right with God the Father.

But as we bow the knee to Christ, we wait, finding ourselves living on the "already" side of the "not yet." In this community of blood-bought believers, everything that we do to serve our neighbor illustrates our hope in this promised future. To Quote Russell Crowe's character Maximus, from the movie *Gladiator*: "Brothers, what we do in life echoes in eternity." Each of us, who have become subjects of the king, are living out our lives in the "already" with every act of love and service on behalf of others being an investment in the "not yet."

Shallow versus Deep Justice

In the meantime, we are free to love our neighbor not from a place of compulsion but willingness. As citizens of the kingdom, we should find ourselves desiring to care for our neighbors in need.

But this is much more than just giving a dollar to the homeless man that we walk by. Kingdom justice looks much different than its counterfeits. As we begin to live out of our newfound freedom and seek to act justly, we must avoid the incipient patterns of shallow "justice." Rather, with the kingdom in our sights, we are enabled to love deeply.

Justice that is shallow tends to give credence to our inner but often unseen "messiah complexes." As I explained earlier, painting ourselves as the hero keeps us from seeing and directing others to the true hero. Therefore, in our attempts to "save" the perishing, we drive them farther away from their true Savior. Pushing ahead with this selfish approach, we may accidentally end up dehumanizing the person for whom we are seeking to care. By attempting to "rescue" people, we end up seeing them as commodities and not as fellow human beings imbued with the same worth and dignity as us. This kind of justice, which is often built around an event of some kind, is something we always tend to do *for* others, expecting immediate results.

But the justice of the kingdom is deep. As we follow a crucified Lord, we take our "messiah complexes" to the cross. For us, justice means that God will do the rescuing. As a matter of fact, he had to rescue each of us and has, therefore, proven that he is the only one fit for the task. Yes, he may use us, but in the end, the results are all his.

This type of justice reclaims and restores the dignity of others as we treat them as "people" from whom we can learn and not "projects" that must be completed. This deeper kingdom justice is more of a lifestyle than an event. Rather than being accomplished in isolation, it is collaborative in nature. Because of Christ, we can love others without any guarantee of reciprocity with the goal to create an atmosphere of empowerment where vulnerable people are encouraged to follow Christ and serve others.[3]

Ken Wytsma, author of *Pursuing Justice*, describes this way of life saying, "the kingdom of God is an upside-down kingdom. It beckons us to gamble all, to trust radically, to come and die so that we might live—to give our lives away. Giving life away is a paradox. It's losing so we can win. It's giving so we can receive. It's risking for security. It's faith. The kingdom of God means living that tension."[4]

The Signs of the Kingdom

As John the Baptist suffered in prison, he sent his disciples to Jesus with a question. "Did I get this right? Did I zig when I should have zagged? Tell me that I was right about the kingdom of God." John's disciples asked Jesus, "Are you the one who is to come, or shall we look for another?" Jesus answered them, "Go and tell John what you hear and see: the blind receive their sight and the lame walk, lepers are cleansed and the deaf hear, and the dead are raised up, and the poor have good news preached to them. And blessed is the one who is not offended by me" (Matt. 11:3–6). To answer John's doubts, Jesus gave him the signs that the kingdom had come to earth in the person of the King.

Living in light of this kingdom, we carry on this focus. We live justly, treating others as they deserve to be treated. A kingdom mentality wars against our desires to pick and choose the "best" from among our community and allows us to love the people God has placed in our path. All the while, in serving others we learn that in many cases the person we were seeking to help is the person God has called to help us.

Commenting on this message of Jesus, Tim Chester, the author of *Good News to the Poor*, shares that "Jesus proclaimed a message of liberation. It is a political message, not in the sense of fomenting revolution now (see Matt. 5:9, 39, 41, 44) but in the sense of witnessing to the hidden revolution that will be revealed at the last day. It is a message of future liberation. But the new regime has begun among Christ's community of the broken. The Christian community is the place of liberation."[5]

An Interview Interrupted

I had arrived early to prep for a meeting with my new friend Joy. As the barista poured my coffee, I couldn't help but look outside through the glass doors of the kitschy coffee shop. It was a beautiful spring day in New York City, so when Joy walked in, we both knew what would happen next: we were going to sit outside. With our coffees in hand, we found what appeared to be the least sturdy table in the entire park and promptly sat down. Once we were situated, we dove right into a conversation.

Joy Farrington, author of *Broken by Beauty*, began to share how she came to dedicate her life to helping those trapped in commercial sexual exploitation. But as she was talking, we were interrupted.

Out of the corner of my eye, I could see a man with a cane slowly making his way toward us. "Excuse me, I don't want to bother you. I'm sorry, I don't want this to be awkward, but do you have any money that you could spare?" By this point, he was standing right next to the table. "I'm sorry, man," I replied, "I've got nothing on me." "It's okay," he assured me, "don't worry about it. Again, I'm sorry that I interrupted you both."

As he walked away, I stopped him. "Sir, what's your name?" He was shocked that I would attempt to keep the conversation going. Turning around to face me, he asked his own question: "Are you a Christian, because only Christians ask me my name?"

"Yes, I am a Christian and so is my friend, Joy."

"My name is Jeff and I'm a Christian as well. God has done a miracle in my life." Intrigued, I asked him to take a seat and join us.

"Jeff, would you be willing to share your story with us?"

Over the next ten minutes or so, Jeff shared how one day he woke up in the emergency room. Of course, this wasn't his plan when he began his shift that morning at a construction site where he worked as a contractor. Apparently, he slipped while using a nail gun. The emergency room physician looked him in the eye as he started becoming more alert. "Do you believe in God?"

"No."

"Well, you should. Because of your accident, there is a nail imbedded in your brain, you shouldn't be alive right now, much less understanding the words that I'm saying." As he was discharged, Jeff couldn't shake the idea that God was somehow at work in his life. From that point on, he began going to church and eventually trusted in Christ.[6]

Looking at the two of us, Jeff said, "I don't have much . . . but I do have a story. I try to tell this story as much as I can to help others."

A Disrupting Pause

God allows disruptions to slow us down and keep us from drifting too far in the wrong direction. As we continue to examine the reality that we are journeying toward a just kingdom, it's a good idea that we pause and reflect for a moment. The problem that many of us face is that as we care for others, we fail to care for ourselves. Tending to allow the weight of the world to rest squarely on our shoulders, we naturally miss the negative impact that working hard for justice can have on us.

Therefore, God has given us a scriptural rhythm in order to slow us down and refocus us. This rhythm of crying out to God reminds us of our inability as we depend on God's ability to bring justice. This act of dependence is a staunch reminder that the world is simply not ours to save.

The idea of petitioning God to alleviate the suffering of others is called a lament. Given that this section is entitled "Recognizing Vulnerability in Scripture," I have couched the next interview within one of David's psalms of lamentation.

Like Jeff, David shares his story to remind others of God's love. If we look at Psalm 41, we will notice that this psalm has an important place in the Psalter. It's the last psalm of the first section of Psalms. Here we find David looking back over his life. He knows how God blessed him as he cared for the poor. He also remembers his own pain and poverty and how God met him in the middle of it. In this psalm, David lays out a paradigm for lament.

A Call to Help

In these first three verses, David reminds us that we are considered blessed as we consider the needs of the poor. "Blessed is the one who considers the poor!" For David, the word *consider* doesn't mean mere mental assent, but practical help. He is saying that we are "blessed" as we get our hands dirty loving vulnerable people. David continues, "In the day of trouble the LORD delivers him; the

Lord protects him and keeps him alive; he is called blessed in the land; you do not give him up to the will of his enemies. The Lord sustains him on his sickbed; in his illness you restore him to full health" (Ps. 41:1–3).

What David is saying here is counterintuitive to everything we know from experience. Naturally, we feel that we can only survive if we protect ourselves and our families from those who would threaten us or our lifestyles. But notice what David is saying: *Your protection doesn't fall on you.* Because of God's grace, you are now freed from the incessant need to protect yourself, and are set free to protect others. As we turn our focus from ourselves, we will be able to focus on the needs of others.

As Jeff walked away, Joy and I were in complete story-telling mode. So she picked up her story from where she had left off. As a child, her family moved to the Red Light district of London. Having experienced the radical grace of God, her parents felt the desire to share it with those in need—specifically with pimps (sex traffickers), sex buyers, and prostituted women.

"It wasn't out of the ordinary for us to invite pimps and prostituted women to share a meal with us," she explained. She shared about one particular day when a neighbor named Val came to visit. When Val left, Joy realized that she couldn't find her phone anywhere. She tells the story in her book like this:

> I soon found myself marching down the street to Val's house. I stood outside the white door and knocked firmly, the ball of upset and anger causing my stomach to churn. After a second knock it opened to reveal Tom, the pimp who resided there, looking a little surprised to see me but smiling nonetheless. "Is Val here?" I looked at him straight in the eyes, giving no room for any attempt at lies. "Yeah . . . she's in her room. I don't think she's able to take visitors though." "She took my phone and I'm here to get it back, please." I was determined

to get what I came for and, after looking at me for a second, Tom let me in. "I'm not sure she has your phone anymore, babe, but you can go up and speak to her if you like," Tom pointed up the stairs, directing me to the right. I began making my way up the steep staircase, in a house that had seen better days, still too fired up to really think about where I was and the surroundings in which I now found myself. I followed the narrow corridor round to the right, past a closed door, to a bedroom with a door that stood slightly ajar. I opened it to find Val sprawled on the bed as if she'd been thrown there by some mightier force and hadn't found the strength to move herself since. Her head was half propped up on the wall that the bed was against, her mouth partly open and what I could see of her eyes revealed emptiness and disconnection. I stood there for a few seconds suddenly unsure what to do. The room itself was small and unkempt, the evidence of drugs and alcohol strewn on the floor. "Val, I'd like my phone back, please. I know you've taken it." I addressed the lifeless form on the bed, my voice sounding quite pitiful against its harsh surroundings. A murmur came from the open mouth and Val stirred in my direction, trying to focus her eyes on me. "I don't have your phone." "She sold it already, babe, to get that hit." Tom appeared at my side, "I'm sorry." He turned to go back downstairs, signaling for me to do the same. I looked again at Val: a mixture of pity, anger and upset surging through me and briefly disabling any movement, before also turning, following Tom back down the stairs. I could feel the hurt stinging at my heart as I walked back up the street to my own home, angry questions steam-rolling through

my mind, and at the same time the image of Val
planted firmly in my memory."[7]

At this point, I looked at Joy in shock, saying the only thing
that came to mind: "Where were your parents? Were you all ever
scared?" She looked me square in the eyes and pointed at me.

"If you are going to be able to do what God has called you to
do, you have to trust that God will protect you and your family."

This protection is what the blessing in Psalm 41 looks like in
real time. In moments of uncertainty and danger, we can trust that
God will deliver us. But in some cases, we will suffer. When we
care for vulnerable people, we are taking a risk. It may end badly
for us—there are no guarantees. But that shouldn't deter us from
loving people. The psalmist wants us to know that even when we
experience the sum of all our fears, God is still blessing us. Because
like David on his sickbed, God will sustain us when we suffer.

A Call for Help

David recounts this time when he was bedridden. He talks
about his enemies, beginning with himself. After recounting his
own sin and struggles, he explains that others are out to see him
fall—even those closest to him. David pleads with God, "be gracious to me; heal me, for I have sinned against you!" (Ps. 41:4).

David's illness is compounded by the fact that his friends are
spreading rumors about him and wishing for his death. Feeling
abandoned and betrayed by those closest to him, David cries out for
justice. Now, let's pause again. Sometimes when we read the Psalms,
we take for granted that each psalm was originally written as a worship song for the people of Israel. Writing this psalm to be sung by
his subjects, David exemplifies what is known as a wounded healer.
This term, created by psychologist Carl Jung, conveys the idea that
a counselor often desires to treat patients because the counselor has
been previously wounded.[8] Most of the time, we can trace our desire
to help others to a time when we were in need of help. Given that

this can trigger our own traumatic experiences, many encourage people to proceed with caution.

Henri Nouwen, a Dutch priest and the author of *The Wounded Healer: Ministry in Contemporary Society,* explains that approaching other vulnerable people from this perspective can actually be a healthy approach. In a letter to a friend, he writes, "There was a time when I really wanted to help the poor, the sick, and the broken, but to do it as one who was wealthy, healthy, and strong. Now I see more and more how it is precisely through my weakness and brokenness that I minister to others."[9] Just as each of us is called to the hurting, each of us is hurting. Our personal messes, in turn, can lead us to our ministries.

A Help for the Called

Putting the finishing touches on this short psalm, David explains: "Even my close friend in whom I trusted, who ate my bread, has lifted his heel against me.[10] But you, O LORD, be gracious to me, and raise me up, that I may repay them! By this I know that you delight in me: my enemy will not shout in triumph over me. But you have upheld me because of my integrity, and set me in your presence forever. Blessed be the LORD, the God of Israel, from everlasting to everlasting! Amen and Amen" (Ps. 41:9–13).

After crying out, David regroups and collects himself. "Raise me up, uphold me, so that I may give them what they deserve." He goes on to say something that comes off slightly peculiar: "You have upheld me because of my integrity" (v. 12). As you might guess, this is a little tricky to interpret. Some commentators believe that David is speaking to his integrity with regards to considering the poor. But even with that, we know that David wasn't perfect. He has said as much. His integrity had been measured and found wanting. His faith could not be in his own performance—it must be found in someone else.

And it would be found in another King in David's lineage. One whose life would by characterized by a love for the vulnerable.

One whose mission was to preach "good news to the poor" (Luke 4:18). One who would focus on those on the fringes of society. Christ "considered the poor" perfectly, without fault, in our place. Whether it was by conversing with a Samaritan woman even though it was socially taboo, healing lepers in spite of the fact that they were considered unclean, or dining with tax collectors though they were considered traitors, he achieved what David couldn't.

However, his earthly ministry would come to an end. As he celebrated what was to be his last supper with his disciples, he quoted Psalm 41. In John 13:18–19, Jesus says to his disciples "I am not speaking of all of you; I know whom I have chosen. But the Scripture will be fulfilled, 'He who ate my bread has lifted his heel against me.' I am telling you this now, before it takes place, that when it does take place you may believe that I am he."

He quotes Psalm 41, so that his disciples—and we by extension—would know that he is the messiah. Christ, like David was betrayed by one of his closest friends; Judas sold Jesus to the Roman authorities. But Jesus, rather than crying out for justice, experienced justice. Rather than wishing that Judas suffer, Christ suffers in his place, in the place of all sinners. He was buried and rose victoriously on the third day for his church, which is made up solely of wounded healers.

But as wounded healers, we are reminded that our motivation can't only come from our past wounds; it must come from the Healer who was wounded for us. The good news of the kingdom is that Christ became vulnerable to death to save the vulnerable from death so that they may love the vulnerable until death.

Now we can say along with David that God upholds us, but not because of our own integrity; rather, because of Christ's integrity on our behalf. We can know beyond a shadow of a doubt that God delights in us and will not let our enemy triumph over us, because at the cross, Christ won the victory. Because of Christ alone, we are set in God's presence forever.

Like Jeff, our story is caught in a greater narrative. Like Joy, we simultaneously feel sad and angry as we think about injustice. Like

David, our pain points to a person who suffered for us. One who didn't ignore us in our hurt, but came down to us to live as one of us. A King, who doesn't see us as a number or a potential voter, but calls us by name. As we lament, we know that God will answer because he loves justice more than any of us do. As we reflect on these truths, we can remember that *as we are called to help, we can call for help, because there is help for the called.*

RECOGNIZING THE VULNERABILITY AROUND US

It is not easy seeing someone trying to survive on the streets of the city, and our reactions can range from pity, to anger, to choosing not to see the person at all.
—The Coalition for the Homeless[1]

CHAPTER 6

ENTER THE DARKNESS

For Rachelle Starr, caring for women and girls impacted by the sex industry is not a passion as much as it is a calling. Since founding Scarlet Hope, she has seen hundreds of women leave Louisville, Kentucky's pervasive sex industry.[1] This is what can happen when you take a risk and start serving people that many would rather avoid than love.

On a weekly basis, Rachelle and company go to where those most vulnerable are in their community: the strip clubs. Armed with a home-cooked meal and the desire to have a conversation, Scarlet Hope helps women locally and nationally transition from the adult entertainment industry by offering them transitional living, career counseling, housing, mentoring, transportation, and drug rehabilitation.

Preparing to Die

But to really understand Rachelle's mission, we need to go back to the beginning. As a toddler, she began to feel slight paralysis in her hands and her feet. Over time, this paralysis affected her entire body. Apparently, Rachelle had an autoimmune disease, for which there was no cure. The doctors were at a loss. By age eight, the medical professionals began preparing her parents for the worst. "This is looking really bad. She is definitely not going to make it," the doctor explained. At this point, they ceased giving her medication to treat her disease.

Having exhausted all other options, her father brought her before the elders of the church that he pastored. Taking their cue from James 5:14, they anointed Rachelle with oil and prayed feverishly for her healing. If the doctors were unable to find a cure, maybe, just maybe, the Great Physician could fix what was wrong in her body. "So they prayed over me," she explains, "and . . . over six months, I started regaining strength in my limbs, my feet, my hands."

Six months later, during a routine follow-up, the doctors appeared perplexed. "I don't know if we have the wrong results, but your disease is gone." Her parents couldn't believe what they were hearing. With tears of joy streaming down their faces, they knew that God alone had healed their daughter. Just to be on the safe side, the doctor kept her in the hospital for another week of observation. By this point, there was no missing this miracle—it was as if the disease had never been there.

As you might have guessed, Rachelle spent much of her early childhood pondering heaven and the afterlife. At the mercy of her doctors, her prescriptions, and her parents, she learned very early on that she was not in control of anything. "I knew better than probably any of my friends at that age that if I died, I wanted to be with Jesus, and so I repented and gave my life to the Lord and then it was within that year that the Lord healed me."

The lessons learned from her childhood have never left her. Having experienced the healing and the love of God at an early age, she knew that she wanted to help people know that God loves them and is able to heal them regardless of what they have gone through. Her experience of vulnerability shaped her into the woman she would become. It would lead her to Theater X.

The Birth of Scarlet Hope

In 2006, an ambitious twenty-one-year-old Rachelle moved to Louisville. Living directly across the Ohio River in Indiana, she quickly became used to her interstate commute. Each day she drove across the bridge into the Derby City to work. Describing this period of her life as a season of "holy discontentment," she became increasingly aware that this marketing position was not a long-term fit. Though her job was fine by all accounts, she felt that she was unable to use the gifts and calling God had placed on her life at an early age. There had to be something else out there for her.

Praying and fasting for God to direct her to those in need of him, she asked God to "send me to those that you want me to serve!" She didn't care if God sent her overseas or across the street, she simply wanted to be able to share God's love with vulnerable people. That's when God opened her eyes to what was happening along her daily commute.

About a year later, on her daily commute, Rachelle noticed Theater X, an adult entertainment establishment. Growing up as a pastor's kid, she had no real frame of reference for strip clubs or the commercial sex industry, but as she drove past Theater X, she says "it was like God just whiplashed me and took . . . my gaze straight to that building and he started impressing upon my heart to pray for them, the women in that place."

Like in the parable of the Good Samaritan, God showed Rachelle the vulnerable people who were in her path. Now she couldn't continue to drive past them without doing something. So as she started praying for them, she sensed God very clearly communicating to her, "Go and share my love and hope with women in the sex industry." She knew without a shadow of a doubt it was from the Lord. So, picking up the phone, she called her husband. She told him she *knew* God was calling her to go to women in the sex industry. Waiting for her to finish her sentence, her husband calmly replied, "That's exactly what Jesus would do." This was further confirmation that she was on the right track.

Beginning that week, she took another step and started researching the sex industry in Louisville. At this point she had little to no knowledge of human trafficking or sexual exploitation. Much to her surprise, she learned that in 2007, Louisville had the fifth largest sex industry per capita in the United States.

This statistic was mind-boggling. She couldn't understand why there could be so much exploitation in a city with such a proliferation of churches. So she started calling churches and introducing herself. "Hi, my name is Rachelle and I'm calling to see if you have an outreach ministry to women in the sex industry." The responses that she received were sobering. Many people would say, "No." And those were the nice people. Others would not even give her an answer. Still others said something to the effect of, "We have a sign in our yard and if people *like that* want to come, they're more than welcome, but we don't go to them."

How could these people going to church *not* want to engage with those working in strip clubs? This happens because, in many cases, we see people not as vulnerable image-bearers in need of love, but as miscreants. I know, because I was just like them.

The first time that I heard about Scarlet Hope was in 2010. I'll never forget receiving a phone call from my friend Kate one Saturday morning. Kate wasted no time in getting to her point.

"Raleigh, I am considering volunteering with this organization called Scarlet Hope. They work with girls in strip clubs."

"Umm. What?"

"Yes, it's this dynamic ministry that addresses the holistic needs of women trapped in the sex industry."

"Yeah?"

"Yeah. What are your thoughts?"

"Honestly, Kate. I think it's a bad idea. I don't think that God would ever call you to do something like that. Also, those women probably make more money than you. They don't need your home-cooking or your charity."

As a Christian, I found it preposterous to even consider doing a ministry of that nature. Like I said, this was 2010. A little more than a year later, I found myself repenting at the aforementioned Passion conference in Atlanta. Shortly after God opened my eyes to the evil of human trafficking, I called Kate and apologized. Seven years later, I would have the opportunity to apologize to Rachelle as well. Without knowing it, I was standing in the way of God using his people to love these often forgotten women.

Stop Praying

Though she had noble intentions, Rachelle was repeatedly rejected by the churches that she called. Finally, she decided if no one else was doing anything, that she could at least start praying. Dragging her friend along with her, she began praying outside of several strip clubs. She mapped out as many clubs as she could find. As she prayed, she continued to reach out to the churches of her community. The answer was still a resounding "no." No matter how much she prayed, it was like the church just wasn't getting behind her vision.

That all began to change on a summer Sunday in August 2008. As she read the first chapter of Francis Chan's book, *Crazy Love*, she froze. The first two words on the page hit her like a brick: *Stop praying.*[2] It was as if God was inviting her to stop praying for a moment and to do something about the brokenness that she was discovering in her community. "Okay, Rachelle, I've already asked you to go. I've already told you. You don't need all the pieces of the puzzle. I just want you to go." And that's what she and her friend did. Fasting for three days, they decided that Tuesday night would be the night when they entered into a club.

And that's how the ministry of Scarlet Hope began. Without a business plan and depending on God for each step, Rachelle watched as Scarlet Hope grew from an idea to a thriving nonprofit, mobilizing Christians to leave the protection of their comfort zones and to find God working in each strip club.

"God calls us to go into the darkness," Rachelle explains. "When we see Jesus interacting with people, he's coming into our darkness with his light." That's the point. Like Jesus, Rachelle and those at Scarlet Hope aren't going to sit around waiting for women to find them; they are actively reaching women in the sex industry and showing up right where these women are. Whether these women are on the street, in illicit massage parlors, or in strip clubs, Rachelle believes that Christians can enter into the darkness to show them God's light.

"We knew that in order for these women to hear the gospel, we had to go to them," she said. "The church sometimes has a tendency to give off a message that first people must 'clean up their acts' and then they're ready to come to the Lord. But of course, this is actually the opposite of the message of the gospel. The gospel meets us right where we are, in the midst of our sin and calls us to our loving Savior."[3]

This radical grace drives Scarlet Hope to serve those people that many would write off as perpetrators. Empowering women through their discipleship program, job training program, and their social enterprise, Scarlet's Bakery, they direct each of their clients to their true value and dignity. Reminding each individual that they are more than the sum of what they have done or what's been done to them.

"They Never Noticed"

"Could he be the one to love and accept me for who I am?"

Everyone is looking to be loved. Anna was no exception. While still in her late teens, she met and fell in love with an older man who gave her what she craved. This longing for love made her vulnerable to her "boyfriend," who had different plans for their "relationship." Over the ensuing months, she would be subtly manipulated into becoming part of his special "art project." Unknowingly, she would be tricked into the world of pornography.[4]

As Anna shared her story with me, I couldn't shake one nagging question.

"How did the local church serve you when you were being exploited?" I asked. I'm not sure what I expected her to say, but I can definitely tell you that I wasn't prepared for her answer. Hearing my question, she began to laugh out loud. "For years," she explained, "I went to church regularly. No one noticed anything. Everyone thought I was happy, so nothing wrong could be going on."

I'll never forget that conversation. As a matter of fact, there are traces of that conversation in every conversation I have had since.[5] In that moment, I realized that on our own, not only do we miss the incidences of exploitation and human trafficking in our communities, but we are in danger of missing vulnerable people right in front of us. Like Rachelle, we need God to open our eyes to the vulnerability right in front of us—on our commutes, in our neighborhoods, and, yes, even in our churches.

Hanging up the phone, I realized that though awareness appeared to be on the rise, our attempts at creating it were simply not enough.

Rethinking Awareness in the Church

In the weeks to follow, I reevaluated everything I had been doing up until that point. Though informative, the panel discussions didn't seem to cut it. Neither were the educational seminars (aptly named "Just Conversations") impacting congregations as much as I had hoped.

I was living in this strange new tension. On one hand, pastors and church leaders were becoming increasingly aware, but on the other hand, there were still people like Anna who were falling through the cracks. This led me to ask myself a question: *Since human trafficking is the exploitation of vulnerability for commercial gain, how could someone mobilize his or her entire congregation to better care for those most vulnerable?*

As I thought about this question, I began to ask each local church with whom I worked to answer a variation of the question that I posed to Anna and that Rachelle posed to all those churches in Louisville: "How is your church responding to the vulnerabilities both in your church and in your community?" With that, the seeds were sown for a new approach.

The mission and direction of Let My People Go was reborn. The focus of our trainings went from locating human trafficking hot spots to finding those most vulnerable. The premise was simple: if we identify the populations who are most susceptible, then we can go beyond simply knowing that human trafficking exists to identifying the underlying vulnerabilities that have contributed to the problem in the first place.

As I mentioned in the introduction, regardless of one's specific area of vulnerability, each person could be, is being, or has been trafficked. Therefore, when we intentionally throw ourselves into the paths of foster children, immigrants, and the homeless, for example, we will find ourselves naturally doing the work of prevention, intervention, and aftercare all at once.

I call this idea the Vulnerability Continuum. The point is that we cannot just find people that have been trafficked, as if it were easy. As we have already established, most of those who are exploited, like Anna, will not self-identify, putting the onus of their identification on each one of us.

This is why focusing on the vulnerabilities represented in our communities is so important. If we actually pay attention, we can recognize the very same vulnerabilities for which a trafficker will look. And as we meet each person where they are, we will find them at some point along this continuum.[6]

Stop Picking Your Neighbors

I'll never forget when a friend in the mayor's office nonchalantly told me, "By the way, I gave your name to the *New York Times*, so just know that you'll probably be receiving a phone call shortly." I stopped in my tracks. "Come again?"

The reason for the call happened the week prior. I had joined seventeen other NYC pastors and religious leaders on a conference call to talk about how we can best address the city's homeless population. To engage the problem, the mayor's office had been introducing family shelters to several different neighborhoods. The reviews were mixed, to say the least.

Five hundred people came to a town hall meeting to protest the opening of a shelter for families in Elmhurst, Queens. In the article entitled "New York City Asks Clergy to Calm Ire over Homeless Shelters," Kate Taylor reveals that the protesters "have cited a string of unsettling incidents, including public urination and thefts from a local supermarket, as evidence that the presence of the shelter is making their neighborhood less safe."[7]

If we look closely at the facts of this story, we may see our reflection in it. Whether we find ourselves like those in need of help (in this case, the families in need of shelter and a fresh start), those desiring to help, or even those fearing the ramifications of what the help would look like, each of us is represented in this *Times* story. Is it possible that when situations like this arise, they can serve to not only convey what's happening in our communities, but also to expose our own fears and xenophobic biases?

I am not in any way attempting to denigrate the concerns of those who attended this particular town hall meeting. Truth be told, their concerns, which should be heard, could be very valid. I'm not discounting that at all. But as Christians, we have the opportunity to respond differently. As those following a Savior who took the mantle of vulnerability upon himself, we are uniquely positioned to step forward and love our new neighbors, trusting that God has a plan. To quote the apostle Paul as he preached in Athens, "[God] made from one man every nation of mankind to live on all the face of the earth, having determined allotted periods and the boundaries of their dwelling place, that they should seek God, and perhaps feel their way toward him and find him. Yet he is actually not far from each one of us" (Acts 17:26–27).

According to Paul, God sovereignly places all of us where we are in the world on purpose, whether we are rich or poor. Ruling over the political whims of the mayor and every other leader, God is sovereignly placing people in our communities for a reason. What will be our response?

In light of this text, this reality should even color the way that we view current world events, like the refugee crisis. Contemplating this diaspora, a friend of mine messaged me on Facebook one morning to share and process some concerns to make sure that she was thinking correctly. "I have such mixed thoughts on this. The momma in me is torn both ways. I want to protect those innocently caught up in all this, but I also want to protect my own children, all the while knowing God is capable of doing both, but unsure of my role and what the role of our country as a whole should be."

"Thanks for your question," I wrote. "Honestly, the majority of the Old Testament admonitions are rooted not in the political identity of Israel alone, but also in its redemption from Egypt. 'Love the sojourners, as you were once sojourners.' There is a recollection that they once wandered in a land that wasn't their own and were mistreated. Again and again, they are challenged to provide for the 'widow, orphan, and sojourner.' The reason again is rooted in the redemption that they have experienced. God is calling them to not merely tolerate their new neighbors, but to protect and provide for them as a family. In the New Testament, we are reminded to love the 'stranger' among us. Honestly, that is why the parable of the Good Samaritan is so radical. The Law demands that we love God and others with everything that we are, but that pesky parable states that even those who 'embody' that Law only keep it on the surface. But a 'sojourner,' a Samaritan, actually loves his sworn enemy—the Jew left to die in the middle of the road . . . to the point of risking his own life. This crisis reminds me that love should cost us something. Though we should be discerning, we shouldn't let our fear or desire for self-protection shackle us and keep us from loving others well."

Rather than reacting out of fear, what would happen if we responded by believing that God is intricately involved in the migration patterns of those around us? Trusting this to be true, we can actually meet our new neighbors. We can listen to them. We can learn from them. If we respond to those vulnerable around us, our lives will be changed, but most likely they will be changed for the better.

If you are anything like me, you find yourself fighting the temptation to choose your neighbors. Face it, there are people with whom you want to spend time and there are people you want to avoid. In selecting those with whom we do life, we tend to choose people that are remarkably similar to us. The danger facing us is that we could live our entire lives and miss the opportunity to know and love our homeless or refugee neighbors. Following Jesus, who himself was a refugee and lacked a place to lay his head, we can step forward in faith to love our new neighbors, trusting that God will meet us as we meet them.

Rethinking Vulnerability

In light of God's sovereignty over everyone who lives within your zip code, it is helpful to know how vulnerability can manifest itself in a given community. Earlier, I mentioned that as I began to see those hurting around me, I began to read the Bible with fresh eyes, seeing vulnerability on every page. But it also works the other way. As you begin to see the oppressed in Scripture, you will find yourself recognizing vulnerable people where you live.

Following is a list of common vulnerabilities adapted from Tim Keller's *Ministries of Mercy*.[8] As you read through this list, check off vulnerabilities you have recognized:[9]

The Poor (Gal. 2:10)

- Homeless
- Substance addicts: alcoholics, drug addicts
- Mentally disabled
- Migrant workers
- Unemployed
- Low-wage earners
- Illiterate

- Cyclically impoverished
- "Deserving poor"
- "Undeserving poor"
- "Working poor"
- "Educated poor"

Disadvantaged Youth (Ps. 68:5)

- Abused and neglected
- Juvenile delinquents
- Learning disabled
- Physically disabled
- Mentally disabled
- School dropouts

Elderly (1 Tim. 5:9)

Disabled (Lev. 19:14)

- Blind
- Deaf
- Mentally disabled

Single Parents (James 1:27)

- Widows/widowers
- Divorced
- Unwed mothers
- Single fathers

Prisoners (Heb. 13:3)

- Inmates
- Formerly incarcerated
- Families with a member on parole
- Children of those incarcerated

Sick (Matt. 25:36)

- Chronically ill

- Terminally ill
- Those unable to pay medical bills

Disaster Victims (Acts 11:28–29)

- Natural disasters
- Acts of terror
- Mass shootings

Immigrants and Ethnic Minority Populations (Lev. 19:33–34)

- Refugees
- Undocumented immigrants
- Documented immigrants
- International students
- Linguistic minorities (the English as a second language community)
- Ethnic enclaves and ethnic minorities

You may have recognized some of these right off the bat, while some of the other categories may have surprised you. Each of these vulnerabilities listed can be hidden in plain sight.[10] Each of us can be impacted by them. We are all one choice or one event away from the unthinkable.

When we assume that sex or labor trafficking can't happen in our towns, we are missing the very thing that makes exploitation possible: vulnerability. Like I said in the introduction, human trafficking is a "catchall" injustice. Each of the vulnerabilities listed here serves as a pipeline to exploitation; if someone has little to no options, they are often powerless to avoid manipulation.

My friend Jonathan Walton says it this way: "poverty plus isolation equals exploitation." One author commenting on a recent 2015 study on social isolation picks up on this idea, saying: "living with air pollution increases your odds of dying early by 5 percent. Living with obesity, 20 percent. Excessive drinking, 30 percent. And living with loneliness? It increases our odds of dying early by 45 percent."[11]

Humans have been created for connection. We need each other, even if we are different than each other. When we are isolated in our vulnerability, we are not only less likely to flourish, but we are more likely to be targeted by those who wish to exploit us.

Rethinking Red Flags[12]

Looking for signs of vulnerability before looking for red flags of human trafficking is crucial. Because often when we are focused exclusively on red flags, we can become so intent on finding certain signs that we miss the vulnerable person in front of us who may be exploited. In other words, the best way to recognize human trafficking is to intentionally look for *signs of vulnerability along with signs of force, fraud, or coercion* in your church and community. Though the presence of only one or two of the following signs may not necessarily point to trafficking, the following list can help you identify those who are potentially trafficked.

Potential Signs of Exploitation

THE VULNERABLE INDIVIDUAL'S PERSONAL DETAILS

- Unable to give consistent information about their schedule and personal details
- Noticeable changes in dress, nails, or hair without explained source of income
- Carries multiple hotel keys, lots of money, or sharp objects
- Has tattoos or other marks indicating ownership or that the individual is hesitant to explain (possible "branding")
- Scripted and rehearsed answers to your questions

FREEDOM OF MOVEMENT AND LIVING CONDITIONS

- Identification/documents confiscated by employer or someone else
- Living in workplace or with employer/boyfriend
- Poor or cramped living conditions
- Isolation from friends or family and unable to visit family
- Inability to speak to others alone
- Respiratory infections or infectious diseases (spread in crowded, unsanitary environments)

SIGNS OF ABUSE OR THREATS

- Signs of sexual, physical, mental, or emotional abuse (burns, scars, bruises at various healing stages, anxiety attacks, extreme shyness, jumpiness)
- Appearing unusually fearful or anxious for self or family members
- Fearful of threats against friends or family members
- Submissive or fearful toward perpetrator

SIGNS OF COMMERCIAL EXPLOITATION

- In a situation of forced prostitution (exchanging sexual services for housing, food, money, or goods by means of force, fraud, or coercion)
- Under eighteen and engaged in prostitution
- Owing large sums of money (debt bondage)
- Works unusually long hours, no access to wages, and/or little, if any, time off
- Unpaid or paid very little
- Children engaging in work unsuitable for their age

- Children not in school or with significant gaps in schooling
- Skin or respiratory problems (because of agricultural products)
- Reproductive health problems, including sexually transmitted diseases, forced abortions, urinary tract infections, or pelvic pain

Common Trafficking Situations

- Strip clubs, exotic dancing, pornography, escort or dating services
- Factories, sweatshops, industrial lines, agricultural work
- Businesses like hotels/motels, nail salons, massage parlors
- Restaurants and bars
- Home cleaning services
- Begging or street peddling

Again, exploitation occurs when there is vulnerability and isolation, accompanied by force, fraud, or coercion. Where there are vulnerable people, there is often exploitation.[13]

Leading Out of Compassion

Regardless of whether you have been going to church your entire life, or you just visit on Christmas and Easter, it's likely that you have seen or heard the following verse: "The harvest is plentiful, but the laborers are few; therefore pray earnestly to the Lord of the harvest to send out laborers into his harvest" (Matt. 9:37–38). Christians love this verse. It clearly reminds us of the priority that we must place on evangelism, or sharing the "good news of the kingdom." For that reason, we include it in everything from banners, to books, to commemorative wall art. It's safe to say that we know the passage.

But do we really? You and I can be so focused on the *mission* of the text that we miss its *motivation*. The verse prior to this divine imperative makes it clear that "when [Christ] saw the crowds, he had compassion for them, because they were *harassed and helpless, like sheep without a shepherd*" (Matt. 9:36, emphasis mine). Not only did Christ see the helpless and harassed, this verse shows us *how* he saw them. It's important for us to know that Christ saw the situation, and rather than dismissing it, had compassion. Christ witnessed firsthand what made these people holistically and habitually vulnerable.

John Nolland, in his commentary on the Gospel of Matthew explains, "compassion involves so identifying with the situation of others that one is prepared to act for their benefit. Apart from [Matthew] 18:27, in a parable (where compassion leads to forgiveness of debt), in Matthew compassion always addresses the physical needs of people, and so it will be in the ministry to which the disciples are called."[14] Christ calls us to join in this kingdom mission, where physical needs as well as the spiritual aspects of life are addressed.

Though unnoticed, Anna, who was vulnerable and looking for love, found the love she desired in the person of Jesus Christ. As those who share in this love, let us notice those who are vulnerable—whether we pass them behind blacked-out windows on our commute or they are sitting in the back row of our congregations as if nothing's wrong.[15]

CHAPTER 7

LOVE YOUR NEIGHBOR: AN INTERVIEW

In our pursuit of a vulnerable approach to human trafficking, we have seen what happens *when vulnerability is exploited*. In Section One, we discovered that before we can answer the call to do something about it, we must discover what human trafficking really is. For this reason, we examined five commonly held misconceptions that ultimately endanger us and those whom we are seeking to help. In addition to unpacking the myths, we also learned the truth about trafficking in a conversation with former Ambassador Luis deBaca.

In Section Two, we took a step back and *recognized vulnerability in Scripture*. To discover the role of vulnerability in God's solution to human trafficking, we searched the Bible to find the scriptural foundation for this approach. We discovered that vulnerability or perceived weakness is actually not a result of the fall, but rather a gift of God to aid us in loving God and serving others. The fall did not produce vulnerability; it produced the exploitation of vulnerability. As citizens of the kingdom of God, Christians are free to invest in the "not yet" as they serve in the kingdom that's here "already." As you may remember, this investment is not always on our own terms. Sometimes there are interruptions, but these interruptions can be divinely disruptive, realigning us to God's purpose. As you learned from my interrupted interview with Joy, Jeff had way more to teach me about God's love in that moment than I had to teach him.

Finally, in Section Three, we have begun to examine how we can recognize those most vulnerable around us. To give us a jump start on the conversation, we saw how Rachelle Starr first saw the needs in her community and then responded. Like Rachelle, each of us can love our neighbors, even if they are different than us. Regardless of our backgrounds, each of us has a story. As we have seen throughout this book so far, God is a master of causing our stories to intersect with the stories of others. But sometimes the narratives of others go unheard because we fail to hear or choose not to listen. For that reason, we learned how we can identify those who can be vulnerable in our communities. In addition, we identified several red flags to help us identify those most at risk of exploitation.

But going with this book's theme of *vulnerable people loving other vulnerable people because Christ was made vulnerable for them*, I still had some questions. For one, we can know categories of vulnerability, *but how do we recognize people on a daily basis? Also, what manner should we adopt in serving vulnerable people?* In other words, *how do we avoid re-exploiting the people that we are trying to help?*

I don't believe there is a better person to help us along this journey than Boz Tchividjian. Boz, short for Basyle, founded Godly Response to Abuse in the Christian Environments (GRACE) in 2003.[1] GRACE began as a response to what Boz was seeing in the cases that he prosecuted as an assistant state attorney in Florida. During this time, he became the chief prosecutor in the Sexual Crimes Division, where he gained experience in cases involving sexual abuse, and later served as the attorney for the Child Advocacy Center in Daytona Beach, Florida. Boz currently works as a law professor and is also the author of a new book entitled *The Child Safeguarding Policy Guide for Churches and Ministries*.[2]

Boz sees his role addressing the problem of child sexual exploitation from a unique perspective because of his upbringing. On one hand, his last name, Tchividjian, points to his Armenian heritage, which has been marked by suffering. Specifically, his great-grand-father and other relatives were wiped out by the Armenian geno-cide. Boz believes this has contributed to the heaviness that he feels for those who have been hurt and oppressed. He sees the role of the church in protecting vulnerable children from a unique vantage point as well. Given that his grandfather was the world-renowned evangelist, Billy Graham, Boz has grown up with both a passion and concern for the local church.

Because I had questions that needed answers, I asked Boz Tchividjian to sit down with me so that I could pick his brain. I took the train from Washington, D.C., and made my way down to Lynchburg, Virginia. As Boz pulled up to meet me, I realized this was going to be a fun trip. Up until that point, I had no idea what kind of car that Boz drove. Hear me, I normally support my friends to purchase whatever automobile makes them happy, unless it's a Mini Cooper or a Smart car. I think my reasoning is solid: I am 6'4" and I can't fit into small cars.

Walking outside, I discovered what I feared most: Boz drove a Mini Cooper. Once I finally was able to fold myself into his car, we drove forty-five minutes outside the city limits of Lynchburg to have lunch at a restaurant with magnificent views of the countryside. As we waited for our food to arrive, we took a few moments to look out of the window and marvel at the beautiful view of the Blue Ridge Mountains. In this tranquil atmosphere, I figured that it was best that I turn on my recorder and begin the interview.

The Interview

Speaking into the recorder, I began: "I'm here with Boz Tchividjian, and we are—"

Boz immediately interrupted me. "I prefer to be referred to as Hugh Jackson."

"As . . . what? Hugh Jackson?"

"I prefer to be called Hugh Jackson."

"So I'm sitting here with Boz Tchividjian—"

"Aka," he interjects a second time.

"Or, as he likes to be called, Hugh Jackson," I said, trying not to smile.

"There you go," Boz laughed, "now we're talking."

I regained my composure and asked "Hugh" my first question: "Could you share a little bit about what you do?"

"I am the executive director of GRACE, which is an acronym for Godly Response to Abuse in the Christian Environment, where we focus on equipping and training the Christian community in understanding and identifying and preventing and responding to all forms of abuse."

"GRACE is an incredible name. Could you tell me a little more about the nature of your mission?"

Boz looked outside for a moment before recounting how he came to start GRACE. "As a young prosecutor, I countered a number of child abuse and sexual assault cases where the church, in some way, shape, or form, was involved—whether the victim was a member of the church, the perpetrator was a member of the church, or whether the victim's family came to the church . . . to seek guidance and direction. And so oftentimes, the church failed in how it responded. . . . Oftentimes the church took a very self-centered approach to these issues. So for example, even the pushing of a victim to reconcile with the abuser oftentimes was self-centered. It's, 'Hey, we gotta get this behind us. What's the best way to move on so we can do cleaner, nicer ministry? Well, let's forgive and reconcile.'"

"Right, right." I nodded in agreement. "Or in other words, 'Let's push it under the rug.'"

"Yeah, or just never see it to completion, because what's fueling that oftentimes is not an ignorance of the issue. Oftentimes it's just self-centeredness. Church-centeredness. And if we learn anything from Jesus, it's to be focused outwardly.

"So I saw that time and time again. So when I left the prosecutor's office, I asked God, 'What do I do with what I've learned in the trenches on this issue as a prosecutor?'" Boz paused for a moment to make his point. "'Cause you learn, when you prosecute or supervise the prosecution of thousands of cases, you learn a lot. You learn a lot that you want to be able to teach others about, [especially] if it's going to protect kids, and help and serve survivors who are so often sitting silently in our churches."

As Boz continued to share, I couldn't help thinking about so many of my friends who have felt either unsafe in the church or unseen by the church.

Multiple Vantage Points and the Need for Collaboration

"So I did that, and through a number of different events it became very clear that I was to take what God had taught me on the front lines, and to go train and equip his church on becoming the greatest advocate for children, and the greatest protector for survivors—in which it's not. In fact, oftentimes children are not advocated or valued much at all in churches. Survivors don't feel safe to speak up in churches about their own abuse stories because of the response that they may get from those around them.

"So we started GRACE in 2003. I reached out to a number of different people God had introduced me to in the previous years, all who were experts in the field with various disciplines, which I think is very important, because we believe a multidisciplined approach to this issue is critical. Just looking at this through a lawyer's lens, you're missing out. If you're looking at it just through a therapist's lens, you're missing out. . . . If you're looking at this through a pastor's lens—so, let's approach this from a multi-disciplined perspective."

"You have to have multiple vantage points," I responded.

"Multiple vantage points," Boz agreed. "The therapists on our board are going to see something differently than a lawyer will. And I need to know that. And they need to hear from my perspective in order to have a more comprehensive understanding."

Boz was actually hitting on something that many of us who are passionate about addressing social ills, at best, undervalue and, at worst, often leave out. In seeing ourselves as the "heroes" of our own stories, we put little to no emphasis on collaboration.

Boz continued, "If the only purpose of GRACE was to 'investigate and prosecute these types of cases,' then okay, just have a group of lawyers. But it's not that. So anyway, we started, and here we are fourteen years later, probably busier than we ever have been in many ways. But busy is not the answer. The ultimate objective is to help contribute to a world that would no longer need an organization like GRACE."

In an attempt to shift the conversation, I took a moment to ask Boz one of the questions that had been weighing heavily on my mind. "Now, we think about this world that you're investing in. This future that you want to see. You want to see a different world where churches are actually safe places for vulnerable people. And I know that that sounds controversial to some, but I think at the end of the day, most of the churches that I grew up in didn't recognize vulnerability as well as they could have. How do we identify people in our community who are vulnerable to exploitation? As well as the people who could be sexually abused, trafficked, or victimized through domestic violence in our own pews? How do we see that?"

Create a Safe Space

"I think there are various answers to that. I would say for me, the first step is *creating a safe space*. It's one thing for pastors and leaders to be able to point to people and identify, 'Hey, this person's vulnerable.' [In doing so,] you're creating [something] in and of itself, that opens up to some exploitation of authority and power that concerns me. It's much healthier to create an environment where people who are vulnerable see it and they feel safe to talk about it, and to share that with other people. And then we can empower them as we move forward. For example, I have a friend of mine, she's a pastor at a small Presbyterian church outside of Philadelphia. She learned a year earlier that a man in the church had molested a child in one of the classrooms. He was awaiting sentencing, but he no longer attended the church. Nobody in the church was really talking about this situation, and this particular friend of mine who's a pastor is also a survivor of childhood sexual abuse. So what does she do? She decides she's going to do a sermon series on abuse. And there's plenty of material in Scripture to pull from to develop such a series, and pastors need to understand that, and know that.

"She preaches for six or eight weeks on abuse. Since that time—now, this is a church of eighty people—she's had twenty-five women from the ages of sixty-five to eighty-five come forward and tell her that they are survivors of either childhood sexual abuse or adult sexual assault. Half of those women had never shared anything about that before until they told her. One of them was an eighty-five-year-old woman. Think about this. Think about an eighty-five-year-old woman, a woman who has spent most of her life in the church, and has never, until she's eighty-five years old, felt safe enough to come forward and share that.

"I praised my pastor friend by saying, 'You're amazing, because you created a safe space.' She created such a safe space by just naming it, talking about it, preaching about it from the pulpit, that they actually came to her. They were empowered . . . Just creating that safe space empowered vulnerable people enough to step forward and say, 'Hey, I want to tell you my story.' To me, that is how we address, and identify, and empower vulnerable people in our midst."

At this point, I was picking up everything that Boz was laying down. He was singing my song, so to speak. For example, as Let My People Go partners with churches, we aim to empower church to 1) identify those most vulnerable in their community, and 2) we encourage each pastor to preach and teach about the biblical themes of justice and mercy, about abuse and redemption. The local church will remain anemic unless we hear the whole counsel of God, which includes God's heart for those most vulnerable.

Season of Learning

Thinking on this "safe space" idea, I asked a follow-up question: "So how could churches both create a safe space, but also intentionally focus on other vulnerable populations in our community that we know are there, but we tend to avoid because they might be too messy?"

"I think that, first of all," Boz explained, "there needs to be a *season of learning*. Churches and leaders have to be humble enough to say, 'We don't know much about this issue. We're bothered by it. It burdens us. But we don't know much about it, so we need to reach out and get help.' We need to be educated about this, to reach out to those, like yourself and others, who know this issue well, to learn. And this is what happens, oftentimes, to our churches, is we hear an issue like this and say, 'Okay, we're going to address vulnerability, so we're going to try to identify people.' And we do it by guesswork.

"Or we think we're the experts because we've read a book about it. No. Reach out . . . If you're going to build a fellowship hall to your church, you're going to reach out to those who know how to design it, who know how to build it, and you're going to ask them questions, and empower them to do that so your church is transformed. It's no different than this. Why would we not reach out to those who know what they're doing, with experience, to help transform our church?"

"Exactly," I replied, "seek out the authorities. The experts."

Nodding in agreement, Boz said, "Yeah. Use the outside experts who have a greater wealth of knowledge on the subject matter. Pastors and leaders . . . God gives them gifts. God gives them a wealth of knowledge in particular areas, but they don't have a wealth of knowledge in everything. And that takes humility to say, 'We need to be taught. We need to learn.' So I think you reach out and learn. That's the first step.

"And the reality is, our churches attract the needy people. When I speak, I'll say, 'Okay. How many of you are needy?' It's funny. Very few hands usually go up. And I go, 'My goodness. I'm needy. Were all needy to some degree. So let's accept that.' But [we need] to know that an environment that attracts needy people will also attract those who want to exploit them.

"So to understand, we need to focus inside of the church. But let it not stop there, because the people who are most vulnerable to human trafficking—most are going to be outside the church."

"Absolutely!" I exclaimed. "I've had friends who were trafficked as they were in church, and some who were trafficked by professing Christians."

Explaining how this can happen, Boz said, "That's the danger of churches; we create environments where perpetrators develop relationships and [the] trust of the congregation, and of parents, and, 'This guy's a great guy.' In regard to the type of perpetrator, don't forget, they are grooming not only the child or the victim, they're grooming those around them. Grooming them to trust, to ingratiate themselves into the social fabric of the church, and as a result of that, they're able to do some amazingly horrific things and get away with it because nobody's even suspecting it. And when somebody does suspect it, or does say something of concern, everybody looks like they're crazy, because this person would never be involved in something like that. We have to start inside the church. That's the starting place, but it shouldn't be the ending point."

Why Do We Avoid "Messy" People?

Theoretically, this idea sounds remarkably biblical and practical. But the problem is that churches that have this approach are more the exception than the norm. For this reason, I asked Boz to explain why he thought that churches were more likely to avoid people whose issues and "messes" were different than their own.

"It's complicated. It's confusing. Oftentimes we're intimidated by it, because we don't feel like we have the tools in our toolbox to meet those needs. We've oftentimes created cultures in our churches where we have to have all the answers. I tell people all the time with abuse survivors, 'Just be there. Be present. Don't have the answers.

Cry with them. Get angry with them. You don't have to have the answers, just be present.' But we feel as Christians . . . that if we don't have the right answers . . . we begin to doubt our own faith. Because, like, 'I don't have the right answer. This is really real.' So they don't even go there, versus saying, 'I don't know the answer to this. These are needy, vulnerable people who are in pain. And I may not know anything except just be present.' And I've found with abuse victims, the mere presence is huge. It goes back to the gospel, where the incarnation of God is God with us. God being present with us.

"I also think the reality is, we're selfish. We have transactional relationships. 'I will do this for you, and I'm not going to say this explicitly, but I'm doing this for this person—if I'm really going to delve into my motives—because I'm hoping to get something back.' With a wounded person, or vulnerable person, we know that that's probably not going to happen. We're just giving, and we're not going to get anything back out of it, and we should be convicted of that. That's wrong. That's not the gospel.

"And the other thing, too, is we can't be the savior to all people. That can be an excuse not to get engaged at all, but on the other end of the spectrum, we can be present, we can connect people with available resources."

Dehumanizing and Rehumanizing

Not only do we need to not avoid marginalized people, we also need to be wise in how we approach them. Speaking to Boz, I said, "I think that the only healthy way to love other vulnerable people is to do it through your own vulnerability. Because if you're not doing it in light of your own fragile humanity, like Jesus did, then you're setting yourself up to quite possibly re-exploit people."

Picking up on this idea, Boz explained, "It's really important for us to know that vulnerable people—whether they be trafficked individuals, sexual abuse survivors, or any vulnerable person—are not projects. And we oftentimes view and treat them as if they're a project. And that is so patronizing and so dehumanizing. I think we should take time to just listen and learn from each other as vulnerable people. Sexual abuse survivors have been my greatest teachers, and greatest inspirers. They've been my greatest heroes, because they know, and they know so much."

This idea was so thought-provoking. While Boz was still speaking, I found myself thinking about how, so often, we approach vulnerable people from the standpoint of power and safety, thinking about all we can do for them, rather than thinking, *What could this person contribute? How is God shaping them to contribute to the community around them? How could this person minister to my needs?*

"But it's more profound than [simply not treating people as projects]," Boz explained. "We avoid [dehumanization] by looking at the situation and acting in it through the lens of our own humanity and our own brokenness. When we begin to think that we're better than somebody else . . . that person becomes a project very quickly. Versus . . . 'Man, I'm messy. I'm broken. And I can only serve . . . you with my brokenness, which means I'm not going to do it perfectly. I'm going to be messy.'"

"This is so true," I responded. "Using our vulnerability levels the playing field and helps us treat humans like humans should be treated."

So we were learning about the dangers of dehumanization, but how can we point to the dignity in these image-bearers of God? Boz gave an example of how we can start seeing people in a more appropriate light: "I think when you see people who are broken as people who can teach, that you can learn from, that is healthy. Because I go, 'Man, this person has so much to teach me.' Oftentimes I walk away from those [interactions] going, 'Who's the real vulnerable one here? It's me. Who's the real broken one? It's me.'"

Hearing his example, I shared an illustration from my ministry. "Some of my heroes are those who are in Alcoholics Anonymous or similar twelve-step programs, because every time I speak at a church—every time—someone comes up to me after the service and they'll say something to the effect of, 'You know what, Raleigh?

I heard what you said, and I've made some mistakes, too. I'm on my eleventh step and I'm at the point where I'm bringing along other guys. They're messed up too, and I'm doing my best to help them.'"

"That impacts me so much. They're no longer hiding. They're no longer focused solely on self-protection. They're saying, 'This is who I am.' They're being vulnerable. And that opens this minis-try up for them. They're able to serve people, and people feel safe around them, because they're like, 'Yeah, I'm broken too.'"

"Groups like AA do that much better than the church," Boz pointed out. "In the church, we have to have it all together. How many times, as a father, we'd be on our way to church when the kids were small, and I'm screaming at them, and they're yelling at me . . . We're all ticked off, and we get to church, and we get out of the car and someone says, 'Hey, how are you guys doing?' 'Oh, we're doing great.' That's that façade. That plastic façade that we live with inside the church. Instead of going, 'Well, you know what? It's been a pretty crappy morning, and I'm not even really happy to be here.' I wouldn't even feel comfortable saying that at my church to people, 'cause they'd look at me going, 'Oh. Okay.' They wouldn't know what to do. But that's being vulnerable and transparent. Because that's the other part of vulnerability, is transparency.

"And again, you have to be careful when you are serving and loving vulnerable people. You have to be careful, because people who exploit and abuse, sometimes intentionally and sometimes not intentionally, will find themselves in those types of work, serving and attracting vulnerable people. So the best position a perpetra-tor can put himself in is in a position where he's serving vulnerable people. So yes, we need to be vulnerable, but I'll be honest with you—when I'm talking to victims . . . a lot of victims of sexual abuse are extremely vulnerable, and they often spend years blaming their vulnerability on the abuse. They blame themselves . . . They're not the ones that need to hear the message about being vulnerable. That's not the message I tell them. 'Be vulnerable.' They'll look at me like, 'Are you kidding me? That's what got me here.' It's the peo-ple who are serving them, who are learning from them, that need that message. So it's really important who gets that message because it can really backfire when you start telling people who have been trafficked or victimized, 'Hey guys, you just gotta be vulnerable.'"

"You're right," I agreed. "We're not preaching, 'You need to be more vulnerable.' No, we're saying, 'They know they're vulnerable, but to those who are trying to help, we ask, do you know you are vulnerable too? Because if you don't, you're never going to be in a place to minister to them well.'"

During our drive back to Lynchburg, I couldn't help but reflect on how God motivates us to love vulnerable people through his own vulnerability for us in Christ. And as we contemplate his vulnerability for us, we begin to see the myriad of ways that we're vulnerable. This acceptance of our own limitations creates a level playing field between us and those we are trying to help. In other words, it destroys the "us and them" dichotomy to which we hold, so that we realize we are all vulnerable people who are in need.

In the next section, we are going to explore how we can better love broken people through our own brokenness and vulnerability.

RECOGNIZING
YOUR OWN
VULNERABILITY

There is no safe investment. To love at all is to be vulnerable. Love anything, and your heart will certainly be wrung and possibly be broken. If you want to make sure of keeping it intact, you must give your heart to no one, not even to an animal. Wrap it carefully round with hobbies and little luxuries; avoid all entanglements; lock it up safe in the casket or coffin of your selfishness. But in that casket—safe, dark, motionless, airless—it will change. It will not be broken; it will become unbreakable, impenetrable, irredeemable. The alternative to tragedy, or at least to the risk of tragedy, is damnation. The only place outside Heaven where you can be perfectly safe from all the dangers and perturbations of love is Hell.

—C. S. Lewis, *The Four Loves*[1]

CHAPTER 8

A FATHER'S LOVE

Looks can often be deceiving. Hearing her accent, one might naturally assume that she was trafficked from Eastern Europe to the United States. But in true New Yorker fashion, Iryna immediately shuts this misconception down. "I am a domestic survivor of commercial sexual exploitation, who came to this country legally."

The Groundwork of Her Exploitation

Iryna grew up in a single-parent household after her father left her mom for another woman. His departure impacted each member of her family differently. For Iryna, she grew up desiring her estranged father's love and acceptance. As she thought about it, she would find herself daydreaming about having the "happily ever after story" that her parents didn't get to experience during their marriage.

As she thinks back to her childhood, Iryna would describe herself as a very "shy and awkward teenager" who always felt a little self-conscious. Her self-consciousness was only further exacerbated as her mother began to react to her own pain. Attempting to care for both of her children on her own, her mother adopted a parenting style that Iryna described as "punitive and aggressive." For Iryna, who describes herself as a "tender-hearted person," this wasn't a good combination.

As she grew up, Iryna became engrossed in her academic studies. "When you come to America from another country your family is like, 'You've got to do good in school. You've got to do good in school. This is why we brought you here.'" So she did everything she could to fulfill her family's academic expectation, but in her heart she continued to look forward to the day when she would meet her "Prince Charming."

Having never dated anyone, nineteen-year-old Iryna was flattered when a handsome stranger approached her on the subway platform asking for directions. Taking note of his charm and his attractiveness, she did her best to hide her excitement.

Even now, she remembers that day when she first met the man who would become her abuser. He played the part perfectly. He maintained his body posture. He was very attentive. He asked her inquisitively, "How do I get to number two train?" She couldn't help but find him attractive, but she figured, "He's just going to go away." Much to her surprise they "ended up" on the same train.

They chatted intermittently while in transit. He was careful to space out his more "personal" questions throughout the conversation. He would ask questions like "How old are you? Where do you work?" between casual topics like the weather and politics, intentionally giving off the impression that he wanted to get to know her more.

When the train came to a stop, Iryna stood up and began to head for the doors. But before she could exit the train, he asked her for her phone number. Since he seemed like a great guy, she gave it to him.

It's important for us to note that he didn't have to stalk or kidnap her, he just had to show interest. He seemed nice and appeared to be engaging, so why wouldn't she give it a shot and go out with him?

Though she didn't think he was going to call, the next day, her phone rang. It was her "Prince Charming." If she had any doubts, they would be soon alleviated when he called her "Princess."

For her, the word *Princess* was the hook. This was something that she had waited to hear her entire life. Each time he said it, she thought to herself, *I'm special. I matter.*

The relationship took off. Within a week, they were dating. To everyone who was watching, he appeared to be a great boyfriend. He would open the car door for her. He would kiss her hand in public. By all accounts, he was a catch. Everyone in Iryna's life was impressed.

The Gradual Nature of Exploitation

But in time, the compliments and kindness gave way to mockery and verbal abuse. Rather than calling her "princess," he starting calling her names, like "scarecrow." Systematically, he began to break her down and strip her of any autonomy that she had, forcing her to become dependent on him for everything. For instance, he intentionally isolated her from her friends and family. As he would put it, everyone in her life was a bad influence—except for him, of course. Using this carefully crafted technique, he sowed seeds of doubt into her mind. Focusing his attention on her relationship with her mother, with whom she still lived, he'd say, "Sweetheart, why does your mother call you every half an hour? Why does she always need to know where you're at?" Thinking back, Iryna asks herself, "Was my mom controlling? Yes, she was. But I think she was coming from a good place. Again, I think everybody does the best they can. Her best, maybe it was her best." He was strategically isolating Iryna from the very people who could and would want to protect her.

Commenting on the abuse she experienced, she said, "I believe that the psychological abuse that happens through verbal abuse, through name-calling, [like] 'you're a nobody and you're a nothing,' and 'the only way you can leave me is going back to your country or committing suicide.' If somebody that you care about repeats these things on a daily basis, you will begin to believe them eventually."

The verbal abuse and his exploitative use of power and control were an attempt to break her spirit, so he could more easily get her to do the things that she hated. Through this process, he began to traffic her for sex. Over time, he would brag that Iryna was his "perfect little slave," telling others that "Iryna will do everything I tell her to do." He never had to physically abuse her because she grew up in a household where obedience was prized above all. In a real sense, the groundwork for her exploitation was laid out years before she even met him. Being a true manipulator, he picked up on her desire to make others happy through her own compliance and used it to his advantage. According to Iryna, her abuser would tell her that he owned her "from head to toe." Case in point, if he called while she was out with her friends, he would interrogate her, commanding her to tell him exactly where she was and who she was with every time. Her friends would often say things like, "Wow, you report everything to him as if he was your father."

After three years, she graduated college with a 3.89 GPA. But for Iryna, she didn't feel like celebrating. "For me, it was just that, 'So what?' I'm graduating because my family expects me to gradu-ate. They're looking for a GPA, they're looking for the grades. I was suicidal. I didn't have a plan. I didn't know if I was going to kill myself or not. But I knew that I did not want to live. I wanted to die every morning waking up, looking myself in the mirror, and saying, 'Why are you still here?' The world did not have a place for me, I was so tarnished, I was so broken, I was so dirty and to [use his] precise words, I didn't have a future."

An Atheist and the Presence of God

Even as a self-proclaimed atheist, feeling hopeless, she began questioning, "God, where are you?" Looking back, she can see God answering her throughout her exploitation. "Even in the darkest place, he was there with me," she says.

One particular moment remains cemented in her mind. Walking up behind her, her so-called boyfriend placed the barrel of his handgun against her skin. "I felt the gun at the temple of my head," she explained. "I didn't beg. I didn't plead for my life. I just closed my eyes and I'm like, 'This man owns me. If he's going to kill me, he's going to kill me.' I heard him press the release button and then heard him pulling the trigger. As he was pulling the trigger, he pulled the bullets out. I didn't know that. I only heard the trigger go off, click, click, and I didn't know if I was dead or alive. I remember touching the temple of my head and trying to see if I had a skull still. I feel like God's hand was holding back the bullets so it didn't fire and I'm still here today."

Another instance where she could see the hand of God at work in her life came after an altercation she had with her trafficker. Refusing to "service" a sex buyer, she stormed out of the house. Her act of defiance not only triggered his insecurity, but impacted his wallet as well. Though she never saw money exchanged, she knew that if she didn't do what was expected of her, he wasn't paid. So he darted outside, chasing her through his neighborhood.

A Vulnerable Neighbor

At this point, a neighbor noticed that Iryna was scared and invited her into her house. This Good Samaritan was not a police officer, a social worker, or even a human trafficking activist—she was a stay-at-home mom.

She didn't know the specifics of what was going on; she didn't need to. All that she knew was that Iryna was scared and in need of help. So she waved at Iryna and encouraged her to come into the house. As soon as the door closed, guess who came knocking. With Iryna hiding behind her, she attempted to mediate the situation. "She's scared," she told him. Recounting this moment, Iryna says, "Before I left, before he got me to go with him, this woman gave me her phone number. She said, 'Call me.' I started calling her and texting her. I didn't have many friends at that point. I lost a lot of friends because I was very much withdrawn at that time. She started taking me out. Just for a girl thing, for a cup of coffee, to talk. Little things mean that much. To people who are going through a lot, little things matter.

"At that point for me it meant so much knowing that this woman wants to take her time out to spend time with me. When I finally told her what was being done to me she said, 'It's not your fault. What he's doing to you is wrong.' She didn't blame me. It was such a big vindication at that moment in time to know that somebody else knows that it's not my fault. If she said, 'Well, it's your fault. You should have known better,' I probably would have stayed with him and I would have killed myself eventually or he would have killed me."

God used a normal, everyday, stay-at-home mother to help Iryna in her time of need. Through this neighbor, who had vulnerabilities of her own, Iryna started to see herself differently.

Over the next nine months, Iryna began the process of breaking away from her abuser. Anyone who has ever been in an abusive relationship knows that this process is not as easy as it sounds. Iryna would experience cycles of leaving and then coming back, but throughout this process, her new friend would remind her, "Iryna, this man is no good for you."

Once she finally broke away, she began thinking about all the things that happened throughout her exploitation. Now that she had time to reflect, it felt like the flashbacks and nightmares would never end. Experiencing post-traumatic stress disorder, she felt that she was absolutely losing her mind. But again, her friend was there to assure her, "Listen, you are not crazy. You're a beautiful young lady. Everything is going to be okay." She encouraged her, "Iryna, maybe you should go to church. I know that you grew up in the church, but maybe you should go back or try a different church."

Why Don't You Go to Church?

At that point, as if it were on schedule, her coworker began inviting her to church. Though she thought her coworker was annoying, one Friday afternoon, Iryna agreed to join her. Iryna couldn't understand why this seemed to make her friend so happy. Regardless, she began attending church regularly and even bought a Bible.

One Sunday, as she responded to "an altar call," something changed. In many evangelical denominations, the pastor will close the service with an invitation for those in the congregation to place their faith in Christ. In her own words, Iryna explains that "there were a lot of people at the altar call. I went, but I was all the way in the back. I didn't like to be crowded. I didn't like to be in spaces where I couldn't easily exit. I was the last person standing. I remember I was having a nervous breakdown. It got to the point where I was like, 'God, these people have probably sinned and they are crying but these people are somebodies and I'm a nobody, God.' I was telling God what my abuser told me. I was just hysterical and then I felt this presence. [This presence] could have just crushed me into molecules. Yet it wasn't there to condemn, it wasn't there to crush me. It was trying to hold me up because I was shaking and almost falling on the floor. I was being embraced. My shoulders straightened out. I still had tears running down my face. I felt peace. It was something that my tormented self had not felt in years. I felt peace and I felt safe."

Without having anyone tell her, she knew that God was there in that moment. Throughout her entire life, she had been in search of a father's love, and it was there, as she cried in the aisle, that she had finally experienced it. "At that moment in time, the little girl, the little Iryna inside my heart, met her Father. That part of me was healed. Until this day, he has opened up many doors for me to speak to others, to share what he has done; the healing that he has done. I don't find my identity in being a survivor of commercial sexual exploitation. I find my identity in being [God's] daughter. The experience of exploitation is something that happened to me. Being his daughter is who I am." Now, as Iryna reflects back on that day, she realizes that she truly is a daughter of the King.

If we look closely at Iryna's story, we can see how God used ordinary vulnerable people like her next-door neighbor and coworker to help and empower her during a time when she needed it most. Neither of these people were certified trauma specialists; they just made themselves available to help her on her healing journey. They were qualified to help her because, like Iryna, they were navigating their own broken paths. Because each "neighbor" understood her own frailty to some extent, they each were able to treat Iryna like a person deserving of love, and not a problem to be solved.

Because two people were courageous enough to be transparent, she was able to finally begin her healing process. Now, Iryna aims to be that person for others. Without making a big to-do about it, she spends her free time caring for others who have experienced commercial sexual exploitation. She looks forward to graduating with her Masters of Social work degree to help her become even more equipped to care for those who often feel unseen in their exploitation.

CHAPTER 9

A VULNERABLE STEWARDSHIP

Y ou need to be vulnerable as you share your story," Grace Thornton, author of *I Don't Wait Anymore*, said to me during one of our brainstorming sessions for this book. "So you're telling me, if I'm writing a book on vulnerable people loving other vulnerable people, then I have to be vulnerable too?" I chuckled.

To be honest, I laughed to keep from crying. I was scared to death at the prospect of being open and transparent with absolute strangers. (No offense.) As we thought through different stories and potential ideas for each chapter, I had to take breaks just to breathe. It felt like the more I processed my own story, the more emotional I got.

You might think, *Well, that's a good thing, isn't it?* Not where I come from. I don't know exactly where I picked this idea up, but somehow, growing up, I learned that it's very important that you don't talk about yourself too much. A little, well that's just industry standard, but not too much. Because if you do, then you are seen as arrogant or prideful. And, apparently, it really matters how people see you.

So with this idea firmly planted in the back of my mind, I grew up always a little afraid of sharing too much. To this day, the thought of being 100 percent transparent is absolutely petrifying.

Don't get me wrong, I say it all the time: "I'm an open book! Ask me anything." But if I were honest, there are things that I don't want you to know about me. There are fears and insecurities that I pray are never exposed. Typically, you and I don't share everything with everyone because we fear how people would react. What would they think, if they knew the real me? Would they attack me? Would they reject me? Or worse—*would they accept me?*

In the introduction of this book, I gave an operational definition for the word *vulnerability*. First, I explained how it can be defined as the experience of an unmet need. The second definition revolves around the idea of our being transparent and authentic with others. Both of these are good definitions. However, at the core of both of these popular definitions lies the definition that we are using for this book. *Merriam-Webster* defines vulnerability as being "capable of being physically or emotionally wounded; being open to attack or damage." In other words, this definition exposes the heart of both of the other more popular conceptions of vulnerability. To be vulnerable is to be exposed, to be open to loss. For many of us, nothing is more terrifying than feeling out of control or helpless.

According to one leading voice in vulnerability studies, "vulnerability is the birthplace of love, belonging, joy, courage, empathy, and creativity. It is the source of hope, empathy, accountability, and authenticity. If we want greater clarity in our purpose or deeper and more meaningful spiritual lives, vulnerability is the path." The author further defines vulnerability as "uncertainty, risk, and emotional exposure."[1] I have felt all of these throughout the process of writing this book.

But in this chapter, we will discover that the thing that we fear the most, that emotional exposure that we dread, is also the thing that we need the most. For us to care for others in a healthy manner, we have to face down our own "perceived weaknesses." We have to stop running and address the elephant in the room that haunts each one of us. Whether you will admit it to yourself or not, you are limited. You are finite. You are not enough to meet your own needs or the needs of others. And that's okay. Jürgen Moltmann, author of *The Crucified God,* says it this way: "Every human life has its limitations, vulnerabilities, and weaknesses. We are born needy, and we die helpless."[2]

But what if I told you that your vulnerability wasn't a curse? That it is actually a gift? As you will see in this chapter, it's something you can "regift" and give to others. To be vulnerable is to embrace your humanity. When we are open with others, and vice versa, we realize that we are not alone; we are not crazy. Though some may hide it better than others, every one of us has issues and we are all in process. So relax, you are among friends.

In chapter 8, we saw how Iryna processed her vulnerability. Now you are going to be in the driver's seat. In the next several pages, we are going to unwrap and explore the "gift" of our own vulnerability.

Rethinking Stewardship

Earlier I mentioned that vulnerability is not only part of the problem of human trafficking, but it's also part of the solution. But before you and I can be part of the solution to human trafficking, we must realize that we are facing a dilemma. Though we actively want this injustice to come to a screeching halt, we have to confess that in a very real way, we are part of the problem. Believe it or not, our personal vulnerability plays a role in the commercial exploitation of others.

You're thinking, *What do you mean? I love my neighbors!* Right. But what about the neighbors that you don't see? The neighbor that picks your coffee beans or the one that sews your clothing? Even the person who catches the fish available in your grocer's freezer?[3]

In our attempts to cover our pain, suffering, and vulnerability, we often find ourselves kneeling at the altar of our "functional saviors," whether this manifests itself through our buying the nicest clothing at the lowest price so as to impress our friends, or through drinking copious amounts of coffee so that we can stay awake to finish writing our great American novel that will finally bring us the recognition that we crave, or through eating as much chocolate as possible as a way to self-medicate after a stressful day at work. Or it may even manifest itself through choosing to watch "just one" pornographic video late one evening after the kids have gone to bed, because the feelings of isolation and insecurity are so intense.

We often forget that as we try to prove ourselves or be accepted by others, we unknowingly can participate in the mistreatment of others—those whom we forget are intricately involved in the process. It's a fact that there are humans, just like us, involved behind the scenes with everything that we consume. Without knowing it, you and I are contributing to the exploitation of others by what we devour on a daily basis. In other words, the way that we spend our money can create a demand for human trafficking. As hard as this may be to believe, we will never be able to truly point others to freedom until we acknowledge our role in their slavery.

With this in the forefront of our minds, we have to admit that "loving our neighbor" can be difficult in a consumer-driven economy such as ours. A consumer economy depends heavily on consumption patterns. If people aren't spending money, the economy is likely to tank. Likewise, if they are spending a lot of money, the economy will be in good shape. This happens because in a consumer economy, consumption makes up a major percentage of the country's gross domestic product (GDP). Economists estimate that approximately 70 percent of the US economy is based on consumption.[4]

Because of the law of supply and demand, the competition for your dollar drives the free markets. But as we will learn, there is not always freedom in these markets. To boost revenue and meet the demand, most companies will buy the cheapest source materials with which to create their product. All the while, we miss—or worse yet—choose not to think about the people who are exploited to make the products we use in our homes.

Almost everything we consume has slavery at some point in its supply chain.

A supply chain is the system involved in moving a product from the supplier to the customer.[5] For example, by the time that you bought the shirt that you are wearing right now, it has already been touched by many people. Someone grew the cotton, another picked it. One person processed it and worked to convert it to fabric, while another person cut out the pattern and sewed it. This is not to mention the person who sewed the tag on or packaged the shirt for shipping. This chain is usually the last thing on our minds when we're shopping for clothes or our groceries.

More often than not, the supply chains of even the most reputable companies are tainted by slavery. The International Labor Organization estimates that 24.9 million people are currently victims of forced labor.[6] In other words, you can rest assured that someone is paying the ultimate cost for your choice, even if you aren't.[7] Men, women, and children around the globe are forced to work in slavery-like conditions so that you and I enjoy a comfortable standard of life.

Love the Neighbor That You Don't See

God addresses an approach to healthy consumption throughout the Bible. This is what is referred to as biblical stewardship—the proper use of the resources God has entrusted to us. In Churchgoer 101, we are taught that we must be good "stewards" of God's resources. However, more often than not, the practical result of this teaching looks more like secular consumerism than anything else. For example, many of us will consider ourselves to be good stewards if we spend the least amount possible for our purchases. But, as we are seeing, our desire to be thrifty often negatively impacts our neighbor. Let us not mistake thriftiness for godliness.

Rather, God's goal for our stewardship is for us to consume goods in such a way that we honor God and bless the neighbor that we see as well as the neighbor that we don't.

Take a moment and ask yourself, "How can I utilize my resources in such a way that I serve the widow, orphan, and sojourner, rather than exploiting them? Is there a way that our consumption patterns can lead to freedom and flourishing, and not to oppression?"

In Deuteronomy 24, we find a nonexploitative approach to addressing our consumption patterns:

> "You shall not oppress a hired worker who is poor and needy, whether he is one of your brothers or one of the sojourners who are in your land within your towns. You shall give him his wages on the same day, before the sun sets (for he is poor and counts on it), lest he cry against you to the LORD, and you be guilty of sin. Fathers shall not be put to death because of their children, nor shall children be put to death because of their fathers. Each one shall be put to death for his own sin. You shall not pervert the justice due to the sojourner or to the fatherless, or take a widow's garment in pledge, but you shall remember that you were a slave in Egypt and the LORD your God redeemed you from there; therefore I command you to do this. When you reap your harvest in your field and forget a sheaf in the field, you shall not go back to get it. It shall be for the sojourner, the fatherless, and the widow, that the LORD your God may bless you in all the work of your hands. When you beat your olive trees, you shall not go over them again. It shall be for the sojourner, the fatherless, and the widow. When you gather the grapes of your vineyard, you shall not strip it afterward. It shall be for the sojourner, the fatherless, and the widow. You shall remember that you were a slave in the land of Egypt; therefore I command you to do this."
> (Deut. 24:14–22)

Though this text was originally written for the people of ancient Israel living in an agricultural context, the ideas contained therein are quite timely and revolutionary. If we look closely at verses 14 and 15, we find God calling his people to care for those who are working for them by paying them fair wages. In addition to paying them in a manner commensurate to their work, they are commanded to treat vulnerable people with the respect they are due: "You shall not pervert the justice due to the sojourner or to the fatherless, or take a widow's garment in pledge" (v. 17). Then God goes for the gusto, commanding them to refrain from exhausting everything that is in their path. Rather than "getting the most bang for their buck," he encourages Israel to leave behind what remains on their fruit trees and their fields for their often unseen neighbors.

Grounding these commands in Israel's own redemptive history, God encourages them to use their resources in a manner that not only meets their needs, but also meets the needs of their neighbors. As those following Christ, we believe that Christ has kept the entire law, including Deuteronomy 24, perfectly in our place. As we ponder our own redemption, we are compelled to spend our money and resources in a way that doesn't leave an exploitative footprint. *So what can we do?*

Take a Survey

Justin Dillon, founder of Made in a Free World and author of *A Selfish Plan to Save the World*, explains that "you can argue morality with those making money from labor exploitation all day long, but it's not until you impact their money that you will see change."[8] In other words, labor exploitation will not come to an end until we use our purchasing power to demand it.

Toward this goal, Dillon created a website called slaveryfoot print.org. Go ahead, type it into your browser. The first thing that you will notice is a question: How many slaves work for you? Take the survey. In taking it, you will be asked questions about your consumption patterns. This helps us to see those left in the wake of our hasty decision-making.

Check the Labels

Another way to stop creating demand is to buy ethically sourced goods. You may not know it, but most likely, you are already halfway there. For example, when you are in the grocery store, you probably look at the nutritional content labels on the boxes of food that you are buying. We do this because we recognize that we need to take care of ourselves. With that in mind, we can also look for other labels that can help us better care for others, specifically those who are producing our food. Fair trade and direct trade labels are used to show that the workers who produced the product that you are holding in your hand were compensated appropriately and treated fairly.

Fair trade refers to a certification process for which producers and distributors of coffee, chocolate, and other goods can apply. The goal is to promote sustainability as those involved are paid an acceptable living wage.

Direct trade, on the other hand, is not based on a certification process operated by an over-arching organization at all. Instead, the only parties involved are the farmers (producers) and the (distributors). Through an interpersonal process with no formal requirements, each party works together to make sure that everyone involved is compliant and people are treated equitably.[9]

As you shop at grocery stores like Whole Foods or Trader Joe's, you'll find that fair and direct trade products are easier to find. But that doesn't mean that they aren't available elsewhere. If for some reason you can't find them, request them. Stores and companies want your money and they will do what they can to make sure that you remain a customer.[10]

Flee Sexual Immorality

The truth of the matter is that every act of consumption is a moral choice.[11] With this in mind, it's important for us to know that it's not just our consumption of material goods like food and clothing that create demand. The day that I sensed a calling to fight human trafficking, I saw for the first time that I was part of the problem. Not only did I do this through the food that I ate and the clothes that I wore, but I had also viewed pornography at different points throughout my life.

Though I knew that it was sinful in a spiritual sense, I never understood the practical impact of my lust. It hurts to admit that up until that point I never thought that the person on the other side of the screen could be exploited. It hit me all at once. I realized that this "private sin" had social ramifications. There I was, sitting in an arena, broken, asking for God's forgiveness.

More than 40 million Americans visit pornographic websites on a regular basis.[12] According to a Barna research group study:[13]

- Approximately two-thirds (64%) of U.S. men view pornography at least monthly. The number of Christian men viewing pornography virtually mirrors the national average.
- Broken down by age, eight out of ten (79%) men between the ages of 18 and 30 view pornography at least monthly, and two-thirds (67%) of men between the ages of 31 and 49 view pornography at least monthly. One-half of men between 50 and 68 looks at porn monthly.
- There are also a lot of men looking at pornography on a daily basis. Three out of ten men (29%) between the ages of 18 and 30 view pornography daily.
- Viewing pornography is not limited to single men. Over one-half (55%) of married men view pornography monthly, compared to seven out of ten single men.
- Broken down by age, one in three (34%) women between the ages of 18 and 30 view pornography at least monthly; one in eight (12.5%) of women between the ages of 31 and 49 view pornography at least monthly; and one

in ten (10%) of women between 50 and 68 looks at porn monthly.

- The number of Christian women viewing pornography is about one-half of the national average. (This data was updated on January 8, 2015.)

Like I learned that day, there is a link between the consumption of pornography and sex trafficking. In his book *The Johns,* Victor Malarek says, "The message is clear: if prostitution is the main act, porn is the dress rehearsal."[14] Even the etymology of the word, *pornography*, points to prostitution. It comes from two Greek words, *pornēia* meaning *prostitution* or *sexual immorality,* and *graphos,* which means "to write."[15] Linguistically, pornography was not viewed simply as recorded sexual intimacy, it was seen as recorded prostitution (in this case, depicted by writing or drawing). In the ancient world most of those who were in prostitution came from classes of people who were vulnerable and left without options; many were enslaved.

The demand for pornography grows the more that we watch pornography. With each video that we watch, we are signaling to the world that we want more of it. And there will be more of it. There will always be a supply made ready to meet the demand . . . and as we are learning, not everyone is there by choice.

But the demand that we create is not the only negative effect. Whether we know it or not, as we watch porn, our own sexual expectations are changing. We are learning what is expected of us in sexual intimacy. In a *New York Times* magazine article, "What Teenagers Are Learning from Online Porn," one teenager interviewed says, "There's nowhere else to learn about sex, and porn stars know what they are doing."[16] On a similar note, sex traffickers often use porn as a grooming technique to teach new recruits what's expected of them. Given the statistics above, it's safe to say that pornography has become the sex education classroom for most Americans.

With this education, we begin to no longer see the person on the other side of the screen (or the person in front of us, for that matter) as a human being, but as an object—an object that stands between us and our sexual fulfillment. Through this act of objectification, our neighbor is viewed as something less than human, a commodity we can consume for pleasure.

In addition, pornography mingles sexual intimacy with violence. Pornography is rarely basic "love making." It is often exaggerated, which in turn exaggerates the sexual appetite of the viewer. Whether it prioritizes violent sexual expression or it eroticizes children and youth, it is normalizing predatory behavior and thus setting the stage for the sexual exploitation of others. At this point, we need to know that our decision to open the browser on our phone and look at images deemed "not safe for work," has consequences.

But there is hope. Here are a few things that you can do right now:

Repent from Seeking Functional Saviors

We go to porn, or prostitution because we think that it will fulfill us or take the "edge off." There is often a woundedness that we are seeking to heal. But it leaves us feeling worse than we felt before. Rather than giving us relief and release, we feel shame. That's because the commercial sex industry cannot deliver on what it promises. No functional savior can.

The point of this section is not to shame anyone that has viewed pornography. Rather, the goal is to think about the consequences and to take a step toward healing. So for us to really address this issue, we have to deal with the thing behind the thing. Why are you going to pornography in the first place? Is it because you feel alone? Unworthy? Angry? Unheard? Broken? Ashamed?

Our unhealthy desires spring from our own sin and brokenness. Start with that pain. Invite God into it. Trust that God loves you even as you are in that moment. Because of what he did on the cross for us, we are assured that he isn't looking at us in disgust, saying, "You need to be ashamed of yourself." He's saying, "I love you." And he will keep on loving you as you struggle and limp toward healing.

For us, repentance means that before we can truly love others and treat trafficked people with dignity, we have to fall out of love with pornography. Falling out of love with porn can happen, but only when we fall more in love with something else. The way to get rid of a desire isn't to tell yourself to let go of it; it's to redirect your heart toward a greater desire. The only way to love porn less is to love something else more, and that something else is God. Unlike our functional saviors, only Christ can deliver on what he has promised.

Make Yourself Accountable by Using Internet Accountability Tools

We like to tell ourselves that we can figure this out on our own, but the stats above prove otherwise. *The good news is that you aren't alone.* White-knuckling your way to sobriety is not freedom. It takes courage to say that you need help. Covenant Eyes offers accountability software that is available for your phones, tablets, and laptops. Its value is found in how it monitors your Internet viewing habits, sending regular reports to an accountability partner of your choice. If you view "adult" content, an email notification will be sent to a friend that you trust. This allows us the opportunity to cast light into the dark recesses of our lives. To experience freedom, we have to invite others into our journey of vulnerability.

Learn about the Link between Porn and Sex Trafficking

There are great resources online, but the best place to start would be with *Stop the Demand: The Role of Porn in Sex Trafficking.*[17] This document produced by Covenant Eyes is a very helpful tool to help you learn more about the conversation. You should download it today.

The problem of global slavery involves us. Whether it is through our consumption of food, clothing, or pornography, our actions create a demand for exploitation. Our daily decisions create a ripple effect. *Are we purchasing freedom or are we consuming suffering?*

CHAPTER 10

VULNERABILITY AS STRENGTH

We have seen that our selfish responses to the pain and suffering we experience can have a negative fallout. The shame of this realization tempts us to avoid vulnerability altogether. But isn't that how we got here in the first place?

Take, for instance, the "Strengths Finder" concept. In the *Harvard Business Review* article, "Strengths-Based Coaching Can Actually Weaken You," Tomas Chamorro-Premuzic, explains:

> A Google search for "strengths coaching" yields over 45 million hits. The top results mostly offer related services, while virtually none question the idea. Amazon sells almost 8,000 books on the subject, including several bestselling exemplars by Gallup, whose StrengthsFinder is now used by 1.6 million employees every year and 467 *Fortune* 500 companies. The word *weakness* has become a politically incorrect term in mainstream HR circles, where people are described as having strengths and "opportunities" or "challenges"—but not

weaknesses. Some businesses are even planning to scrap negative feedback.[1]

For Chamorro-Premuzic, though our passion for discovering and working out of our own "strengths" shows no signs of stopping, we "would be better off if it did." One reason is that there is no scientific evidence available to back up the idea that strengths-based personality profiles or coaching actually works. Evidently, we collectively assume that it must work, and thus we depend on it without question. This leaves us thinking that our "weaknesses" are at best worthless and at worst an impediment to our progress. So we shelve them and do our best to find and maximize our strengths.

Another reason for us to rethink this approach is because strengths-based coaching can give us a false sense of proficiency. He says, "it conveys the illusion of ability even to those who lack it. Since most people already have an inflated self-concept (especially leaders, who tend to be more narcissistic than average), it is likely that strengths-based feedback will only enhance people's deluded self-views."

The third danger is that "overused strengths can become toxic." Most of us are absolutely unaware of our most toxic behaviors. Unbeknownst to us, as we "overuse" our strengths and natural gifting, we are setting ourselves up to ride right off the rails.[2]

What we don't know is that our experience of adversity, weakness, and limitation is really a blessing. To prove my point, we need to look no farther than the American bowling alley experience.

I love bowling alleys. Let's be honest, bowling alleys are the perfect place to think through the concept of vulnerability. Because here, no one is really trying to impress anyone. It's definitely a "come as you are" environment. If you, perchance, were seeking to impress, your lofty expectations will come crashing down to earth as you walk up to the counter. Regardless of our station in life, you take on the "mantle of vulnerability" as you put on the worn-out, seventies-era bowling shoes, which on their best day can be described as hideous looking. In "someone else's shoes," you make your way over to your lane and commence setting up the game. If you are like me, you may have to admit that you aren't exactly the best bowler. Case in point, a 100-point game for me is a feat worthy of a parade. So I typically bowl at least one game with the bumpers up. Don't judge. This is how I avoid gutter balls and pick up spares like it's my job.

In this analogy, the bowling ball represents our particular strength. We take the ball and fling it down the lane with all of the strength and focus we can muster. Like the ball, if we keep using our strength, alone, we are destined for the gutter. The bumpers, however, represent the weaknesses that we typically want to jettison from our lives. Are they embarrassing? Absolutely. However, it's only by having the bumpers up that we are guaranteed to knock down some pins every time. The point is that our weaknesses, though they feel unsightly, are integral to our growth as human beings.

If anyone knew this principle, it was the apostle Paul. As he writes to the church at Corinth, which he founded, he faces a smear campaign. Leaders have risen to power, who are calling into question his physical appearance as well as his speaking ability. Paul, in their estimation, doesn't have the look or the presence of an effective leader. In their eyes, he is neither credible nor qualified to lead the Corinthian church. To cast further doubt on his character, they question his apostolic credentials, basically, arguing that he has lied on his résumé.

Writing to the church, Paul explains how, as a true apostle, he has seen visions and revelations that would make even the most humble swell with pride. "So to keep me from becoming conceited because of the surpassing greatness of the revelations," he says, "a thorn was given me in the flesh, a messenger of Satan to harass me, to keep me from becoming conceited" (2 Cor. 12:7).

The fact that Paul uses the phrase "to keep me from being conceited" twice in verse 7 conveys a lot about his understanding of the purpose of his weakness. God had given him amazing visions, but to keep him from becoming self-centered and image-focused, he was given a thorn. The picture here is not of a tiny thorn like what we would find on a rose bush. The "thorn" in Paul's mind is much larger; it's as if he's had a wooden spike driven through his chest. This is not a minor inconvenience; it is debilitating.[3]

Picking up on this idea, one pastor explains that this verse in the Greek is to be read not as a "thorn in the flesh," but as a "thorn for the flesh," existing to kill the proud tendencies of Paul's sinful humanity (what the Bible calls our flesh).[4]

Countless sermons have been preached on the particular identity of this "thorn." Did Paul have poor eyesight or physical health? Was he facing intense sexual temptation? Was it anxiety or depression? Let's for a moment push those questions to the side and try to read this text with the immediate context in view. Paul was brokenhearted over the crisis facing both himself and the Corinthian church. Looking at the "thorn" through this lens illustrates that his thorn could very well be his vulnerability and accusations he's facing.

Paul's point in bringing it up is not to simply complain or vent his frustration. Rather, it's to cast light on the idea that though facing our "thorns" can be challenging, it's ultimately a gift. Our perceived weaknesses are a gift because they possess a unique ability to teach us humility. Just like bowling with bumpers, they keep us in alignment with God's purposes for our lives.

Have you ever noticed how when you experience adversity, you start to notice things to which you were blind before? You start seeing other people in a fresh way in light of your pain. You may even find yourself becoming a little more compassionate and a little less self-righteous or arrogant. This is by design. God's solution to our problem with pride and self-glorification involves living in light of the things that seem to constrain us.

Rather than always looking out for number one, those marked by humility grow in the ability to put themselves in the passenger seat, to look to the needs of others before meeting their own. The beauty of this gift is that we don't even have to ask for it. If Paul's experience is any indication, God will give it to us freely. But he does so through the process of suffering.

As soon as I began writing this book, my life went haywire. It was as if everything happened all at once and I wasn't prepared. After sharing my woes with my friend Erick Sorenson, a Lutheran pastor in Manhattan, he said sarcastically, "It's almost like God is helping you write on the subject by allowing you to experience the content." I believe Erick was right on the money. Like a potter, God molds and shapes us through both our individual and collective experiences of vulnerability.

As God shapes us, he also uses this "gift" to invite us into prayerful dependence on him. "Three times, I pleaded with the Lord about this, that it should leave me" (2 Cor. 12:8). Here we see why God never took the thorn away: it drew Paul closer to the God. Paul was literally begging God. He was in anguish. All the while, he was learning the secret art of prayer. Though difficult, this crisis he faced brought Paul to his knees. As he cried out to God for assistance, he knew that he alone couldn't fix what was wrong.

Sometimes, in order to grow in our prayer lives, we attend conferences, read books, or start journaling. Paul didn't take this approach. Instead, he had developed a foolproof method. He suffered. The more he struggled, the more he prayed.

Our experience of suffering attacks our predisposition to rely on ourselves. Paul hinted at this idea earlier in his letter. "Not that we are sufficient in ourselves to claim anything as coming from us, but our sufficiency is from God" (2 Cor. 3:5). Paul learned firsthand that our vulnerability compels us to depend on the God who became vulnerable for us.

Have you ever noticed how when our circumstances are comfortable, we tend to put our lives on autopilot? We coast through life. We start working from our own strength. It's as if we tell God, "It's okay, man, I can take it from here." This is something of which I have been guilty. Though I never intentionally set out to live the Christian life out in my own strength, I find myself doing it more often than I'd like to admit. And for that reason, God allows me to experience turbulence. He allows each of us to hit the bumper rail.

But our suffering is not simply meant to drive us to a deeper relationship with God; there's still more to it. The apostle continues: "But [God] said to me, 'My grace is sufficient for you, for my power is made perfect in weakness'" (2 Cor 12:9a). In other words, our vulnerability is also a gift because when we are at our weakest, we begin to trust God *for his strength*.

Throughout this process, the power and love of God is on display. For this reason, Paul says, "Therefore I will boast all the more gladly of my weaknesses, so that the power of Christ may rest upon me. For the sake of Christ, then, I am content with weaknesses, insults, hardships, persecutions, and calamities. For when I am weak, then I am strong" (2 Cor. 12:9b–10). To tap into a strength that endures, we don't need to take the latest strengths test. As we depend on God's strength, in our darkest moments of exposure, we will find that we have access to God's power.

Finally, this gift of weakness qualifies us for ministry. Despite the accusations that were hurled at him, Paul was qualified to serve the church. But his qualifications were not the kind you would list on a résumé. His weaknesses were the very thing that made him viable as an apostle. Maybe he wasn't as skilled or impressive on the exterior as the others, but he had suffered more for the cause of Christ than any one of them. Speaking to his qualifications, Paul says:

> Are they Hebrews? So am I. Are they Israelites? So am I. Are they offspring of Abraham? So am I. Are they servants of Christ? I am a better one—I am talking like a madman—with far greater labors, far more imprisonments, with countless beatings, and often near death. Five times I received at the hands of the Jews the forty lashes less one. Three times I was beaten with rods. Once I was stoned. Three times I was shipwrecked; a night and a day I was adrift at sea; on frequent journeys, in danger from rivers, danger from robbers, danger from my own

people, danger from Gentiles, danger in the city, danger in the wilderness, danger at sea, danger from false brothers; in toil and hardship, through many a sleepless night, in hunger and thirst, often without food, in cold and exposure. And, apart from other things, there is the daily pressure on me of my anxiety for all the churches. Who is weak, and I am not weak? Who is made to fall, and I am not indignant? (2 Cor. 11:22–29)

Paul uses a time line of his personal history of vulnerability and suffering to showcase how it's precisely through our "weaknesses" that we are qualified to love our neighbor. As fellow sufferers, we can love vulnerable people because we are also vulnerable.

A Vulnerability Time Line

In the book of Genesis, fourteen chapters are dedicated to the story of a human trafficking survivor named Joseph. Like modern victims, Joseph, the biblical patriarch, was trafficked by those he trusted—his own brothers sold him for twenty shekels of silver (Gen. 37:28). Once in Egypt, he would again be sold, this time to Potiphar, the captain of Pharaoh's guard, to labor as a domestic servant.

Despite these circumstances, the Lord "was with Joseph and he became a successful man" (Gen. 39:2). God continued to guide and bless him. But his life was not without difficulty. Joseph's God-given success attracted the affection of Potiphar's wife. "Lie with me," she continually demanded, but Joseph resisted (Gen. 39:7–9). When she could take his rejection no longer, she grabbed him, ripping his clothing as he ran away. She then accused Joseph of attempting to rape her (vv. 12–18). So he was imprisoned for a crime he didn't commit. Although his situation grew more difficult, "the LORD was with Joseph" (Gen. 39:21).

While in chains, Joseph interpreted the dreams of two fellow prisoners, the Pharaoh's cupbearer and baker. The cupbearer would be restored, while the baker would be executed. "Remember me, when it is well with you," Joseph told the cupbearer, "and please do me the kindness to mention me to Pharaoh, and so get me out of this house" (Gen. 40:14).

Two years passed, and Joseph waited for a miracle. Then one evening, Pharaoh had a baffling dream. With no one else in Egypt able to interpret it, Joseph was brought before him. Recognizing Joseph's wisdom in foreseeing a worldwide famine, Pharaoh made him his top adviser.

Many years later, Joseph found himself face-to-face with his brothers. Sensing their fear, he told them not to be "distressed or angry with yourselves because you sold me here, for God sent me before you to preserve life" (Gen. 45:5). Rejected by his brothers, God chose Joseph to be their deliverer. In this way, Joseph foreshadows Christ, the true and better deliverer who would save those who rejected him (Acts 4:27–28). Joseph's story is a reminder that no matter what some may mean for evil, God still means it for good (Gen. 50:20).

This is good news for us as we discover more about the extent of our own vulnerability. Joseph's story prompts us to remember that though traumatic and difficult, nothing that happens in your life is ever wasted. God is too good to allow that to happen. It's through our pain that we grow. The person that you are today is the result of what you have experienced.[5]

Hebrews 12:6–11 has much to say about how God molds us through our suffering. The writer of Hebrews says it this way:

> "For the Lord disciplines the one he loves, and chastises every son whom he receives." It is for discipline that you have to endure. God is treating you as sons. For what son is there whom his father does not discipline? If you are left without discipline, in which all have participated, then you

are illegitimate children and not sons. Besides this, we have had earthly fathers who disciplined us and we respected them. Shall we not much more be subject to the Father of spirits and live? For they disciplined us for a short time as it seemed best to them, but he disciplines us for our good, that we may share his holiness. For the moment all discipline seems painful rather than pleasant, but later it yields the peaceful fruit of righteousness to those who have been trained by it.

Bill Mounce, Greek scholar, asks the following question of the passage above: "Does this passage apply only to God's children when we sin?" The answer is no. Mounce says this passage "is a means of encouragement for all followers of Jesus Christ who are going through difficult times (not just sinful times). Just as an earthly father does not always smooth out the road for his children but rather allows them to experience life and grow through those difficult times, so also our heavenly Father is at work in all situations, whether they be the consequences of sin or the consequences of life. And as we experience life, we are reminded to not grow weary or fainthearted. The saints who went before us endured the same difficulties and remained faithful. Jesus endured great suffering that had nothing to do with sinful actions he committed, and yet for the joy set before him he endured the cross."[6]

The things we have experienced, including the vulnerabilities of which we are most embarrassed, fashion us into something entirely new; they train us to better love God and love others. It is no question that we are who we are because of the things we have experienced.

I challenge you, in light of this reality, to look back over your life, through your most painful experiences. What are the moments in your life when you couldn't take it anymore and you cried out, "God, where are you?"

As you embark on this journey, I have found the following questions to be quite helpful: *What vulnerabilities did I experience during my childhood and early adolescence? At what times during my life did I feel particularly vulnerable due to extreme pain, suffering, loneliness, or loss? What aspects of my life now regularly cause me to feel vulnerable? What struggles do I find myself continually bringing back up to God?*

Take a moment and sketch them out in the form of an outline.

Though I have used much of my time line already in this book, here is an example of my own vulnerability time line.[7]

In elementary school, I didn't fit in. I was two feet taller than most of my classmates and not as athletic. Going outside each day for P.E. was torture. Every time we played dodge ball or kick ball or anything with a ball for that matter, I was the last to get picked. I longed to be accepted by my peers.

In fifth grade, I contracted spinal meningitis and eastern equine encephalitis. Rushing me to the hospital, we waited as doctors struggled to discern what was wrong with me. Thinking that it was probably just the flu, they attempted to send me home. But before I could make it out of the emergency room, I threw up everywhere and passed out. The next thing that I knew, I woke in a hospital bed with several physicians wearing masks standing above me. In the span of a week, I lost seventy pounds. But one specific thing stands out from that difficult week. My parents left me in the room as they went out for a really quick lunch. They hadn't been gone five minutes when a nurse came in to do blood work. As a twelve-year-old, I was scared to death of needles. She looked me in the eyes and calmly said, "I know it hurts, but think about how you will feel when it is over." This advice has helped me through many a trial since.

My experience at the local church as a child and youth shaped me as well. While I was still in elementary school, my parents sat me down to talk with me. They explained that my Bible study leader, to whom I looked up to, would no longer be my teacher as he was in prison. He had committed a crime. I remember trying to process my feelings as I put pen to paper and began to write my Bible study leader a letter. As I wrote the prison's mailing address on the enve-lope, I was genuinely curious. "Why did this happen?" For a third grader, this was a simple question, deserving of an answer. This moment taught me very early that even the people that I respect can fall because each of us is trying to process our own brokenness at some level. But I would also begin to have a passion to see the church better care for people who were hurting.

I would watch as another church leader that I loved and respected made certain decisions that left destruction in his wake. Though I will not go into detail, from that moment on, I began looking with suspicion at those in authority, especially church leaders.

While in college and seminary, I noticed that my mother's health was in decline. I'll never forget receiving a call from my father my first semester in seminary. My father, being of the sort that never cried in public, cried as he told me, "Your mom fell and shattered her leg. The doctors told us that she'll most likely never walk again." Her mobility was only the tip of the iceberg; given other medical complications, like heart and renal failure, we spent six months in fear that she was not going to make it. Vulnerability became a part of life. I see how God taught all of us to savor the time that we had with each other and to not take life too seriously. Life is hard enough on its own.

As I look back at these dark times, I can now see all of these things working together to mold me into who I am becoming. All of these things played a role in my own development. I would probably not be working with churches around the idea of vulnerability had these things not occurred.

After you finish sketching out a basic time line, pause for a moment. Invite God into your suffering. I know that sometimes it's impossible to see God in light of what we have experienced, but I'd argue that in hindsight, this where he is most clearly seen.

You may feel that God skipped town during your childhood, that he was "out to lunch" when you needed him. Joseph experi-enced the presence of God in the middle of his exploitation. God never abandoned him. The Bible shows us time and time again that it's in the worst moments of suffering that God is present. Take, for example, the crucifixion: Jesus—both fully God and fully man—died at the hands of sinners. Through his suffering, those who place their faith in him are saved. God uses vulnerability and pain to not only change us but to change the world.

What would lead God to move toward us in the cross of Christ? Love. Through a cruel wooden cross, Christ dealt with your past, present, and future sins two thousand years ago. If you trust in him, you can be certain that before you were ever even close to being born, God took your salvation out of your hands. Therefore, as we process through the things that make us feel broken beyond repair, I ask you to look for God in those places. As you look, remember two critical things: 1) he's there, and 2) he loves you. Ask yourself as you write down your time line: "How did God meet me in that moment? What does the love of God have to say to that vulnerability?"

Finally ask yourself, "Is the gospel enough to meet me where I am?" If we can learn anything else from the trials the apostle Paul faced, it's that the good news of God's love for us is indeed more than sufficient to meet us where we are.

Jesus lived, died, and rose to heal us. His life counts for us. With his strength, we are reminded that it's okay to be weak. In light of his victory over sin, we learn that failure is an option. We are not only shaped by God, we are defined by his work on our behalf. This truth motivates us to love others through our own vulnerability. Our path to healing involves us facing the things that scare us most. These vulnerabilities that we do our best to ignore are the very things that qualify us to love other vulnerable people.

Whether you feel like it or not, you are loved as you are.

CHAPTER 11

A VULNERABLE CONVERSATION

If given the choice between flying or driving, I'd take air travel hands down. I enjoy the whole process. It's an adventure of sorts. I love the drama of locating your seat, cramming your oversized carry-on underneath the seat in front of you, and sitting down as fast as you can, so you can put in your earbuds before the "all call" and "flight check." As you might have guessed, this is my preflight ritual.

Flight attendants have preflight rituals of their own. Prior to takeoff, we are greeted by the flight attendant who has specific crew member instructions for us. To be honest, though important, most of us are too busy on our phones or untangling our headphones at this point to really pay attention.

But the information that we are ignoring could actually save our lives. For example, immediately after hearing the best practices for putting on your safety belt, we learn about the oxygen masks located above our seats. "If cabin pressure should change, panels above your seat will open, revealing oxygen masks; reach up and pull a mask toward you. Place it over your nose and mouth, and secure with the elastic band, that can be adjusted to ensure a snug fit. The plastic bag will not fully inflate, although oxygen is flow-ing. Secure your own mask first before helping others."

The last sentence always captures my attention: "Secure your own mask first before helping others." In other words, if we don't address our needs first, then we won't be able to help others in the moments that really count. Though we understand this principle when it applies to air travel, we don't tend to apply it to other spheres of life.

As we care for the "widow, orphan, and sojourners" around us, it's important for us to "secure our own mask first" and prac-tice "healthy selfishness." This is what my friend Neal Salzman, the founder of The Rest Initiative (TRI), is asking those who are actively working with vulnerable populations to take seriously.

A few years ago, Neal gave me a call. Though we went to college together, we hadn't spoken much over the years, so I was really excited to catch up. "I love what you are doing, man," he said, "but I want to see it last twenty years instead of two years."

I was intrigued. "What do you mean?"

He went on to explain that oftentimes those who lead socially aware not-for-profits are so focused on other people that they forget to care for themselves.

After seeing what LMPG was doing, he reached out to see if I had a plan for "self-care." On that call, he cautioned me to be aware of "compassion fatigue."

At the time, this sounded like a lot of jargon, and I'm aware you might feel the same way as you read. According to the American Counseling Association, "compassion fatigue" is also known as vicarious or secondary trauma:

> It is believed that counselors working with trauma
> survivors experience vicarious trauma because of
> the work they do. Vicarious trauma is the emo-
> tional residue of exposure that counselors have
> from working with people as they are hearing
> their trauma stories and become witnesses to the

pain, fear, and terror that trauma survivors have
endured.

It is important not to confuse vicarious trauma
with "burnout." Burnout is generally something
that happens over time, and as it builds up, a
change—such as time off or a new and sometimes
different job—can take care of burnout or improve
it. Vicarious trauma, however, is a state of tension
and preoccupation of the stories/trauma experiences described by clients.[1]

Neal, a trained counselor, knew the dangers of doing ministry firsthand. He dealt with his own vulnerabilities head-on
when he moved to India in 2005. "I was almost on the brink of
a nervous breakdown because of the stress. I was alone, and had
panic attacks, a lot of anxiety, and I didn't have a support system.
I had no plan. I was supposed to be there a year and came back
two weeks later with my head down, tail between my legs." Neal
experienced shame as he thought about "failing" to do the ministry
to which he had been called. He came to realize, though, that just
as God called him to India, he called him back two weeks later. "I
think a big part of that was to learn that if I don't care for myself,
that's what's going to happen," he said. At this point, his eyes were
opened to those who were burning out and exhausted. He began to
ask himself, "What can we do proactively? What can we do ongoing to support people who were, I think, doing some of the greatest
work in the world?"

Out of this experience, The Rest Initiative was born. The Rest
Initiative's vision is "to support clergy, church-planters, mission-
aries, humanitarian workers, and caregivers both nationally and
internationally as they care for others. Organizations and churches
that have staff either in high stress, cross-cultural assignments,
or domestic, ministerial positions have a responsibility to care for
them—those who work with the traumatized, hurting, poor, destitute, and emotionally broken."[2]

They accomplish this vision by helping people actively engaged in serving those most vulnerable to incorporate healthy rhythms into their lives, so as to promote resiliency. For Neal, self-care is all about rhythms. "If you wait until it's time for your vacation, you've already waited too long." For Neal, we need to move away from a "50 weeks/2 weeks" vacation model and move toward a more biblical model.

This is possible as we focus on creating regular rhythms of rest. The weekly Sabbath is an example of this idea. Knowing humanity's tendency, even before we knew it, God called his people to set aside one day a week to rest. Though I believe that Jesus has become our Sabbath rest by fulfilling it for us, I still believe that we would be wise to take at least one day a week where we can rest, recharge, and remember.

Much of the experience of Israel in the Old Testament revolves around this idea of resting and remembering. Each festival, each celebration, was an opportunity to rest and reflect on what God had done for them. This was a healthy disruption, which helped them to refocus weekly and periodically throughout the year.

In addition to resting and remembering, we can also incorporate rhythms of relationship into our busy schedules. Like hypertension, isolation is a silent killer. Just as "it is not good that man should be alone" (Gen. 2:18), it's never good to do this work alone. We need people speaking light into our darkness. Whether this takes the form of weekly counseling sessions or regular intentional conversations with friends that love you, we need people who care enough about us to check in consistently. And we need to be that person for others as well. The work of justice and mercy is impossible without community. In other words, justice can fail when it's just us.

As we think through what these rhythms should look like in our lives, we need to be careful to not fall into the trap of "living for the weekend." This approach drastically undervalues the work God has called us to do, placing a premium on two days a week where we likely will not be resting adequately or actively. No, these rhythms of rest, remembrance, and relationship need to be proactive, rather than reactive. Rather than working *for* rest, we should work *from* rest.

Ask yourself, *What is the first thing that Adam and Eve did after they were created?* They rested in God's presence.

In this way, they were marching in tune to God's cadence. Like our first parents, we were created to value rest and to live in the right rhythm with God and others.

Consider other questions: When do you start getting shaky? Stressed out? Exhausted? When are the times throughout the week, month, and year that you begin to feel worn down? With these times in mind, plan your rhythms. Remember that we won't survive this work unless we rest in a manner that is both preemptive and proactive.

Truth be told, the only person who doesn't need to create regular consistent rhythms of self-care is someone that has it all together. And if you say that you've got it all figured out, you are either standing in the physical presence of Jesus or you are a self-deceived liar. Given our choices, if you are reading this paragraph, then there are probably a few things you can do to better love and care for yourself.

In this chapter, we will continue to think through how our brokenness impacts us and those around us. Remember, each reminder of your own brokenness is a reminder to take care of yourself, because you will never be able to properly care for others unless you are seeking to be in a healthy place.

The pain of others often exposes the pain we feel deep within. This "vulnerability mirror" shows us as we truly are. It glosses over nothing. Staring into this mirror, you will find every inadequacy that you have. Therefore, it's important that we keep our fingers on the pulse of our emotional, physical, spiritual, and psychological health. To learn more about how we can best care for ourselves in the midst of our own perceived weaknesses, I reached out to Dr. Diane Langberg.

An Interview with Diane Langberg

Dr. Diane Langberg is a practicing psychologist whose clinical expertise includes forty-five years of working with trauma survivors and clergy. Her books include *Counsel for Pastors' Wives; Counseling Survivors of Sexual Abuse; On the Threshold of Hope: Opening the Door to Healing for Survivors of Sexual Abuse*; and *Suffering and the Heart of God: How Trauma Destroys and Christ Restores*. She is also a clinical faculty member at Biblical Theological Seminary where she co-leads the Global Trauma Recovery Institute with Dr. Phil Monroe.[3]

At 8:00 a.m. on a Friday morning, my phone rang.

"How are you, Diane?"

"I'm fine."

"Thank you so much for making time."

"You're quite welcome."

After chatting for a couple minutes, I gave Dr. Langberg the gist of this book. "[It] assumes a simple yet clear definition of human trafficking, which is basically the exploitation of vulnerability for commercial gain. In light of that, the theme of this book is that vulnerable people can love other vulnerable people because Christ became vulnerable for them. For this chapter, I would love to get your thoughts on how, as we're caring for others, we can recognize our own vulnerability and address it in a way that is appropriate. Diving in, could you start out by sharing a little about who you are and what you do?"

"I'm a licensed psychologist," Diane explained, "and I worked with all kinds of trauma and the abuse of power for forty-five years."

She continued, "If I hadn't figured out the self-care thing and all these other things you were just talking about, I'd have died a long time ago. I started out in the early to mid 1970s. PTSD was not even a diagnostic category at the time; it wasn't a diagnostic category until 1980. There were very few women in the field of psychology. I started working with Vietnam vets and women who began telling me their stories, which were about childhood sexual abuse. Had a woman who had been trafficked, though nobody knew what it was at the time, of course. Then domestic violence cases. I realized that the vets and the women who were being battered and the women who'd been abused all had the same [thing in common]. They all lived in war zones. They all didn't have power. I spent some years at the beginning of my career being a student of traumatized human beings, because there were no books, there was nothing. I ended up reading books about the Nazi holocaust, that's where I learned about trauma. I read Elie Wiesel and Primo Levi and all kinds of people like that. They were the ones who taught me, along with my clients."

I was amazed. I had no idea that the study of trauma was a relatively new concept.

"It's a little bit of a weird story," she said.

I said, "That's incredible . . . those are tangible examples of traumatization that no one can argue away. Yes, we see the experience of Vietnam War veterans, we see the experience of those who were in the holocaust, as experiences of extreme traumatization."

Diane agreed. "Yes, and those who are reluctant to say people are traumatized at least allow those to be real."

As we were talking about the trauma of others, I remembered how easy it is for us to discount the trauma that we have experienced. "As we're caring for people who've experienced intense trauma and intense vulnerability, like those, it's important for us to process where we are, to process our own vulnerability. How do we do that?"

Being Aware of Our Own Power

"You not only have to process your own vulnerability," Diane answered, "you also have to process and be aware of your own power. You have to do both sides. I do think there's something inherent in human beings that [we] feel shame about vulnerability. It is equated with weakness. I think particularly in the West, because in the West, we tend to believe that if you do the right thing, and just make the right choices, everything will turn out fine. If your life's a mess, if you're trafficked or an addict or whatever, it's because you didn't make the right choices. It's not because of what's going on around you and it's not because of trauma and it's not because of lack of power and those kinds of things.

"People are very uncomfortable, I think, looking at their vulnerabilities. I also think just theologically, it's inherent in humans, because once we ruined everything, we became vulnerable in a way that was not safe. Before that, we were vulnerable, but we knew we were safe, because of the right relationship with God. That got lost. The whole thing got messed up. I think your definition in terms of trafficking is excellent, when I work with abuse-of-power kind of things, which we're seeing plastered all over the news and churches now and things like that, it's always the exploitation of vulnerability for self-gain. It isn't always commercial. That's certainly something that motivates many people. It's always using the one with less power, in order to feed myself.

"Vulnerability is not exploited without someone abusing power."

"Right. One-hundred percent," I agreed.

"Otherwise," she said, "vulnerability is safe."

She was right. Like we saw in the second section of this book, there is a such thing as safe vulnerability. I responded, "Adam and Eve were naked and unashamed. They were vulnerable in the presence of God. But as soon as they exited the garden, exploitation became the norm. You see that as it works itself through the family, you see power differentials and how they play themselves out."

"If you think about trafficking," Diane shared, "in particular, it's the work of rescue, rehabilitation, and restoration. If I'm going to do that work, I want to feel competent, which means I want to feel powerful. I do that because I want to rescue the vulnerable, which is a good thing. But, people are often not aware of the fact that that's usually not 100 percent good. I often say to particularly young therapists, but old ones too, there is a Messiah. I am not he. There is always, I think, in us—which is how we try to throw God off the throne—something messianic. When you do work that is rescuing, rehabbing, and restoring, it's there. It has to be there. If we don't understand it and know how to submit it to God and have obedience to him . . . we'll go under. We just see our desires, our hopes, our wanting to help people, as just good. It's not . . . Nothing human is *just* good.

"Everything we do is tainted. If we deceive ourselves or if we're just ignorant about the tainting, then we become a danger to those we want to rescue. Certainly, the work becomes a danger to us. . . . If you work with trafficking, you know there's a revolving door for many. You can't rescue everybody. You can't restore everybody. You can't rehab everybody. What are you going to do with that?

"That's where people get twisted up. There was a study, and I couldn't tell you where now because I read it forever ago, but there was a study about therapists who work with trauma, and they start out with the same high ideals and hopes and good plans and everything else, and they burn out in less than seven years. Five to seven is about what people can stand. Then, they have to find something else to do that doesn't make them feel not competent.

"I think those things have to be really clear from the beginning, and dealt with all the time. It doesn't matter, I'm still doing those things with myself after forty-five years if there's no arrival point."

"That's very helpful to hear," I replied.

Diane went on, "I think that people have to understand that and accept that as a reality. You will be perpetually a student. You will be perpetually not at the arrival point.

"The other thing I often say to therapists . . . is I've seen a lot of black things. I travel internationally, so I just came back from Cambodia. I've been back and forth to Rwanda many times, I've been to Auschwitz. I'm going to Eastern Europe at the end of the month to speak to heads of trafficking organizations about trauma. I've walked a lot of killing fields. Which is enough to make you curl up in a ball and never want to do anything again. I say to people, 'Look, with all of this darkness and ugliness that I've seen, I have also seen redeemed lives, and mine is one of them.'"

Approaching Self-Care

Thinking about the darkness that we will come into contact with as we care for those who are vulnerable to human trafficking, I asked, "What are some tangible ways that as we're doing this, through our vulnerability, that we can actually take care of ourselves?"

"I don't know, maybe twenty years or so, maybe more, I wanted to quit," she answered. "I sat down one day and I wrote a list of the characteristics of the work that I do. Wasn't a pretty menu. It's dark and it's ugly and it's evil and it's on and on and on and on. It's chaotic; lives are chaotic when they've been traumatized. Anyway. I pretty much held the list up and said to God, 'This is why I'm quitting.'

"I felt nudged to take the list and write the opposites of it. It's ugly, [he's] beauty; chaotic, [he's] order, things like that. I did. What I learned that day from him is that he is those things. They're all him. The other piece is . . . you need an antidote. It comes from that list. But, being a finite, frail human being, many of those things can't just be thoughts and ideas, or even spiritual exercises, though they are a vital part of what I do.

Diane began listing antidotes that she takes on a regular basis. "I . . . need to go walk in the woods and listen to Bach, who's never disordered. I have to purposefully ingest the things that are the antidotes on a concrete human level." She also explained that being a spiritual being, she must also make time for common spiritual practices, like prayer. In her own words, "You can't constantly feed on poison, and not take antidotes. If you do that, you will die."

"I've also learned in teaching that to people who do things like this, there's something about what he taught me that day that gives people permission to do self-care without feeling selfish. Which is a cockeyed way to think about it, but lots of Christians do. How can I go do something, how can I go walk on the beach and absorb the beauty of that, when people are being trafficked? How can I do that? Doesn't feel right. The fact is, if you don't do that, you can't help them."

Taking note of the point that Diane had made, I said, "It's interesting, because Jesus did not heal everyone he came across." There are times when we feel guilty because we can't help everyone. Looking at the example of Jesus, Diane seconded this idea.

"He did not," Diane said. "No, he left a lot of dead people behind too."

"Yeah. He took days off. He rested."

"Where did he go?" Diane answered her own question: "He went into nature."

This made me think about my friend Neal and his organization, The Rest Initiative. "Neal was on the phone with me and was like, 'Here's the deal, man. Most of the people that are engaged in work like this have their own issues—'"

"That they've never looked at," she interjected. "They're escaping them by doing the work."

"Exactly," I said. "He's like, 'We have to practice healthy self-ishness.' That's the phrase that he used. 'As we do this, we have to take care of ourselves.' It's interesting, because as we talk about this, I'm reminded of the idea or of the concept of the wounded healer. Could you explain that for me a little bit?"

Diane obliged. "First of all, there is no other kind. You can't be the *un*wounded healer. There is no other kind."

"But we want to be the unwounded healer," I said out of slight frustration.

"Yes," she said. "But the one that we follow, who was perfection itself, is a wounded healer. It's not a flaw. It's necessary. Part of it has to do with, you have to be little to help little. You just think about it at an ordinary human level, if you have a little person in your house, and you want to be the little person who's sitting on the floor, what do you do? Get on the floor . . . Part of it is being with, which is the incarnation. That's *Immanuel*, God with us, that's God becoming little. Literally. Talk about vulnerability. He was an infant. There was nothing he could've done to protect himself. Part of woundedness is littleness. . . . It is righteous to be a wounded healer, because it's like him. And, part of what awareness of that does is keep driving us back to him. We know we're not sufficient. We know we don't understand how to do this thing, because we think of healing as having no wound. The trafficked victims that you work with, no matter how wonderful the story ends up, they will always have wounds and scars. Always. They're never going to have a life that looks like a life that's never been trafficked. You and I are never going to have lives that look like the life that never was wounded. The problem is that many people are drawn to work like that, and my work as well, because they're escaping their own histories of trauma and abuse and things like that. Number one, they assume because I was [like them], I understand—which is a lie, because everybody's unique. Number two, they'd rather think about other people and help them, which will make them feel good, which is a feeding off of. It'll blow up, because it's not healthy. It's not right. If we accept the fact that the only way to heal is if we were also accepting of our own woundedness, then we can deal with our own woundedness in the ways that we need to."

Commenting on her previous point, I said, "That's powerful, because I agree, it's so easy to try to run away from your own problems by running to the problems of others."

"Absolutely."

"We feel that by helping others, we're in a sense maybe redeeming our own brokenness," I persisted. "In a sense, operating from your own wounds, I think, as you're saying, can be healthy, but it can also be extremely unhealthy if we're not unpacking it; for instance, we're not addressing it if we're not working through our own wounds with other people."

I asked her my next question: "How can were appropriately care for others through our own perceived weaknesses?"

Reflecting on what I said, Diane responded, "Let me just say in terms of what you were talking about before, if I do not deal with my own weaknesses or woundedness or whatever, and I think that because I was wounded, I can help other people without processing my own, it's really rather arrogant, because what I'm doing is saying to other people, I'm going to help you do what you most fear, which is look at the truth about your life, but I'm not doing that for me. I think we call that hypocritical. Again, the model is Christ. What did he do? He became little like us; he became wounded like us. He's the only one in heaven who's going to have scars. I'm not going to have any scars, he's going to have scars.

"If I'm going to follow him, I have to go the way he went, which is to become like [the ones I'm helping], but not be ruled by [them]. He was always ruled by the Father. We get ruled by other people's needs and everything else. Or we get ruled by our own history or whatever. He was relentlessly ruled by one thing only. I think that the 'best' helpers . . . are the ones who truly follow him . . . in dealing with the truth about themselves.

"There has to constantly be an ongoing assessment, not in a self-absorbed way, but because we know that we are an instrument, tool, but it is a tool that has to be kept sharp, or it will do more damage. If I don't really, on an ongoing basis, ask God to search my soul, talk to other people, get input about what I'm doing, . . . then I'm not safe.

"If you take it out of the realm of trafficking and just think about all the headlines, this pastor and this ministry leader and this person, whatever, and all of a sudden, the light gets turned on and you see things that everybody thought couldn't possibly be true about them. They didn't want to think they were true about them either, for a long time. They were running from themselves, which resulted in perhaps building ministries or a church or whatever, mission field, and they ended up doing damage, not only to the little ones, but to the body of Christ and to the name of Christ.

"You can't tell other people to look without learning how to look yourself. You have to do what you ask of people."

I took a moment to share how I had begun to process on my own brokenness within the last five years. "It just took a lot of things happening at once several years ago to drive me to not just mention things that I'd experienced, but actually really deal with them and take some tough tangible steps toward healing. To quote one of my friends who is a survivor, she says, 'First, God doesn't heal

you of everything at one time, because if he did, you would disinte-
grate. You can't take it. He heals you little by little.'"

"You think about it on the physical level," Diane noted. "You
break a bone. Then it has to heal. How does that feel? Awful. It
takes a lot longer than you want, it's very slow, and it hurts like
crazy. That's what healing looks like. Which is why a lot of people
run from it."

"It's interesting," I responded, "because as we're talking about
this, you and I both recognize that there are a lot of well-meaning
Christians who want to respond to issues of injustice, like human
trafficking, and as they do it, they often operate from the wrong
posture. Sometimes, we don't take the traumatic experiences of
others into account like we should. With that said, how can those
of us who want to care for those who've experienced trauma be
more trauma informed?"

On Being Trauma Informed

"Lots of study and training needs to be ongoing," Diane
informed me. "Years ago, when trafficking was just on the map,
Donna Hughes, one of the most well-known researchers in trafficking in the world, taught a class on it, and there were no classes on it
at the time. And [she] graciously allowed me to audit it. At the end
of the class, we had a conversation, and she said to me, the piece
that's missing in the trafficking world is the trauma piece. You need
to talk to trafficking people all the time about trauma, because if
they don't understand that, they're going to have a revolving door.

"What happens when you have a history of trauma, and you
don't deal with it, is you have to find ways to feel better. You do
that by things like addictions, which cost money which you don't
have. . . . Most people think of trauma as an event. Trafficking victims have trauma that's not an event; it is a lifetime. It is a life that
was developed as a child, marinating in trauma.

"Everything about that person has been shaped by trauma.
People get the stats, with histories of abuse in the homes they came

from, histories of addictions in the homes, all of that kind of stuff, they leave home, many of them, most of them, to get away from bad things.

"I have a YouTube video online on complex trauma. It's a whole different thing than post-traumatic stress disorder. It has to be understood by people. This is whole-person, lifelong trauma. It's like all the files in a child's head when they grow up like that have to do with protecting themselves from trauma. How do I stop the pain, how do I get away from the person? . . . There's no creative thinking, there's no learning, there's no flourishing—all the things humans are meant to do.

"If you go and 'rescue' somebody and get them through rehab and they're off the drugs and you don't deal with the trauma, you've left them with the pain of their history and a total lack of understanding of themselves and how trauma's affected them, and a lack of understanding about how to make different choices. And guess what will happen?

"It's because the trauma's never dealt with. I think it is a central thing to trafficking work. It's not a thing that [simply] also needs to be done; it's like one of the legs of the stool."

Pausing a moment, Diane asked me. "Do you know who Jeanne Allert is? She gets this. Her place is in Baltimore called the Samaritan Woman. She put on a conference in October called Sheltered and had people from trafficking organizations all over the United States come. I was one of the speakers, and I spoke on this issue of trauma and the kind of trauma it is. [The talk is] called 'Standing in the Presence of Trauma.' Everything is recorded, but the point is, there were lots and lots of people in the room who had started trafficking work, and it had folded. There were scores of that. Then there were others who felt like folding, and there were others who weren't folded, . . . It was clear that almost 99 percent of the people in the room didn't understand anything about the trauma that goes on in the lives of these women, all of their lives.

"One of the things I did when I spoke down at the Samaritan Woman was take everybody through a brief thing about child development and the different stages, and what you're supposed to be learning in that stage and what you're learning if you're in an abusive home. . . . If you're going to predict their behavior and understand their motives and everything else, you need to understand how that development occurred over time—shaped their brain, shaped their behavior, shaped everything. People don't understand that. There is redemption, but it doesn't look like pushing a button."

God's Working Both Sides

"The other piece I find—which is one of my other things I keep saying to young therapists and old therapists—when God sends you somebody and takes you to somebody, to get involved in their lives, he's working both sides. He didn't send you to teach them and help them and fix them. He sent you to teach and help and fix each other."

I could no longer stay silent. "That's incredible," I exclaimed. "This is a thought that I have hinted at throughout the book thus far. In my interview with Boz Tchividjian, this is something that he brought up as well. We need to continue to hear that it's not about us fixing someone else, but that the person that we're working with could be who God sent to help us."

"Yes," Diane acknowledged. "If I look back over forty-five years, there are people who walked away from help, who went back to whatever, all those things. [But] I changed. There's always redemption offered, if we'll bow to it. Even if the other people don't, it doesn't mean we can't. The failures can be redemptive in our lives as much as the successes, or whatever you want to call them. I hate those words, when you talk about people."

On this note, we wrapped up our phone call. Throughout the rest of the day as I reflected on our conversation, I couldn't help but think how much I had been challenged. We are not only shaped by what we experience personally; we are also shaped by the experiences of those around us.

RECOGNIZING YOUR VULNERABLE MISSION

I am struck by how sharing our weakness and difficulties is more nourishing to others than sharing our qualities and successes.

—Jean Vanier, *Community and Growth*[1]

CHAPTER 12

EMILY'S VULNERABLE MISSION

Recognizing our vulnerability is an important first step as we process our own journeys toward healing. However, it's not only important for us; our recognition of our own limitations directly impacts those with whom we are serving. God calls each of us to minister to the vulnerabilities of others through the lens of our own emotional exposure. To guide us in exploring this idea of "vulnerable mission" in more depth, I asked my friend Emily to share her story in her own words. Some of the content below was shared in conversation, other parts are taken from her excellent journal article, "From Victim to Healer."[1]

> Looking back, I can see how my childhood experiences led me to become a very vulnerable target for a trafficker. I was raised in a wealthy home in the Houston suburbs, went to respected schools, and was a competitive ice skater by age twelve. From the outside, everything seemed perfect. I was quiet, modest, and never wore makeup. I never dressed in a way to attract attention. I was the shy girl next door.

No one saw what happened inside my home. I was adopted and my family lived in constant chaos. My mother was severely mentally ill. She displayed symptoms of paranoia, prosecutorial complex, and lack of empathy for others. Most days she was confined to her bed or reclining chair—too over-medicated or depressed to interact. When she was up and about, our home was filled with violence. I would later understand that this was a mixture of borderline personality disorder and schizophrenia.

I began working at age fourteen to stay away from home as much as possible, and managed to be gone from 5:00 a.m. to 9:00 p.m., including school. When I left home at seventeen, I had no plan. I began to work more and more, using methamphetamine to stay up for twenty-two hours straight, five days a week, for two years straight. I took a few classes at a local college, and began to think I was stabilizing. At eighteen, a friend asked me to go on a blind date with her one night, and we ended up separated along a creek bank in Houston, drinking and using drugs. I was raped, beaten, and left for dead. I crawled up from the ditch where I was thrown and knocked on many doors until I found someone who would answer. They left me standing bloody and mostly naked on their doorstep as they called a cab for me to return to my apartment. This is how I lost my virginity.

Even after enduring extensive child abuse, I still believed that trust and love were possible, but the experience of rape killed my hope. I concluded I was completely worthless, as I had long been told; now, I thought, it was clear for everyone to see. I began a sharp downward spiral. The first man who trafficked me was a drug dealer who gave me drugs for sex acts, which quickly involved servicing men other than him. A group of men from Europe came to manage the hotel I worked in, and I began performing the acts for guests at their direction. My coworkers and managers clearly knew what was happening—the primary trafficker was in upper management—but did not step in. What's essential to know: I was incredibly vulnerable at this point in my life. I had no home, and nowhere to turn. I was eighteen, living on my own, and broke. I used drugs and alcohol to numb; the effects of negative childhood experiences, and having heard from my parents I was a [expletive] and [expletive] since childhood, the abuse did not seem undeserved.

Within a few months, though, I began to get scared. The sex buyers became more violent, and crossed lines I had previously thought were established. Threats began—they threatened to tell my friends and university what I was doing, and to harm me—although I was much more frightened of being exposed than of mere pain. After spending my entire childhood covering up abuse at home, imagining this new abuse revealed, terrified me. I was told as a child that if anyone knew what happened at home, I would never be able to get a good job, and that it would stigmatize me for life. This is why I never told. Eventually, fear and an overwhelming sense of degradation took over, and I told the men that I wanted out.

That night, in February 2001, the original trafficker and others held me in a room for eight hours and repeatedly assaulted me, ending up fracturing two vertebrae and stabbing me twice.

A few weeks later, with the help of a friend, I simply disappeared. I bought a plane ticket to another state, and after numerous harassing phone calls, I changed my number, and the traffickers never found me.

After the initial rape at age eighteen, I shut down emotionally, and used drugs and alcohol as a way to keep moving. After a childhood of pain and abuse, one more thing had been taken from me. My self-esteem plummeted and I became numb: it took everything that I have to keep getting up every morning and not attempt suicide. During the time I was trafficked, I lived in a constant state of panic and hyper-vigilance, which lasted for more than ten years.

My experience was a classic form of complex trauma. Not only did I experience multiple sexual assaults, mental manipulation, and violence from trafficking, but I also experienced several forms of child abuse. As part of my treatment, I worked with trauma therapists who used eye movement desensitization and reprocessing (EMDR) and trauma-focused cognitive behavioral therapy (CBT) as techniques to work through my experiences and help with diminishing flashbacks and triggers. These techniques also helped me to understand that the abuse was not my fault.

I spent a total of seven months in a treatment center for post-traumatic stress disorder (PTSD) at age nineteen—three months in-patient and four months in a sober living environment. This was not specific trafficking treatment, but was the best treatment I could find in 2001, especially since I did not recognize myself as a victim. I believed I was a "prostitute" who was frequently raped and degraded. The elements of force in my case are clear: beatings, gang rapes, death threats, as well as the threat to expose my activities on campus or to other employers. The elements of coercion, involving drug and alcohol addiction, became more clear later.

As a result of intense therapy, honest relationships that allowed me to grow and become comfortable with my authentic self, and developing a spiritual life, I was able to deescalate into the "window of optimization," where the brain is most chemically stable. This is the state of the brain where the prefrontal cortex is "online," as psychologists say, and rational thinking and logic prevail. I remain in this place today, although I still carry a diagnosis of complex PTSD.

Being a survivor strengthens my ability to help those exiting a life of exploitation in several ways. First, understanding the complex trauma, triggers, and flashbacks that are common for trafficking victims—which constitutes a different framework for working with complex PTSD—is vital. Understanding, on an intimate level, how triggers of loneliness, money, and sexual relationships affect survivors, and how being trafficked distorts the sense of self and healthy boundaries, allows keen insight into another survivor's reality, and helps us begin to undo distortions and negative self-talk.

We are able to remind ourselves that the abuse was not our fault, and we are able to turn off the self-blaming "tape" that can play on repeat in our minds on stressful days.

Second, understanding the difficulty of navigating interpersonal relationships is extremely valuable. Establishing healthy sexual boundaries is a skill that sex trafficking obliterates. Helping another survivor determine how best to disclose abuse to potential partners is an aspect of healing I share. It can be a difficult road to navigate with romantic partners, and even more difficult to guide someone through if the clinician is not a survivor. While experienced trauma clinicians can certainly make an enormously positive impact with clients, many survivors report an added benefit when the clinician is also a survivor.

Third, being able to assist in a shift from self-blame to empowerment of self is more easily addressed when a survivor is serving in a clinical role, with a deep connection and understanding of the issue. This is what my survivor sisters, especially those farther along in their healing process, have been able to do for me.

Sex trafficking clients can present with PTSD and co-occurring disorders. We are often diagnosed with either the co-occurring disorder or a manifestation of PTSD as a primary diagnosis. To put it simply, trafficking survivors are often misdiagnosed with mental illnesses other than complex post-traumatic stress disorder (C-PTSD). A benefit of having an experienced clinician, especially one who is a survivor, is the ability to delineate the pathology behind the behavior and glean the primary trauma to be treated. Survivors who have become clinicians, or other very experienced trauma therapists, will be able to understand the different manifestations of PTSD in trafficking survivors because they most likely will have experienced it themselves. Essentially, survivors will understand on a crucial level the behavior and

actions of other survivors who are in the beginning
of their healing process. While they may be misdiagnosed by an inexperienced clinician, a clinician
who is a survivor should readily recognize the presenting problems and know how to address them.

The ability of a clinician to walk with a survivor from her first hours out of "the life" through
the long journey to healing is most aptly found
in clinicians who are survivors, or experienced
trauma therapists who understand that this client
demographic differs significantly from other PTSD
clients. Recognition of trafficking trauma by the clinician can increase the chance of proper treatment
because the clinician has a greater understanding of
her needs. My trafficking survivor clients can always
reach me outside of office hours. This is not a breach
of boundaries, but a concrete understanding that
this clientele has experienced a full degradation of
the human psyche, and a 2:00 a.m. phone call may
at times be necessary.

Even after working in the anti-trafficking field
for over eight years, I did not disclose that I was a
survivor until 2013, when a woman who became
my mentor sat with me in three hours of Houston
traffic. She had flown in to speak as a survivor
at a fundraising event held by my organization.
Stalled on the highway, she asked me why I worked
in the field. I detailed the anti-trafficking work
I had done overseas and for the treatment center
in Houston. A few minutes later, we happened
to drive by the hotel where I was exploited, and I
murmured, "I was a prostitute there." She asked
me to explain my understanding of force, fraud,
and coercion. After I did, she asked why I didn't
identify as a survivor of trafficking. I told her so

many had experienced much worse—unbelievable cruelty. She looked me straight in the eyes and said, "That doesn't mean it didn't happen to you."

In that moment, I received a new lens on my victimization, and a better understanding of what had happened to me. This assisted my healing tremendously. I was also able to understand so much better the therapeutic processes I instinctively used with clients, and approaches other clinicians had used with me.

Disclosure is sometimes helpful, but it is also important to establish boundaries that allow the whole therapeutic focus to be on my clients. I have disclosed my experience with only a handful of clients in approximately ten years of practice. Typically, this is done with younger clients who are beginning their journey of healing. Breaking through a young person's sense of isolation and adjusting the expectation of feeling broken forever can be a powerful tool. That said, I never disclose in detail: I only communicate that it happened to me too. The treatment is centered solely on the client, and the client's journey, with disclosure only appropriate if it would put the client more at ease and assist in establishing a positive therapeutic relationship.

Working as a clinician has allowed me to gain a better grasp of the pathology regarding my own behavior and triggers. Working with other survivors who have entered the clinical field, we have shared the struggles and the joys of our cases, and have even better managed our own flashbacks and panic episodes when they arise.

I feel an immense responsibility as a survivor of trafficking to help others who have suffered.

I know that many will not have the resources or opportunity that I did to disappear—going abroad to begin my work in the anti-trafficking field. The road to full healing is long and arduous; it has been so strengthening for me to come across others who have traversed the same path. I have worked with hundreds of survivors over the past ten years, and hope I have demonstrated the compassion and courage that others have shown me.[2]

Like Emily, each of us is charged with an "incarnational" calling. Embracing our own personal histories, we are fueled to meet people right where they are. Though our vulnerability time lines may differ, each of us have experienced pain. As you process and begin your healing journey, you'll discover that your own story can be the very thing that gives you keen insight in walking with your most vulnerable neighbors.

In this section, we will discover that Christ, whose incarnation personified vulnerability, calls us to count the cost as we risk our lives to love those for whom he died.

CHAPTER 13

LAMBS AMONG WOLVES

As she readied herself for another day at the childcare center, Lissa had no idea that something as benign as her daily commute could ultimately change her life. Turning the corner, she noticed how erratically those in front of her were driving. She figured that they were most likely swerving to avoid hitting a dead animal. Within seconds, however, she realized that she was wrong. To her shock, an emaciated woman lay in the middle of the road, the flesh having been ripped off her body after falling out of a moving vehicle.

Being a registered nurse, Lissa's training took over. She intentionally parked her car so as to block the oncoming traffic and create some space so that she could administer first aid.

With the keys still hanging from the ignition, she hurriedly ran up to the woman. After evaluating the woman's condition, Lissa called 911. As she waited for the EMTs to arrive, she cradled the woman's head in her lap; her hands covered in the woman's blood.

Shortly after the ambulance arrived, the woman's "boyfriend" drove up. Those at the scene would later learn that he actually pushed the woman out of a car going at least forty-five miles an hour. But at this point, he was attempting to assist the medical personnel gathered at the scene. With his head bowed down, he looked at the woman. "She's HIV positive," he said.

The words took Lissa by surprise. For the next six months, I watched as Lissa, my mother, endured a battery of tests to determine whether or not she had contracted HIV. I couldn't understand it. At age fifteen, this made absolutely no sense to me. *Nothing bad should happen to you if you are trying to help people,* I thought. *Why would God let this happen?* It didn't seem fair.

I couldn't wrap my head around the fact that this woman's "poor decisions" were impacting my mom. Of course, I had absolutely no idea of the woman's exact circumstances or any right to judge her in the way that I did. But that didn't stop me. The abrupt nature of the pain that I was feeling apparently had unearthed my own xenophobia. Could my mom die all because she wanted to help someone?

Recently, my mom, whom I consider to be a genuine Good Samaritan, told me, "It never even occurred to me that the woman could have HIV. What did occur to me, however, was that someone was hurting and in need of help." I asked her, "If you had it to do over again, knowing what you know now, would you have kept driving in hopes that someone else would handle it?" Without hesitation, my mom said, "Absolutely not. You can't leave someone in the road to die."

From Lissa's story, we learn that we can't love people well when we are standing at a safe distance. Though situations may vary, when we meet people in the middle of their pain, we will often find ourselves exposed to risk. There is a cost associated with loving other people.

This is something about which Jesus was very clear during his earthly ministry. For example, as Jesus and his disciples were walking together, someone said to him, "I will follow you wherever you go" (Matt. 8:19). Jesus, never missing an opportunity to show people that this mission is not for the faint of heart, said to him, "Foxes have holes, and birds of the air have nests, but the Son of Man has nowhere to lay his head" (v. 20).

Jesus illustrated that the way of the cross is not safe. On this journey, you will experience discomfort. Suffering is not only a possibility, it's an inevitability. Regardless of your attempts to avoid it, you will suffer when you place a primacy on Christ's kingdom message. By his own profession, Jesus was saying that though he was God incarnate, he was "functionally homeless." If you are to follow this Messiah, you have to count the cost prior to making your decision.

We see two examples of Jesus saying as much in Luke 9:

> "To another he said, 'Follow me.' But he said, 'Lord, let me first go and bury my father.' And Jesus said to him, 'Leave the dead to bury their own dead. But as for you, go and proclaim the kingdom of God.' Yet another said, 'I will follow you, Lord, but let me first say farewell to those at my home.' Jesus said to him, 'No one who puts his hand to the plow and looks back is fit for the kingdom of God.'" (vv. 59–62)

Earlier in the same chapter, we find Jesus sending out his twelve disciples to take the "good news of the kingdom" to those in surrounding villages:

> And he called the twelve together and gave them power and authority over all demons and to cure diseases, and he sent them out to proclaim the kingdom of God and to heal. And he said to them, "Take nothing for your journey, no staff, nor bag, nor bread, nor money; and do not have two tunics. And whatever house you enter, stay there, and from there depart. And wherever they do not receive you, when you leave that town shake off the dust from your feet as a testimony against them." And they departed and went through the villages, preaching the gospel and healing everywhere. (Luke 9:1–6)

Notice how this text absolutely crushes our modern conception of "comfortable and safe" ministry. In reality, his disciples were anything but comfortable and safe. Intentionally charging them with carrying the message of the kingdom, Christ sent them out with nothing. "Take nothing for your journey." Excuse me? Wait just one moment. How can they do ministry without a budget? How can they take the gospel to the masses without Bible study curriculum? Or a building?

This imperative is mind-boggling. All of the standard items on which they could rely for protection were taken away. Christ was remarkably specific. He commanded them to leave their backpacks, snacks, emergency cash, and extra clothes at home. I won't even agree to a road trip unless I have all of those things and Jesus was saying, *You don't need them.*

He even went as far as telling them to not bring a staff. A staff was not simply used for propping oneself up; it was used for protection. Throughout their journey they may encounter robbers or wild animals. In that case, a big stick would come in handy. But they were made to be as vulnerable as humanly possible as they carried out this mission. In keeping them from depending on their "reserves," Jesus forced his disciples to depend on God's power and authority. Moreover, through the process, they were also compelled to rely on those whom they would meet along the way.

When we have nothing to distract us, we are freed to depend on Jesus and focus on his mission. With each step along the way, we are compelled to trust him to provide us with what we need when we need it. In faith, we risk everything for the sake of our neighbor. Is it scary? Absolutely. Is it uncomfortable? You betcha. But God will provide.

Our own vulnerability is integral to how we serve others. Though we like to insulate ourselves from risk and scarcity, Jesus is calling us to embrace it.

In Luke 10:1–12, Christ sends out seventy-two of his followers, saying, "I am sending you out like lambs among wolves" (v. 3 NIV). You don't have to be a biblical scholar to understand the imagery that Jesus is using. His followers were intentionally to be vulnerable as they cared for other vulnerable people. "Carry no moneybag, no knapsack, no sandals." They were at the mercy of those that they were aiming to help. Rather than operating out of their own self-sufficiency, they were made to be exactly as those that they were serving. They were on common ground.

This is what we see Emily doing so well in chapter 12. By focusing on her own healing and then putting herself out there, she is able to connect with others on a level that most couldn't. This is the point. If we would stop hiding from the vulnerabilities that we have experienced or are experiencing, we may just discover that they are the very things that empower us to do the work to which we are called. He is equipping us through our vulnerabilities. It's only from this posture of weakness that we are actually driven to trust in his strength.

Saint of Darkness

If anyone knew what it meant to be on a vulnerable mission, it was Mother Teresa. "If I'm going to be a saint, I'm going to be a saint of darkness, and I'll be asking from heaven to be the light of those who are in darkness on Earth," Mother Teresa wrote. Not only did she live with those whom she served, she suffered beside them as well.

Following Teresa's death, her personal correspondence was discovered, highlighting a previously unknown struggle. For nearly fifty years, she felt isolated from God, experiencing doubt and deep sadness.[1]

According to David Van Biema, in his *Time* magazine article, "Mother Teresa's Crisis of Faith," "that absence seems to have started at almost precisely the time she began tending the poor and dying in Calcutta, and—except for a five-week break in 1959—never abated."[2]

Almost the entirety of her ministry, she was suffering deeply as she cared for Calcutta's poor. With a broken heart, she cared for the broken-hearted. Her life proves the point that we will be exposed as we get our hands dirty in the lives of others. If you choose to accept this mission, you will experience "dark nights of the soul." There is no way around it.

A few years ago, I had the opportunity to go to the Mother House in Calcutta, India, with others who were actively engaged in addressing human trafficking. In the middle of an open room filled with pilgrims there to pay their respects, I will never forget seeing her tomb. On top of the marble lid, written in bright orange flowers, were the words: "Love until it hurts." Mother Teresa knew this well. She said, "I have found the paradox, that if you love until it hurts, there can be no more hurt, only more love."[3]

A Good Samaritan

God is calling us to love until it hurts. Following the sending out of the seventy-two to be lambs among wolves, an expert in the Jewish law asks Jesus a question: "What must I do to inherit eternal life?" In a way that only he could, Jesus answers the man's question with a question. "What is written in the Law? How do you read it?" He answers, "You shall love the Lord your God with all your heart and with all your soul and with all your strength and with all your mind, and your neighbor as yourself." Jesus agrees. "Do this and you shall live." Realizing the impossibility of carrying out God's righteous standards in his own strength, the man attempts to find a way to justify himself. "Who is my neighbor?" he asked (see Luke 10:25–29).

Jesus answers with a parable. A Jewish man on his way to Jericho was robbed, beaten within an inch of his life, and left to die in the middle of the road. By chance, a priest and a Levite walked across his path. But instead of stopping, they deliberately crossed the street and continued on their way (see vv. 30–32). Then along came a Samaritan.

A little background may be helpful here. Samaritans and Jews were not exactly on speaking terms; they were enemies. Seen as "half-breeds" whose own ethnic identity pointed to their idolatry, Samaritans were to be avoided at all costs. In a sense, Jesus is already making a provocative statement, when he says that the Jewish leaders left one of their own behind. But he truly upped the ante when he says that the only person who would stop was a Samaritan. Though this Samaritan man had every reason to keep walking, he stopped.

You may have heard this story hundreds of times, but let's not miss the fact that this man put himself in harm's way as he cared for the man in the road. Out of compassion for this man that he had never met, he picked him up and transported him to an inn, where he could receive care. Giving the innkeeper two days' wages, he said, "Take care of him and if it costs any more, I'll pay you when I come back this way" (vv. 33–35). In the words of Mother Teresa, he loved until it hurt.

After finishing the story, Jesus posed a question for the Law expert: "Which of these three, do you think, proved to be a neighbor to the man who fell among the robbers?" Unable to even utter the word *Samaritan*, he said, "The one who showed him mercy." And Jesus said to him, "You go, and do likewise" (vv. 36–37).

As we embark on this vulnerable mission to love other vulnerable people, we are reminded that we will face opposition and pain. However, we are not alone. Though we may feel like we are alone and that God has abandoned us at times, the Scriptures show us otherwise. Jesus Christ, the only human capable of perfectly loving God and others, is coming to fix all that is broken. In this, we can have hope.

CHAPTER 14
A VULNERABLE MINISTRY

Without testing our assumptions, we can accidentally fall prey to the insidious nature of our own unchecked biases. To subvert this, it is best to flee isolation and bounce our ideas off of one another. Community can be an antidote to our own deep-seated prejudices. I believe strongly in working with others, even those who may see the world from a different perspective than I do.

One friend with whom I talk regularly is Darryl Williamson. Darryl is the lead pastor of Living Faith Bible Fellowship in Tampa, Florida, and a council member of The Gospel Coalition. Having been a bivocational minister for years, he has keen insight on the adversity that we can face as we seek to love our neighbors. With regard to loving those around him, he has been outspoken regarding the gospel, racial justice, and community outreach.

Generally, when Darryl and I talk on the phone, there is nothing that is off the table. Gun control, immigration, race, politics. Nothing is too taboo.

What I love about our conversations is that no matter what we talk about, we both feel completely free to ask each other any questions that we may have. It's a safe space to process how we are experiencing the world.

The assumption is that, given our own limitations, we can't see everything from every angle. So we need good friends to walk with us. Darryl, an African-American man several years older than me, is able to help me process my blind spots as a white "Xennial" evangelical, and vice versa. Each time that we connect on the phone, the goal for both of us is to truly hear the other person and try to understand from the other person's perspective. If you don't have friends who can challenge you like this, you are missing out.

The Place of Vulnerability

When I called Darryl to talk to him about this book, we both figured that we would have one of our normal conversations. So my first question for Darryl was: "In your experience as a pastor, how do you see God calling Christians to serve from a place of vulnerability?"

"Wow," he said. "Man, that is such a fundamental question. Our vulnerability is really kind of built in to the fact that we can't really see and do anything the Lord is calling us to do on our own. There's this fundamental sense of inadequacy that we have so I think right out of the gate, if we're going to serve, we're not [going to be] self-reliant. We're just not self-reliant, which means we're apt to make mistakes. We're certainly not . . . able to pull this thing off without a large measure of grace.

"So, whatever it is that you're doing, what the Lord is trying to achieve in it is not something that we can kind of get our hands directly on. We need him to do it. And so I think we try to really emphasize that we are relying on him. We need him, we need the Spirit, and not to lose sight of that. So, I think that, without talking about things like risk and exposure and stuff like that, I think a good place to start is just recognizing my inadequacy in and of myself—my inability to pull off what I am called to in and of myself—provides this kind of inherent vulnerability, just by virtue of fact that I can't fulfill what God is calling me to do on my own. . . . He has to actually do the transaction. I think that's one of the things that we try to really emphasize so that folks know that they're inherently weak when it comes to how they are trying to serve."

Reflecting back on something that he said earlier, I said, "You mentioned risk and exposure. Why would you think that is important to our mission as Christians?"

"Yeah, that's a fun one. I think the most basic reason . . . is Philippians 3, which focuses on how we fellowship with Christ and how we serve. . . . In the most basic way, my risk and vulnerability in pursuing gospel mission allows me to fellowship with Christ and to kind of share with him more deeply the big three (justification, sanctification, and glorification) . . . so I think that's the most fundamental thing. This is what it means to be in partnership with Jesus. This is how you really know Jesus. You know Jesus really through vulnerability and exposure. That's the only way you can truly know him. This is how we actually connect with him. He really shows himself in us.

"And so I think that piece is first. If you think about Romans 8:17, which says 'and if children, then heirs—heirs of God and fellow heirs with Christ, provided we suffer with him in order that we may also be glorified with him,' that his whole promise [is] that because we're heirs with Christ we'll inherit basically everything that is given to him, but then Paul emphasizes all this happens [provided] we share in the sufferings. It's like, 'What is that?' Yes, this inheritance is yours because you share in his suffering. And so I think every kind of connection with, partnership with, fellowship with Jesus, is connected or is conjoined with vulnerability and risk because Jesus risked and succumbed to that risk right on the cross and there is this clear sense that we've got to do the same thing."

Talking about a period in his ministry when he discovered that he was called to a mission of vulnerability, he said, "The Lord really just took me very quickly . . . to Colossians 1:24 and he just kind of said, 'Darryl, this is your passage. You need, like Paul, to rejoice in your sufferings for the church and know that you have to complete what remains or what is lacking in Christ's suffering for the church.

That is how, as a pastor, you are meant to minister. You are meant
to minister from that posture. You're going to be vulnerable, broken,
hurt, injured, for the church.'"

Risk and suffering are essential if we are to follow God.
Following Christ will always entail pain and exposure. It's unavoid-
able. Though this sounds great in theory, Christians can find ourselves at times rejecting this idea functionally. With that in mind, I
asked my friend: "How do we as Christians vulnerably join the rest
of our outside community in its suffering?"

"That's a really good question," he responded. "I think it starts
with us kind of moving the center of gravity of all that we do [as a
church from inside to] outside of our walls. And I think fundamentally and in a very basic sense, we've got to think about it. It doesn't
mean that we're necessarily out on the street corner sharing the gospel, which is not a bad thing to do at all, but I think it's probably a
bit more organic. I think it's really saying that the normal kind of
pattern of our faith rhythm has us really reaching out, connecting
with those who are outside of our faith community. It could be as
simple as us connecting with our neighbors and getting to know
them. What's interesting and in some ways discouraging is that
everybody is experiencing trials. It's just a universal . . . And so if
we can connect with our neighbors and coworkers in an organic way
and an 'I'm really interested in you' way, we will connect with their
vulnerability. We're going to find out what they're dealing with.
We're going to discover that there's either health issues or relationship strain or who knows what it is.

"If we want to connect with the vulnerability that is outside of
our gospel community, that's outside of church, then we've got to
push outside of the walls of our church. We've got to push out into
the public square, man. We've got to be out there, and if we are
and we relate to folks, then we will by default get pulled in to that,
which allows folks to see how the Lord loves them and their vulnerability. That's a great question, man."

"It's interesting," I said, "because I never thought about any of
this until I worked with students at a historically black college and

university in West Virginia. As I would speak at our Thursday night meetings, I tended to focus more on the proclamation of the gospel than the demonstration of it. Then several friends and bishops within the community began to ask me questions. 'What are your thoughts on justice, injustice?' Truth be told, I hadn't really focused on it much at all at that point. From the Christian experience that I had, we appeared to focus [only] on personal salvation. It appeared myself and others had almost become Neoplatonic in that because we focused so much on the spiritual aspect of salvation we forgot the social aspect of salvation. It was as if I was out of balance. I focused on proclamation of the good news at that expense of its demonstration. And with that I have a question: Why, in your opinion, do you think that the African-American church experience focuses more on justice and mercy than maybe the white evangelical church?"

A Focus on Justice and Mercy

"Your question, I think, brother, puts its finger on the real thrust and core I believe as to why the Lord providently brought African-Americans, in particular Africans and other marginalized people in the various kinds of diasporas in general, why he brought them through such deeply undesirable times. Deep oppression. And I think one of the things the Lord did with that is that he implanted in our hearts just deep sensitivity to this core aspect of the gospel . . . I think for African-Americans and for other people who have a legacy of marginalization, this longing for relief, for liberation, this seeing God as a deliverer, is core to who they are. They . . . can't have a prayer life, without praying for that fundamentally. It's not like I've got a way to tell there's a problem, there's a job loss or a physical health issue, it's like there's this overarching theme of 'God help us.' I think the hearts of black people, Latinos who have come out of their kind of marginalized situations, they just feel it, man. They're just always looking for it.

"It's also a thing that speaks to the whole New Testament context. The first-century Jewish community was a vulnerable community and so Christ came to a vulnerable community. This community that was marginalized and longing for God's men to come. And so I definitely think that's one reason why the Lord has done what he's done historically amongst African-American people is so this kind of message about the priority of redemptive vulnerability, that message would be brought out."

Thinking about how the Good Samaritan crossed the road to love his neighbor, I said, "It's interesting because, as humans, regardless of our ethnic identity, we protect ourselves. It's very easy for us to give in to our own xenophobic biases and we both know that we cannot love our neighbor, we cannot do justice or mercy without addressing our own xenophobia, or fear of the other. For example, I grew up in a town not too far from you that is divided by one state road. This road goes right down the middle of the town. On the west side you had the majority of the African-American community, on the east side you had the majority of the white folks. Though we all went to high school together. It was interesting because I didn't really see too many people crossing the street, so to speak. So, how do we who have grown up in our own cultural expression, cross the street to love others who may not look exactly like us, who may not have our same background?"

The Vulnerability Bridge

"I think the angle that you're taking with this focus on vulnerability becomes the bridge to cross the street, because I think vulnerability is the thing that should connect us. It is the thing that really should show us that we have this experiential commonality, right? I'm broken; you're broken. I'm vulnerable; you're vulnerable. And I think if that bridge can be built, if reconciliation can have a profound focus on, I wouldn't call it mutual vulnerability, but certainly common vulnerability, across the various communities, I think that can be. And that vulnerability is not necessarily primarily in relation to each other. There's a vulnerability that we have that's not a mutual threat."

The idea of crossing the street forced me to think of how, throughout history, there have been Christian denominations that have preached a gospel of freedom, but supported such inhumane institutions as slavery. This led me to ask my next question: "In your opinion, how does race factor into exploitation and how can we come together to eradicate exploitation?"

"I think by eradication you mean to be really committed to eradication and we're acting toward it and not indifferent or only talking about it," he pointed out. "It's a real fundamental question. It's not one that has an easy answer. We can only try to throw out some things for consideration. The history of gospel-proclaiming people having this tension between their history of profession and their history of oppression is, brother, more than tension. It really is a contradiction. It's a fundamental contradiction. And so it's like a violation of logic. There's just no way to get around that and I think that there are a couple of things here that really come to mind. One I know that we have talked about before is, I think that the first thing that Christians in our country, especially Southern Baptist Christians need to embrace, this also would be true for PCA brothers and sisters, is we have to embrace or accept that there is no way we can excuse where the evangelical church of the nineteenth century was on slavery and the evangelical church was largely, especially in the South, on Jim Crow in the twentieth century.

"It's indefensible, theologically. And so I think if folks can say, 'You know what? To do such a thing is to act out of what I expect grace to do.' I don't see grace actually producing that kind of conduct. I don't see it. . . . It's a contradiction to genuine faith. . . . And so I think if we can start there, one step toward eradicating exploitation is realizing exploitation is fundamentally antithetical to the knowledge of God. We've just got to say, 'I'm sorry, man.' God was very clear. If you don't love your neighbor, you don't love God. Full stop. That's it. It's done. This is over. And you can recite all the verses you want, you can give all the biblical truths, unless you believe that knowing biblical truths means, entails, an inner presence of the Spirit of God, unless someone wants to say that, then you have to say, 'Sorry. Lack of love or hatred toward others is a sign of no knowledge of God. Done.' So, I think if folks can feel that . . . it could bring people conviction, which is the thing that leads to action."

"And there's this inner change, man, that's got to happen if we're really going to . . . make some real progress on eradicating exploitation and getting to the real community. There's some folks who've got to have real heart transformation. And if they can admit where they are, that's your vulnerability, you don't have to admit it to anybody, you have to admit it to the Lord. 'Lord, you know this is how I feel.' I think if they can do that then the true-to-self man might be getting to a new place.

"So, brother, I know that was a long kind of journey in answering your question, but I think if we can do those two things, we can see it theologically and also be honest and sincere with how we feel, because our feelings are involuntary. If I have a conversation with somebody who admits some prejudices, the first thing I'll say to them, I say, 'Listen, that's just how you feel. I'm not going to blame you for how you feel. I don't think you're choosing it. I think that's where you are and so we can start from there. You're just expressing what's going on in your heart.' . . . If we can admit that . . . I'm not offended."

Darryl, giving a practical example of his point said, "I will say to folks, if I were to have a conversation with a hard-core racist that's not trying to do anything criminal or anything like that . . . I would say to them, 'I am not offended. I'm not offended just because you're saying what's going on in your heart. I'm not going to judge you or look down on you. Now, if you would try to [hide] that racism . . . and deal with the gospel, now you're dishonoring the Lord and you're lying about what it means to be possessed by the Spirit in my mind. That I do have an issue with.' But if you're just saying, 'I'm sorry, I don't like black people, I don't like Jewish people, I don't like Latinos, I feel like they're taking over, I see Spanish all around town.' Okay, then I'm happy to keep talking with you. . . . You can come over to my house. That's no big deal. But I think that if we can just admit those things, I think the Lord will meet us there, man. I think he will.

"I just think isn't confession the first step, like the opening door to transformation? Doesn't it start there? My gosh! People that just say that. I think that's where your vulnerability begins. . . . I think we could really make some progress. Don't start with, 'I'm not really racist,' or, 'I'm sorry, but that's not really who I am.' . . . No, just go ahead and admit it. It's okay . . . We can deal with it. We can talk it through. I think the Lord might actually change us.

"It's interesting because as we think about this idea of having a vulnerable mission that every Christian, regardless of their ethnic background, is on, we're on this same mission, if we really think about this then issues of race and systemic injustice are not a problem to be pushed under the rug."

"Amen."

"They're more of an invitation to get to know your neighbor and to work with them together to eradicate the injustice around you."

RESPONDING TO THE VULNERABILITY **OF OTHERS**

Everyone can be great, because everyone can serve.
—Martin Luther King Jr.[1]

CHAPTER 15

THE GOOD SAMARITAN AND VULNERABLE NEIGHBORS

A fter preaching the parable of the Good Samaritan at my church, I headed to Harlem to have dinner with my girl-friend. As we climbed the stairs to exit the subway, I saw him—a homeless man, begging for change. "Can I have a dollar?" he asked passersby, who looked down at the ground instead of into his eyes, refusing to acknowledge his humanity.[1]

I, too, looked away and continued walking. With each step, though, my feet got heavier and heavier—to the point that I could no longer continue moving forward. I heard two voices. One was the faint, defeated voice of the man asking for change. The other was my own, reciting the remnants of that morning's sermon. Immediately, I was crushed by the law of God. Convicted of my sin, I realized I was failing to love my neighbor as myself. I thought to myself, *You are the priest and the Levite who walked by.*

The Reality of Dehumanization

People vulnerable to exploitation are everywhere, but they are sometimes hard to see because their vulnerability masks itself as poverty, hunger, homelessness, or something else. When we do not see them, though, we dehumanize the people God loves and values. In *Generous Justice*, Tim Keller writes, "Jesus taught that a lack of concern for the poor is not a minor lapse, but reveals that something is seriously wrong with one's spiritual compass, the heart."[2] In other words, a heart not bent toward grace and mercy has not experienced true compassion. When we ignore the poor, we show that we have not yet understood our own poverty.

Dehumanization, the active refusal to recognize the image of God in others, is at the heart of every form of exploitation. Although it's especially obvious in the commercial sex and labor trade, we show that the seeds of dehumanization live in our own hearts every time we ignore the image of God in our neighbors.

The Good Samaritan

In the parable of the Good Samaritan, Jesus does not explore possible reasons for which the priest and the Levite walk by the vulnerable man. He does not say, for example, "Maybe they do not want to be taken advantage of," or, "Maybe the priest wants to remain ritually pure." Their reasons are irrelevant because they are actively choosing to walk away and not show compassion. They do not love their neighbor as they love themselves. Self-protection, fear, and apathy are not excuses for passing by; they are indicators of our sick hearts.

Jesus wants us not only to identify with the priest and the Levite; he also wants us to see our own neediness in the vulnerable man. That man might be half dead, but we were completely dead—dead in our sins (Eph. 2:1). Yet Christ did not leave us to be the living dead. On the cross, he did not merely risk his life to help us; he freely gave it. Today, he speaks life into our death—even when we cannot love him or anyone else. He comes to us in our brokenness and vulnerability to rescue us by his grace. In this way, Jesus himself is the Good Samaritan.

Timothy Revisited

With this parable in mind, I turned around and began talking to the man—whose name, I discovered, was Timothy, though he preferred to be called "Dreads." As I looked in his eyes, his face brightened up. I asked him what he wanted, and he told me he just wanted a sandwich. So we went to the local convenience store, and I told him to order whatever he wanted. As we ate together, I couldn't shake the realization that Timothy reminded me of people in my own family. Though I attempted to disregard his existence, he was actually a human being who had much to offer. The more we talked, the more we both wanted to continue spending time together. He invited us to swing by his shelter for a Fourth of July barbecue. He gave us the number of his new prepaid cell phone.

As he shared his story with us, I began to notice a change in my own heart. After experiencing the conviction that came as I realized that I had broken God's law, I fled to the security of the grace of God. In response to God's free grace, I found myself naturally responding with compassion and generosity. The gospel freed me to protect him, not myself. It opened my eyes to see him as someone God loves, which empowered me to acknowledge his dignity. I would like to say that we became great friends at that moment, but the truth is that we lost touch.

A year later, though, I was standing on the street, waiting to go into a meeting, when I noticed a man begging on the side of the road. As he looked down, he asked each passerby for change. He seemed weak, weathered by a harsh life. I walked up to him and talked with him. "I love this town," he said. Shocked, I asked, "Why?" He replied, "Because people like you stop and talk." Something about him seemed eerily familiar. I asked his name, and he said, "Tim." I smiled. "We've met!" He replied, "Yes, I thought it was you. I remember when you bought me that sandwich last year."

Return the Dignity

The gospel reminds us that Christ loved us when we had no capacity or desire to love him back. In light of Jesus' life, death, and resurrection on our behalf, believers in Jesus are not defined by what we have done or what has been done to us. We are seen as righteous in the eyes of God. This transformational love sets us free from the shackles of comfort and self-protection to care for our neighbors.

In this last section of the book, we will explore how we can respond to those most vulnerable around us. With the gospel as our motivation, we can give value to those whom we have devalued. We can show mercy because we have been shown mercy.

Mister Rogers: A Vulnerable Approach to Neighboring

"Mister Rogers was a marine corps sniper in Vietnam," my friend said to me when we were in elementary school. Without question, I believed this juicy morsel of schoolyard gossip. "As a matter of fact, he wears the cardigans to cover up all his tattoos!" That's all I needed to hear. I bought this urban legend hook, line, and sinker. In my eyes, America's favorite neighbor was not one with whom to be trifled.

To be honest, there is something really intriguing about this idea. We love the thought that someone so gentle, like Fred Rogers, could experience the trauma of war and come back to dedicate his life to loving children and helping them know that they matter. That's really a beautiful picture.

However, at the heart of this story line lies a dangerous assumption. Namely, that one must show specific acts of heroism to really "matter." For the kids at my school, the man in the cardigan was easier to accept if he was a combat veteran. In other words, if Mister Rogers had been Liam Neeson in a previous life, then we could really understand him more. His "masculine" battlefield experience would negate his taste in clothing and passion for singing, "It's a beautiful day in the neighborhood," giving him the right backstory to truly be a hero in our eyes.

In the article "Why Are There So Many Urban Legends about Mr. Rogers?" Erin Blakemore quotes Trevor J. Blank, an assistant professor of communication at the State University of New York at Potsdam, who specializes in folklore and urban legends. Answering the question posed by the article, Blank says that "'He's an individual to whom we trust our children. . . . He taught kids how to take care of their bodies, associate with their community, how to relate to neighbors and strangers.' This makes Rogers the perfect target for urban legends—especially ones that counter his upstanding public image."[3]

But misrepresentation never stopped Mister Rogers. Like clockwork, he would take the trolley into the neighborhood of make-believe, and connect with his [puppet] neighbors, King Friday, Daniel Tiger, Prince Tuesday, and last but most certainly not least, Ana Platypus. To this day, I am seriously impressed with how he addressed their "felt" needs. (I'm sorry, I couldn't resist.)

In his purposeful yet fantastical conversations, Mister Fred McFeely Rogers modeled healthy relational boundaries and communication styles for the children viewing at home. For us, this was a safe place.

Rogers embodied healthy conversation as he consistently made it a point to listen and show deference to his neighbor, no matter what they were experiencing. In that way, he gave us a master class in "active" listening. Every time that I rewatch an episode, I am impressed with how he seems genuinely interested in everything that he is hearing. Though each episode had a running time of only twenty-eight minutes, he always seemed to make time to listen to his friends.

In a simple yet profound manner, he conveyed the truth that *everyone* mattered; regardless of your background, you had a voice.

Though he went to seminary to train to be a pastor, Pittsburgh's own Fred Rogers found his voice on public television. For Mister Rogers, it was in his "neighborhood" that he could best exemplify what it meant to be a good neighbor. Amy Hollingsworth, the author of *The Simple Faith of Mister Rogers: Spiritual Insights from the World's Most Beloved Neighbor*, explains that "his definition of neighbor was simple: the person you happen to be with at the moment—whether that person is a Samaritan, a hermit bearing gifts, or a television viewer. This is even more the case if the person you happen to be with is in need, as was the waylaid traveler in Jesus' parable. At the center of Fred's theology of loving your neighbor was this: Every person is made in the image of God, and for that reason alone, he or she is to be valued—'appreciated,' he liked to say."[4]

According to Rogers, "evil would like nothing better than to have us feel awful about who we are. And that would be back in here [in our minds], and we'd look through those eyes at our neighbor, and see only what's awful—in fact, look for what's awful in our neighbor. But Jesus would want us to feel as good as possible about God's creation within us," Mister Rogers said, "and in here [in our minds], we would look through those eyes, and see what's wonderful about our neighbor. I often think about that."[5]

Children and adults alike can learn a lot from Mister Rogers. Though we may not be "heroes" in the traditional sense, we can love those around us. No matter who we are, we can be a "good neighbor."

How Can We Respond to Our Most Vulnerable Neighbors?

Though I at first ignored him, I tried my best to respond helpfully to my vulnerable neighbor "Dreads." I couldn't shake the parable of the Good Samaritan—I just preached it, so it had to inform how I acted as a neighbor. The same parable informed how Mister Rogers viewed neighboring. In this chapter, we will learn how the art of neighboring enables us to fight human trafficking. As we will discover, the trick to being a good neighbor is to operate from a posture of vulnerability.

A Posture of Prayer

When we hear about injustice, we tend to react rather than respond. What would happen if we took a moment to collect our thoughts before rushing to action or retreating into the safety of inaction?

As we assume a posture of prayer, we are immediately reminded that it's not our job to save the world; that job is already taken. Rather than looking for the answer to society's problems within ourselves, we look to another—someone greater than us.

I learned this the hard way shortly after moving to New York. Having only been in the city a couple of days, I wasted no time getting involved. I was like a sponge, soaking up whatever I could to learn more about human trafficking. Over time, I started to notice something that troubled me. It seemed that no matter how much my friends and I made others aware, the problem continued to persist. I felt useless and beat down. "We're not even making a dent," I confessed to a friend. Within six months, I was on the verge of burnout.

Having exhausted all my options, I realized that I hadn't prayed much about what I was seeing. I was awakened to my prayerlessness.

Believing that God loves justice more than I do, I started praying over the illicit massage parlors and brothels in my community. I had never done anything like this before, but I figured that it couldn't hurt. So with intentionality, I chose one particular establishment for which I prayed specifically. Once a month, I would make a special trip to the thirteenth floor of a nondescript building in midtown Manhattan.

As I exited the elevator, I noticed an ill-fitting wooden door with peel-and-stick numbers fixed to it. Alongside of the door was a buzzer. Apparently, the only way to gain entry into the room was to press the buzzer and look at the camera in the right corner of the hallway.

Each time that I visited the floor, I would walk down the hallway like I was lost and ask for divine intervention. "God," I prayed, "I ask you that no one would exploit those who work here anymore." I did this for about three months, until one day, I noticed something different. The crude wooden door was gone. The original glass door had been reinstalled. Peering through the new door, I noticed that the entire room was empty. Returning home, I commenced researching. There was nothing online to give me any indication that they had relocated. I would later discover that the phone line was no longer connected. Researching further, I found that the person who bought the domain name represented a group in a developing nation that offers "employment opportunities in America." Feeling that this was a little fishy, I ran my discovery by a friend in federal law enforcement. Taking one look at it, he confirmed my hunch that this was most likely the result of organized crime.

A week or two later, I went back to the neighborhood. As I looked at this building, I noticed something that I had never seen before: a giant painting of a lion's head. Beneath this beautiful picture were the words, "Call to me and I will answer you." The reality of what had happened flooded my mind. God heard my prayer. This was a turning point for me.

God will hear you as you cry out to him for justice. Though things may feel dark now, rest assured that he will bring justice in due time. As you pray, I encourage you to learn about the needs of your community and then present them to God. Pray also for those in your community who are already engaged in this work. Ask God to help your church see these needs and respond appropriately. But most of all, as you pray, expect God to answer you.

A Posture of Intentionality

You will never drift into compassion. In order to love your neighbor, you must make a conscious choice. Choosing to be compassionate is a life-altering decision. Often when we learn about various societal ills, we feel completely inadequate to do anything about them. The enormity of the problem overwhelms us.

In seeing the forest, we can fail to see the trees. Mother Teresa gives us a unique perspective, reminding us to "never worry about numbers. [Rather to] help one person at a time and always start with the person nearest you." "I do not agree with the big way of doing things. To us, what matters is an individual," she wrote.[6]

Recently Laura Galt, the NYC Director for Safe Families for Children, shared the following illustration of this principle with me. Each day, at a neighborhood Chinese restaurant, Charles stands opening the door for clientele and asking for change. Laura and her children had become familiar with him as they passed by him multiple times a day.

On one occasion, they were talking to Charles and asked him if he wanted them to bring him anything to eat. Given that he was missing most of his teeth, they opted to give him something soft. He requested a peanut butter and banana sandwich.

This act of kindness turned into a daily ritual of asking Charles if he wanted food, going home to make a sandwich, and then walking back up the block to deliver the peanut butter and banana sandwich. Her children were always involved and loved to see the excitement written on Charles's face when they handed him his sandwich.

One day, as Laura turned the corner at the Chinese restaurant, she noticed that Charles wasn't looking in her direction. Being tired after a long day, she decided to turn down her block and head home without stopping to talk to Charles. As soon as the stroller turned, her toddler son began demanding, "Nana, bread. Nana, bread. Nana, bread!" From the vantage point of a stroller, he noticed that his mother was avoiding Charles that day. Convicted by the compassionate pleas of her son, she turned around and asked if Charles would like a peanut butter and banana sandwich.

We don't have to go far to find the ministry that God has for us. With that in mind, make a decision to intentionally love the person in front of you. Talk to the stakeholders in your community like social services, local law enforcement, and local not-for-profits. Ask them to tell you who they are seeing. Ask God to open your eyes to your neighbor and then start meeting the needs that present themselves. To one person you may give a "nana sandwich," to another a listening ear. But what's key is that you start meeting needs nearest you. Continue to pull that thread and see where the Lord leads you.

A Posture of Empowerment

When asked the question, "What is the key to understanding poverty?" Brian Fikkert, coauthor of *When Helping Hurts*, explains that "the key is to diagnose, 'what is a human being, what are the effects of the fall on that human being, and what is Christ's good news for the whole human being?' Most of us in the West have reduced human beings, in essence, to candy machines, in which we pump quarters in and we expect something sweet to pop out. Human beings aren't like that. The church has done this; the average American has done it. The discipline of economics has done it in a profound way. The entire paradigm of Western economics is to treat human beings like rational, consuming, material agents that we can describe in mathematical terms. And the reality is, they're relational."[7]

Our desire to give charity to those in need is often anything but relational. Assuming the needs of those most vulnerable are solely material, we throw money at the problem, hoping it will go away. Digging deeper, we find that a lack of financial means is just the tip of the iceberg. Hidden beneath the surface of each presenting need of our neighbor is a fear of isolation as well as a God-given desire for community and relationship.

With that said, when we blindly give charity, we can create an unhealthy sense of dependence and refuse to give people the very thing they need most. Robert Lupton, author of *Toxic Charity*, reminds us that "when we do for those in need what they have the capacity to do for themselves, we disempower them."[8]

Empowerment, on the other hand, involves recognizing the dignity of those we are trying to help by giving them power or authority to make decisions for themselves. In essence, we empower others by assisting them in discovering the tools they need to provide for themselves. Rather than doing this for them, we join them in their journey and work alongside of them.[9]

Instead of simply giving donations or handouts, we can start by building an enduring relationship with those who are down and out. In the context of an actual relationship, we can focus on communion over charity.[10] As we commune with others, we are positioned to recognize their dignity. In this posture, we can actually get to know the name and the story of the person with whom we are connecting. The goal here is not to solve their problems or even fix them. Rather, it's to be with them. To join them in their struggle and walk beside them. For this approach to bear fruit, we must transition from asking the question, "How can we help you?" to asking, "How can you give back? What can you do?"

Remember, human trafficking exists because of the sinful misuse of power and control. If we are not careful, we can do further damage to people by keeping the power firmly in our grasp.

A Posture of Collaboration

It all started with a link. On their neighborhood Facebook page, someone shared the website of a local illicit massage parlor. The person who posted it was shocked to realize that this was happening in their own backyard.

As a pastor in the community, Nathan clicked on the link to see what all the fuss was about. He did not like what he saw. One glance at the pictures on the site was enough to convince him that these women were being exploited. As he was about to click away from the site, something stopped him in his tracks. He recognized one of the girls.

About two months prior, a young woman came to Nathan's church for a coat drive on her first day of work at a seemingly legitimate massage parlor right next to the church. He gave her a coat and hat and hoped that they would see her again.

But not like this.

Nathan, one of the first pastors to partner with Let My People Go, gave me a call soon after. "What do we do?"

I said the first thing that came to mind: "Have you contacted local law enforcement? Have you alerted your local precinct?" Nathan was already on it.

"The Lord had just really opened some doors to have great access to the local precinct," Nathan said. "I had become friends with the captain and when I shared my concerns with him, he didn't just dismiss it, he really took it very seriously."[11]

The local police precinct responded by parking a car in front of the massage parlor, where the girl was likely exploited.

What began with one pastor's concern has led to the closing of twenty-four illicit massage parlors in a community.

We can't fight human trafficking in a healthy way without collaborating with others. Here are four reasons that we should prioritize collaboration. First, regardless of how smart or talented we are, none of us knows everything that is happening in our community. Second, collaboration keeps us from creating something that already exists. Before you say, "I want to start a homeless outreach, see if there is one already active. If there is one, volunteer your time. Third, as we partner with others we will discover that each of us has something different to contribute. We don't have to know everything—what a relief! Finally, it's only by working with others that we are able to gain a clearer picture of the needs of our neighbors. Essentially, we can do more together than we can do in isolation.

A Posture of Advocacy

Justice is more than meeting the physical and spiritual needs of the weak and vulnerable. We often miss opportunities to advocate for our neighbors. In order to truly stand for the oppressed, we must stand against the systems that hold them in vulnerable positions.

One easy way to start is by visiting the Polaris project's website. Here you can find out what anti-human trafficking policies are in place or are pending in your state. You are also able to have your voice be heard as you sign petitions for legislation. Go here for more information: https://polarisproject.org/policy-legislation.

Also, the more that we see what is actually happening, the more difficult it becomes to stay silent. If you are seeing something you believe needs to be changed, let someone know. Nowadays, it's easier than ever to contact your elected representatives. You can directly email them by visiting usa.gov/elected-officials.

From a posture of vulnerability, each of us can love our neighbors. But this love will be short-lived unless we have the right motivation. We will learn more in the next chapter.

CHAPTER 16

A GOSPEL MOTIVATION

Whatever you do, don't share the gospel with me." Those were my exact words to my slightly mystified seminary professor. As he set his coffee down, I could tell that he was holding back in an effort to allow me to process what I was thinking. "To be honest," I said, "I don't think God loves me. I feel like he is angry at me. I feel like I have prayed the 'prayer of salvation' over a thousand times and he won't hear it."[1]

As I continued to share, I figured that this couldn't be the "norm" for incoming students like myself. I mean, you don't have to be perfect to be enrolled in theological seminary, but you should at least, at bare minimum, be a Christian . . . right? Here I was baring my soul to my professor over dry bacon and watery eggs. In my head, I figured that the only recourse would be for the school administration to send me home. This would make sense to me because, ultimately, I can't tell people about the love of Christ if I am not sure that I have received it.

Surprisingly, my professor didn't condemn me. As a matter of fact, he didn't do much at all. He just sat there silently listening to me as I poured out my heart. He didn't respond with Christian clichés or platitudes, nor did he give me any advice on how to "fix" my problem. He just sat with me as I struggled to finish my breakfast. After waiting for me to gather myself, he calmly asked to pray for me. He encouraged me to stay the course and to seek him out as I processed my current crisis of faith.

Truth be told, this "current" crisis was not a new problem for me. This issue had hounded me for as long as I could remember. Growing up in church, I had been conditioned to consistently examine my faith. If I failed to pray or read the Bible regularly, I would immediately doubt that my faith was genuine. If I struggled with a particular sin too long, I would find myself thinking that I hadn't truly been saved. I would spend hours searching the Scriptures, and praying constantly that God would love me, all, it seemed, to no avail.

But you wouldn't have known it, because I was in church every time the doors were open. I was a leader in my local congregation and my campus ministry; I once worked in the music section of a local Christian bookstore. Outwardly, it looked as if I had it all together, but inwardly, I was falling apart.

During my shifts at the bookstore, I would steal evangelistic tracts, take them into the back room, and study them word for word to make sure that I had done everything right. (Yes, I understand how that sounds.) With that said, I'm proud to say that I have memorized Billy Graham's "Steps to Peace with God." I just needed to know I had prayed the prayer correctly, that I had done everything in my power to be saved.

So there I was at seminary deciding to stay the course. During this semester in 2003, I would be introduced to Martin Luther. Not only was I enamored by his theology, but I was captivated by his doubt and his fear. The Father of the Protestant Reformation didn't have it all together either. For that reason, his struggle to find peace with God was oddly reassuring. With that said, I jumped at the chance to write a paper comparing Luther's understanding of "justification by faith" to the Council of Trent's formulation. The problem with this assignment, though, was that it was given to the entire class, so by the time that I made it to the library, almost every book was gone. Only a couple of books were left, one of them an old, dusty copy of Gerhard Forde's *Justification: A Matter of Death and Life.*

As I began to read, Forde's words moved me:

> We are justified freely, for Christ's sake, by faith, without the exertion of our own strength, gaining of merit, or doing of works. To the age-old question, "What shall I do to be saved?" The confessional answer is shocking: "Nothing! Just be still; shut up and listen for once in your life to what God Almighty, creator and redeemer is saying to his world and to you in the death and resurrection of his Son! Listen and believe!"[2]

I was shocked: "Do nothing? The strength of my faith doesn't matter?" I couldn't put the book down. Forde continued his argument by posing the question:

> "But we have to do *something*, don't we?" "Are there not, after all, *some* conditions?" . . . Don't you at least have to "decide"? The difficulty is exactly with the unconditional nature of the decree: you are justified for Jesus' sake! . . . The gospel of justification by faith is such a shocker, such an explosion, because it is an absolutely *unconditional* promise. It is not an "if-then" statement, but a "because-therefore" pronouncement: Because Jesus died and rose, your sins are forgiven and you are righteous in the sight of God![3]

At that point, I realized that I was justified *by* my faith, not *because* of it. My own feeble attempts to "get saved" were not enough. My salvation could not rest in the strength of my faith, but only in the *object* of my faith—namely the perfect life, death, and resurrection of Jesus in my place. Finally, I could embrace my inner accusations.

Of course I am not good enough to be saved.

Yes, my faith may be weak, but Christ is my strength.

After this realization, sharing the gospel was no longer a chore. It was an opportunity to tell others what Christ had done for a sinner like myself. But the gospel is not just for those who are yet to trust in Christ. It's for Christians as well. Now as I meet with other Christians, I am quick to share the gospel. Not because I think that they are not saved, but to remind them that they are loved.

We need this reminder daily, because we are forgetful people. An example of this is found throughout first five books of the Bible. Moses is constantly reminding Israel of their redemption from slavery. Each time, he grounds their good works in the work that God had already done on their behalf. They were reminded of their redemption as a nation to motivate them to love God and others.

As Christians, we know that guilt, though effective in the short term, will not motivate us for the long haul. To love our neighbors, we need a motivation that lasts. We need to hear the good news that we are saved, not because of anything that we have done, but because of everything that God has done for us. As we ponder this freedom, we will find ourselves taking risks unlike ever before because we know that God is for us.[4]

To learn more about how the gospel motivates us to action, I spoke with Dr. Michael Horton, professor of Systematic Theology and Apologetics at Westminster Seminary California. He holds an MA from Westminster Seminary, a PhD from University of Coventry and Wycliffe Hall, Oxford, and completed a research fellowship at Yale Divinity School.

In 1990, he launched the nationally syndicated radio show *The White Horse Inn* to help people "know what they believe and [know] why they believe it through conversational theology."[5] He is the author of more than twenty books, including *The Gospel Driven Life*, *Where in the World is the Church?*, and *A Place for Weakness*. He is also an ordained minister of the United Reformed Churches in North America. Dr. Horton speaks and writes about the need for the American church to fully understand and live out the gospel of Jesus Christ.

An Interview with Dr. Michael Horton

It was an overcast day in Marion, Alabama, where I had spoken the night before. Having just woken up in the guest room of the Judson College dormitories, I was ready to start the day. Finding my handheld recorder, I called Dr. Horton. As soon as he picked up, I could hear the birds chirping in the background. Apparently, it was a beautiful day in Southern California. I was only slightly bitter.

After the pleasantries of weather and my attempt to enjoy the sunshine vicariously through him, we jumped right in. I shared the story of how I came to embrace the gospel and how that eventually drove me to take a leap of faith and start Let My People Go. Explaining the turning point that I experienced, I said, "I told the Lord, 'I'm done. I'm going to go wherever you call me,' and three months later, I would end up selling everything I own to move to New York City to fight human trafficking, even though I didn't know what that meant."

"Wow. You're crazy," he laughed.

"That's what my pastor friends said. As a matter of fact, that's what most everyone said," I explained. "And you know the beautiful thing, Dr. Horton, is I don't think I'd ever been called crazy for following after Jesus. But I'll tell you right now, I was scared to death."

"Yeah," Horton said in agreement. "No, I mean, from a human perspective, it is completely nuts. But isn't it fun too?" he asked.

That's something I couldn't deny. Though the last five years have been uncertain and difficult, I've had a blast. "In my own experience," I explained, "I have learned that God uses vulnerable people to love other vulnerable people, because Christ's vulnerability was exploited for us. And really, that's the thought that I'm tracing throughout this book. So I am really excited to talk to you, because, I mean, you've written a few books."

"Well, nothing as practical," he replied. "Of course, I think theology's practical, but I mean nothing as 'in-your-face, daily headlines,' as this. And so, I'm a pupil; you're my tutor on this one. This is a big one, and it's something that I'm, of course, very concerned about, but have not been involved with as an issue personally at all, and I'm looking forward to this as a chance to actually find concrete ways of getting involved, and getting our church involved."

A Place for Weakness

Though he said that he had never dealt with the issue personally, I disagreed slightly.

"Well, out of the books that you've written, two . . . have a very immediate bearing on how we can respond to human trafficking, as vulnerable people loving vulnerable people. Take your book, *A Place for Weakness*, for example. It really hits at the heart of what I'm trying to say, because I don't know if you're anything like me, but I try to avoid my own weaknesses. That's just my natural default. I want to operate out of strengths, because in a sense, I'm afraid of my own weaknesses. But I've noticed that God says that our weaknesses are a gift. It's precisely in the middle of our perceived weakness that we experience God; it's through these limitations that we depend on God. Thus, we are better positioned to witness God at work, because we are not depending on our own strength."

Agreeing with me, he said, "Well, I think the categories that I draw on there are pretty familiar, theology of the cross and theology of glory. Whereas I think in good times, especially, a lot of Christians are quite happy to feed off of theology of glory, they don't have firm ground to stand in times of great crisis. And by contrast, people who have been abused and exploited have a sort of 'theology of the cross'—they understand what it's like to be an underdog, to be on the losing end of life—but they don't have any hope [in] Christ, who for the hope set before him, endured the cross and the shame."

He continued to explain that some go to unhealthy extremes in processing our perceived weakness. "So there's something different between despair, [which is the] cross without the resurrection, and triumphalism, the resurrection without the cross. So I think that's where I would take my bearings, my coordinates, for talking to people about this issue from a theological standpoint, anyway."

Echoing his sentiment, I said, "I think that is so key, because naturally, we are going to have a theology of glory. We are going to say, 'Well, if I'm doing what I'm supposed to be doing, then bad things aren't going to be happening to me.' But as we kind of transition to this theology of the cross, we realize we're following a crucified savior on a cruciform walk. Suffering is inevitable, but it will shape us. It's in our sufferings that we're able to be who God has called us to be, and to experience joy, and to love others. There's a beauty in this brokenness."

"Mm-hmm," he mumbled in affirmation. "Exactly, exactly. And it's not a 'there's no pain, no gain,' a kind of stoic outlook on life, where [we say], 'Well, this is just the way it is. You gotta buck up, and if you get through this, won't you be glad you learned some lesson out of this?' That's not what we're saying. It's what a lot of people think that we're saying, perhaps, but [that's] not at all [what we are saying]."

Picking up on this idea of a theology of the cross, I decided to ask Dr. Horton to explain in detail how the gospel motivates us to action.

Which Gospel Motivates?

"Dr. Horton, could you explain to me the content of the gospel that would motivate us to love others without a guarantee of reciprocity?"

"I'm thinking of Jesus telling the disciples," he answered, "'and when you have a banquet, invite those who can't repay you,' because isn't that what God does with us, actually? And he wanted a banquet hall full of people who can't repay him, but actually he is repaid in a sense, because he has the company of people he's chosen from all eternity, created in his image, retrieved, resurrected, restored, living with him forever as his children. You know, God does in a sense get something out of it. He doesn't give gifts to get things in return, but he does get the satisfaction of fulfilling his merciful plan, and receiving all of the glory from it.

"The gospel that drives people, I think, in these circumstances is there's a kind of patient endurance through the cross, in the hope of the resurrection, that says 'I can endure all things because of Christ,' 'Greater is he who is in me than he who is in the world,' 'I count these sufferings to be meaningless in comparison with, or puny in comparison with the glory that will be revealed in us.' There's that kind of theology.

"But then there's kind of a platinized gospel that says this life doesn't matter at all because salvation is fluffing off this mortal coil, and so why on earth would you care for somebody now who is just on the way to death and decay anyway? Of course, the same person will go to a doctor and will hope to cure cancer, so they can live a little longer, but when it comes to solving problems that people think are just so big, we often say, 'Yeah, well, it's just not going to be taken care of here and now, and so we're just going to have to wait . . . It's all going to burn anyway.'

"And so, if you have that kind of outlook, I don't know why you would really care at all about [people]. So on one hand, a theology of glory says we can save the world if we just get enough people together, enough action programs, enough lawyers arguing before the Supreme Court. If we could just get enough people in the White House, or in the Congress, and the right people in the White House, then we can usher in the kingdom of God, and we can bring an end to these things.

"But then, a kind of resignation to the cross says, 'Well, we don't really have a resurrection. There is no resurrection of the body, and life everlasting. It's all going to burn, so let's just not really take the concerns of the body, our embodied nature, including politics, which is just concern for the body corporately. Let's just ignore the body and its needs, and focus on the spirit.'" After explaining this unbalanced platonic view of service, he asked the question, "If we believed this, then why would you even have vocations? Why would a mom even change a kid's diaper? Why would you even go to work and run those numbers again for the company? Why would you care at all about getting out of bed, or any concerns of the body? Why would you go to the bathroom?"

"So anyway, we're either enduring this, and then we're going to die, which is a kind of Christian nihilism, or there's a continuity between this body that is decaying and dying, and the one that will be raised such that this world will not be destroyed, including my body, including human society. Beauty, goodness, and truth in the world will not be destroyed, but will be restored without the pain, suffering, death, evil, without, in short, the turning away from the sun, s-u-n, that warms us."

"So you're arguing for a middle approach between triumphalism and nihilism?" I inquired.

"Don't you find that triumphalism and nihilism sort of feed each other?" he asked me. "Today's triumphalists are tomorrow's nihilists."

I couldn't help but agree.

He continued, "People who are 'Rah, rah, we can handle this, we can beat this, we're ushering in the kingdom of God,' a week and a half later are sitting in their hammock paralyzed with a sense of meaninglessness, thinking that they can't do anything. It's really the tortoise and the hare here. We have the long view, because we are like the spies who have seen the good land that the Lord has for us. We know how this story ends, or rather begins, and so we don't have any fear that we can't solve all the world's problems here and now. That was never promised to us. But we do have the promise that Christ will be with us, even to the end of the age, and that we can love and serve our neighbors in ordinary, everyday ways. I wrote this book, *Ordinary*, kind of encouraging this sort of practice of patient hope.

"God gives us different callings, even at the same time in our life. I have a calling as a dad, as a husband. I have a calling as a seminary professor. I have a calling as a neighbor. I have all sorts of callings simultaneously, and furthermore, God gives me different callings at different times in my life. So he might remove one calling, and give me another one in its place, and sometimes God does give us a vocation of a radical kind of role in providential history.

"Now, it's not a radical role in the history of redemption. I'm not a co-redeemer with Christ when I'm opposing human trafficking; rather I'm witnessing to that redemption that Christ has already won, and will one day consummate when he returns bodily. I'm witnessing to that, I'm testifying to that, but I'm also just loving my neighbor, and that itself is a calling, even if nobody sees or hears the testimony to Christ and the resurrection. I have an obligation to my neighbor right now, right there, right in front of me; to this particular neighbor, right now in front of me, who-ever that person might be. God has placed that person as a pack-age, a gift, wrapped up in a big bow, right in front of me for me to be a neighbor to, 'cause they're going to be a gift to me just as I am hopefully a gift to them."

"It's interesting," I said, "that's what Mother Teresa would say. When people would ask her, 'Well, how did you impact global poverty?' she would say something to the effect of, 'Start with the thing that was in front of you.' Don't do this triumphalist thing, just start loving people where you are at and see what happens." We transitioned to talking about Mother Teresa. "And it's interesting, because I've been in the community where you will find the Home of the Destitute and Dying. If you stand on the front steps of the center and look to the left, you will see the sacred river Ganges, or a tributary of it. And then, as you walk down the street from the home, you see rampant vulnerability. In the middle of all of this vulnerability, you start seeing shack after shack after shack, and they're all brothels."

He agreed, saying, "Yep, I saw them, I saw them. It's heartbreaking."

"What's interesting to me," I explained, "is that wherever you find vulnerability, you find exploitation. At the end of the day, if we are to fight an injustice like human trafficking, addressing vul-nerabilities is key, and loving your neighbor, that's really what we're called to do. It's messy, it's frustrating, but at the end of the day, we're called to do it."

The Two Words: Law and Gospel

"Now here's the problem though," I said, "I think you would agree here, justice and mercy, that is the law of God. The Law commands us 'do this, and you will live.' It's not a suggestion. It demands perfection.

"I think sometimes when we're encouraging people to respond to the needs around them, we are using law and guilt [to motivate them] and not grace. And so, how can we avoid this trap? How can we differentiate between law and gospel, and its relation to loving our neighbor?"

Horton answered with enthusiasm. "Great question, great question. I do think you're right, almost everybody who's involved these days in concern for neighbor, on a wide scale, political and social justice, confuses law and gospel. You hear it all the time, you know, *doing* the gospel, *being* the gospel, and so forth. Well, that gives us no hope whatsoever. If my works, my doing justice, loving mercy, if that is the gospel, then I'm going to give up right now, 'cause I can tell you that I don't love my neighbors well enough to be able to pull that off. *But I am loved well enough to be able to begin to love my neighbors.*"

This last sentence caught my attention. He drew a great distinction between law and gospel. He describes his inability to keep the law when he says "I can't love my neighbors well enough to pull that off," but then he points to the emancipating power of the gospel: "But I am loved well enough to begin to love my neighbors." Because we are so forgetful, we need to be reminded of this on a daily basis. Martin Luther said it this way: "Preach the gospel to yourself every day."

Each day we need to see ourselves in the mirror of God's righteous standards. As we compare ourselves with his perfect law, we will see every blemish and imperfection. We will rightly see that, on our own, we fall short of the glory of God. This is what it means to preach the law to yourself. But then in the moment where we feel that all is lost, we hear that second word—*grace*. Thankfully, our salvation is in God's hands. Yes, we have sinned and fall short of the glory of God, but we are justified freely by his grace, through faith in Jesus. Out of a sense of gratitude, then, we will find ourselves freely demonstrating and proclaiming the good news to others.

Dr. Horton continued: "I think you start with creation in the image of God, not with a fallen redemption, but creation in the image of God. What does it mean for even the most unlovely? Not just vulnerable, but unlovable people. You need them. John Calvin has a great line where he says, 'If we really believe that each person is loved by God, then even when they treat us badly, we will love them not for their actions, but for the image of God that is stamped on them that we share with them.'

"So we start with the image. Of course, that's not the gospel, but we start with nature, and then we go [to] redemption and all that that entails. The application of redemption, justification, sanctification, adoption. Then we go to glorification, what we're looking for up ahead ultimately with the consummation. Glorification [is] that we will be as much like God as it is possible for a creature to be. That's mind-blowing. We will be perfectly conformed to God's holiness and righteousness, love and integrity. We will be as much like God as it is possible for any creature to be, without actually becoming God's essence.

"Romans 8, that's the plotline, that's what we're looking for, not the late, great planet Earth."

I agree that Romans 8 is a wonderful place to start thinking about how the gospel can motivate us. The chapter begins with the declaration: "There is therefore now no condemnation for those who are in Christ Jesus. For the law of the Spirit of life has set you free in Christ Jesus from the law of sin and death" (Rom. 8:1–2). In other words, though we are lawbreakers, you and I are free from condemnation, because Christ was condemned in our place—the Just for the unjust. Verse 3 picks up on this idea and shows us why this is so important: "For God has done what the law, weakened by the flesh, could not do."

Let's take a moment and unpack this idea. Guilt, which the law produces, could never motivate us to love God or our neighbors—that's the point. You will never fight human trafficking in a way that endures if you are guilted into it. Whether that guilt comes from within or without, it's not going to last and for good reason. The law does not have the power to change us. It is unable to enable what it demands.

This is why Christ came to live, die, and rise for us. "By sending his own Son in the likeness of sinful flesh and for sin, he condemned sin in the flesh, in order that the righteous requirement of the law might be fulfilled in us, who walk not according to the flesh but according to the Spirit" (Rom. 8:3–4). Christ dealt with our sin problem by becoming sin for us. Since the law is powerless to free us from ourselves, Christ came to us and did what we couldn't. Filling us with the Spirit of God, he set us on a trajectory. All those who are predestined, are also called, justified, and finally glorified (cf. Rom. 8:30).

The more we meditate on these two words, *law* and *gospel*, the more we see our helpless estate, the more our theology of glory begins to crumble. But looking to the cross, we also see that Christ took the law out of our hands. He has fulfilled it for us. You are no longer enslaved to the law; because of Christ, you are free.

In addition to allowing the plotline of Romans 8 to guide us, Horton added that we should also make a clear distinction between the two kingdoms. "People who affirm the distinction between the kingdom of Christ and the kingdoms of this age, are not giving up on the world, not giving up on our callings in the world. On the contrary, it has been the people who believe that most strongly who have developed a really strong, robust doctrine of calling, vocation."

Two Kingdoms

"Why? Because we know we're not redeeming the world. We know that this passing evil age really has its days numbered, and there is not going to be a kingdom that we can build. It has to be a gift. It is your Father's good pleasure to give you a kingdom. 'Fear not, little flock, it is the Father's good pleasure to give you a kingdom.' Wow, that's a gift too? Yeah, even the kingdom is a gift. We're not building it; we're receiving it. . . . But that doesn't mean that my callings to my neighbor in this world are unimportant. On the contrary, it says, 'What'll I do in the meantime?' Paul told the Thessalonians, 'Work with your hands, mind your own business, and have something to give to those in need.'"

As citizens of two kingdoms, we wait in the "already" for the "not yet" kingdom of God. During this intermediate period, believers can meet the needs of the person in front of us in a truly holistic manner. Not only can we can meet their physical and material needs, but pointing them to Christ, we also remind them that things are not as they will always be.

"So there's a clear distinction between the kingdoms," he asserted, "but the two kingdoms overlap at the individual Christian. Every believer is simultaneously a citizen of heaven and earth, of Christ's kingdom and the kingdoms of this age. So negotiating that is what we have to do between Sunday and Monday, taking all of the gifts that we've been given on the Lord's Day, and distributing that to our neighbors throughout the week.

"It's a short bucket list. Don't live self-indulgent lives, live for your neighbor. But don't imagine when you're doing that that you're building the kingdom. You're not—you're testifying to the kingdom that is a gift, to life that is a gift, to the fact that we can't even lift a finger apart from the God in whom we live and move and have our being."

I interjected. "I think understanding the proper reception of this good news of the kingdom is very pivotal for doing anything, because we realize that justice came and was poured out on Christ at the cross, and it flows out of that cross to us."

"Yes, yes, yes," he confirmed.

"And having that as a mind-set," I continued, "where we're thinking, 'Okay, God has brought justice, my vertical debt has been taken care of, now I'm free to focus on the horizontal approach, where my neighbor is there.'"

As the conversation came to a close, I brought up Martin Luther, who famously said, "God doesn't need your good works, but your neighbor does." His point is clear. God doesn't need us to "pray the prayer right," or for that matter, "do anything right," to be saved. We are saved by the finished work of Christ on our behalf. The more that we come to grips with the fact that our salvation is not found through introspection, but rather lies outside of us in the person of Christ, the more that we will naturally begin to care for the other. Once we finally lay our futile attempts at self-justification down at the foot of the cross, we can rest in the fact that we are justified by faith alone. As a result, we are set free to love our neighbor through our vocation; we can love the person in front of us as we go about our ordinary lives.

EPILOGUE

My phone vibrated and lit up.

As I reached for it, I saw I had a Facebook message from my friend AJ. From the look of it, this wasn't a social call. Witnessing a peculiar exchange on his subway commute, he wrote, "What should we do if we suspect something fishy going on with an older guy/couple and a younger girl that doesn't look like she wants to be with them?"

Whether this was human trafficking or not, this person was being visibly pressured by those with whom she was standing. The fact remains that though she was most likely not being trafficked, she was vulnerable. This is exactly what caught AJ's attention.

I immediately fired off two messages back-to-back.

"Call 911. Report it. That's the best you can do on short notice. Do you still see the girl? Where are you? Call for a welfare check," I wrote quickly.

A few minutes later, he sent another message. "He looks and is acting very demanding."

In turn, I replied. "Still near them? If so, follow them . . . at a safe distance. Find out where they go and then call 911 or 311. Either way, you explain what you are currently seeing."

Over the next ten minutes, AJ messaged back and forth. He continued to send me updates as he followed them at a safe distance. "Possibly under the influence of something," he noted.

I sent four more messages:

"Still on the train?"

"Okay. Be prepared to convey what you see to the police . . . not what you think you see."

"Follow them . . . but be safe. Do not attempt to be the hero. That could endanger her. Give the police all the info that you gather."

After a few more minutes, he responded, "Okay, I got off at the station, no one is with me, cops are on the way. I was walking in front of them but they stopped in the subway station. [They are] still in there. I'm outside on the street."

Like AJ, we all want to do something for those most vulnerable to human trafficking. But it's easy to feel unqualified or "in over our heads."

Defining human trafficking as the "exploitation of vulnerability for commercial gain," we are reminded that traffickers target those people who have their backs against the wall. They intentionally look for those who have exhausted all of their options.

Thus, the aim of this book is for each of us to realize that we can fight human trafficking by loving those most vulnerable. Operating from a standpoint of vulnerability, we realize that each person is on a continuum. In other words, they may/are/have been trafficked.

With that, you are invited to invest your life in those who live in the margins. Because, truth be told, they aren't any different than you. As a friend of mine says, "We are all one medical emergency away from being on the street."

Therefore, as vulnerable people ourselves, we love other vulnerable people, because Christ was made vulnerable for us.

You don't have to be a superhero (or Liam Neeson, for that matter) to make an impact. You can be . . . you. Like those for whom we wish to care, each of us has God-given dignity and a voice worth hearing.

Together we can end human trafficking.

100 WAYS YOU CAN FIGHT HUMAN TRAFFICKING TODAY[1]

Please note that some of the recommended films and books in this appendix contain mature and at times disturbing content related to human trafficking. Please use discretion before watching or reading, and do so according to your own conscience.

1. Get informed and know your facts! Read the book *Ending Slavery: How We Free Today's Slaves* by Kevin Bales to further your understanding of slavery.

2. Become aware and learn the warning signs and red flags of human trafficking and slavery. This way, when you see something, you can say something. To learn more, visit PolarisProject.org/signs.

3. Get informed and know your facts so you can be a better abolitionist! Read the book *A Crime So Monstrous: Face-to-Face with Modern-Day Slavery* by E. Benjamin Skinner to further your understanding of slavery.

4. Save the Polaris Project's National Human Trafficking Hotline number in your phone so you know how to report tips if you see slavery or trafficking occurring in real time: (888) 373-7888.

5. Get informed and know your facts! Watch the documentary film *Very Young Girls* to further your understanding of slavery. Also, visit the website of the organization featured in the film, http://www.gems-girls.org.

6. Know the National Center for Missing and Exploited Children CyberTip Line so you know how to report tips if you see children in need: (800) 843-5678 or CyberTipLine.com.

7. Get informed and know your facts so you can be a better abolitionist! Read the book *Terrify No More: Young Girls Held Captive and the Daring Undercover Operation to Win Their Freedom* by Gary Haugen to further your understanding of slavery.

8. Volunteer to post the Human Trafficking Hotline or the CyberTip Line number in your workplace, school, or house of worship.

9. Have a conversation with someone who is different than you.

10. Experience what it feels like to be a slave. Ask permission to accomplish any task where someone else is present. If entering a building, ask someone near if you can enter. If in a coffee shop, ask permission to order. If at work, ask permission to be seated. Share your experience with others.

11. Reflect on the good news of Christ and allow that to motivate you to love others.

12. Talk about slavery and inform those around you. You would be surprised how many people do not know that modern-day slavery exists here and now.

13. Address demand by going and learning how supply chains are impacted by modern-day slavery at https://www.responsiblesourcing tool.org.

14. Join the Nexus HTMS anti-slavery selfie campaign to help raise awareness about slavery by tweeting a picture of yourself, your friends, coworkers, or family members holding a sign that says #EndSlaveryNow #WeAreNexus to @NexusHTMS.

15. Learn how your church can fight human trafficking. Go to lmpgnetwork.org.

16. Address demand by downloading Covenant Eyes online accountability software to your computer, phone, and tablet.

17. Read Diane Langberg books on trauma; start with *Suffering and the Heart of God: How Trauma Destroys and Christ Restores.*

18. Help create jobs for survivors and women at risk of human trafficking. Visit BuyHerBagNotHerBody.com and purchase your handmade, slave-free bag to help spread the message.

19. Buy a scarf or accessory from rethreaded.com, a company that aims to renew hope, reignite dreams, and release potential for survivors of human trafficking locally and globally through business.

20. Most products we wear, eat, use, or buy have slavery embedded in the supply chain. Find out how much you contribute to global slavery by visiting SlaveryFootprint.org.

21. Get informed and know your facts! Read the U.S. State Department's annual *Trafficking in Persons Report* to further your understanding of slavery. Visit www.state.gov/j/tip/rls/tiprpt.

22. Sign up for Google Alerts on "human trafficking" or "slavery" to educate yourself. Also, set Google Alerts for the vulnerabilities

in your community. If you do not know what a Google Alert is, Google it.

23. Don't let the enormity of the problem overwhelm you. Start with caring for the person in front of you.

24. Learn what laws exist at the state and county level and where the deficiencies are. To learn how your state needs help, visit PolarisProject.org/what-we-do/policy-advocacy.

25. Be informed about trauma. Read Chris Lim's book, *The Heart of a Healer: Trauma Informed Biblical Counseling.*

26. Call your congressman or senator's office and ask them what they are doing to end slavery in your state and support those representatives that are strengthening anti-human trafficking laws. Start here: https://www.usa.gov/elected-officials.

27. Get informed and know your facts! Read the book *Not for Sale: The Return of the Global Slave Trade and How We Can Fight It* by David Batstone to further your understanding of slavery.

28. Make your voice known to the lawmakers by voting for candidates who are tough on traffickers. You are also able to have your voice be heard as you sign petitions for legislation. Go here for more information: https://polarisproject.org/policy-legislation.

29. Learn the art of empowerment; read *When Helping Hurts: How to Alleviate Poverty without Hurting the Poor and Yourself.*

30. Support initiatives to change local, state, and federal law so that underage girls in prostitution, slavery, or who are victims of trafficking are treated as victims and not criminals. They need rescuing, rehabilitation, and vocational training, not jail time.

31. Get informed and know your facts! Read the book *Half the Sky: Turning Oppression into Opportunity for Women Worldwide* by Nicholas Kristof to further your understanding of slavery.

32. Find anti-trafficking organizations anywhere in the world using the Global Modern Slavery Directory: http://www.globalmodern slavery.org.

33. Watch the documentary film *Nefarious: Merchant of Souls* to further your understanding of slavery.

34. Seek out and "like" or follow anti-trafficking/anti-slavery organizations on Facebook and Twitter. Not only will you be showing your support for abolition, but you will learn more about slavery and trafficking from their updates as they appear in your social media feeds.

35. Check out the Walk Free Foundation's annual *Global Slavery Index* to further your understanding of slavery. Visit GlobalSlaveryIndex. org.

36. Take up trafficking as a topic for academic study. There is still much work to be done and we need your intellectual capital on this problem.

37. Learn more of what the Bible says about justice; read *Justice Awakening* by Eddie Byun.

38. Seek out internships and volunteer opportunities with anti-trafficking/anti-slavery organizations.

39. For a look at Christian social action, read Mae Elise Cannon's *Social Justice Handbook: Small Steps for a Better World.*

40. Learn about the vulnerable populations in your community with the Distressed Communities Index: http://eig.org/dci.

41. Watch the movie *SOLD* or read the book of the same title by Patricia McCormick to further your understanding of slavery. Then text SOLD to 51555 to join the SOLD campaign and stay informed about local screenings and events.

42. Do not support the commercial sex industry in the television you watch, the magazines you buy, the places you visit. If it offends you, put it down, turn it off, walk away (then write a letter of complaint).

43. Learn about inequality and privilege in Ken Wytsma's book, *The Myth of Equality.*

44. Volunteer in a prison system or spend time working at survivor housing, survivor community centers, or a program for victim rehabilitation and create relationships that can change someone's future.

45. Demand the President stand by the 2008 Child Soldiers Prevention Act by instituting sanctions against, or pulling support from, those states and substate groups that continue to recruit, train, and use individuals under eighteen years old in any military capacity.

46. Listen to survivors and support survivor-led empowerment organizations, like mentariusa.org.

47. Promote a chocolate-free Valentine's Day or Easter and spare the West African children who are enslaved to make over 90 percent of the chocolate sold in America or buy fair trade chocolate.

48. Get informed and know your facts so you can be a better abolitionist! Watch the documentary film *The Dark Side of Chocolate* to further your understanding of slavery.

49. Be a conscientious consumer and switch to fair trade products in order to increase the demand for slave-free labor.

50. Investigate the products you buy to ensure that they are free of slave labor and fairly traded. Download fair trade apps on your smartphone and become aware of what you buy.

51. Ask your retailers if they know where their products come from and if they support slave-free supply chains. Then find out what they are doing about it or call on them to make changes in how their products are made.

52. Get informed and know your facts! Read the book *Sex Trafficking: Inside the Business of Modern Slavery* by Siddharth Kara to further your understanding of slavery.

53. Buy socially minded products and gifts that support the abolition movement or provide relief to victims or potential victims.

54. Read real-life stories of those who have committed to the mission of vulnerability. Start with *Let Justice Roll Down* by John Perkins.

55. Bring a group from your church or your university to NYC and learn how you can fight human trafficking in real time with Let My People Go. Go to lmpgnetwork.org for more details.

56. Support survivors of human trafficking by buying products that are survivor-made. To learn more, visit MadeBySurvivors.com.

57. Get informed and know your facts! Read the book *Girls Like Us: Fighting for a World Where Girls Are Not for Sale, an Activist Finds Her Calling and Heals Herself* by Rachel Lloyd to further your understanding of slavery.

58. Invest in the lives of children, particularly those in poverty and at-risk.

59. Get informed and know your facts so you can be a better abolitionist! Watch the documentary film *Food Chains* to further your understanding of slavery.

60. Talk to bus drivers, cab drivers, pizza delivery person, cable installers, etc., about human trafficking and slavery. These workers have a vantage point that few have and may be able to identify potential victims.

61. Ask the managers and staff at hotels you stay in to take steps to care for those most vulnerable in their hotels. For more information, check out https://www.ecpatusa.org/hotel/.

62. Take the Human Trafficking 101 Awareness Training at https://www.state.gov/j/tip/training/.

63. Buy produce from distributors or dine at restaurants that have signed on to the Fair Food Program. Encourage those that have not to do so. Learn more at CIW-online.org/fair-food-program.

64. Get informed and know your facts! Watch the feature film *The Whistleblower* to further your understanding of slavery.

65. Buy or consume products that are fair trade. Encourage your favorite products to sign on if they have not already. Learn more at FairTradeUSA.org.

66. Get informed and know your facts! Watch the documentary film *Not My Life* to further your understanding of slavery.

67. Speak out! Write about this issue and how it is affecting your community in your local newspaper or news blog. The power of a pen has never been more true.

68. Get informed and know your facts! Read the book *Not in My Town: Exposing and Ending Human Trafficking and Modern-Day*

Slavery by Dillon Burroughs and Charles Powell to further your understanding of slavery.

69. Host a fundraiser for a local anti-trafficking organization.

70. Donate to organizations that are addressing the vulnerability that traffickers are likely to target. For example, those working with the homeless and immigrant communities.

71. Get a small taste of having no voice. On a given day only speak if you are asked a direct question. Answer with only a small phrase. The following day, share your experience with friends and coworkers. Then get them involved in giving a voice to the voiceless.

72. Watch *I Am Jane Doe* on Netflix to learn more about how people are trafficked online on websites like Backpage.com.

73. Raise awareness by celebrating the United Nation's World Day Against Trafficking in Persons on July 30.

74. You can't walk with vulnerable people without having others walk with you in your vulnerabilities. Look into The Rest Initiative. Go to http://therestinitiative.org.

75. Raise awareness by celebrating the United States' National Slavery and Human Trafficking Prevention Month in January.

76. Get informed and know your facts! Watch the feature film *12 Years a Slave* to further your understanding of slavery.

77. Change the conversation about buying sex. Pimping is not cool. The person is not a prostitute, this word conveys identity; rather they are prostituted.

78. Pray for all those involved in human trafficking, pray for those who are at risk of trafficking. Pray for the traffickers. Pray for the

buyers. Pray that ordinary people, like you and I, would stand up and say, "Enough!"

79. Diamonds are a source of funding for authoritarian regimes and violent substate groups all across Africa who frequently use slave labor (both children and adults) to mine them. Make sure when buying precious gems that they are guaranteed conflict-free.

80. Get informed and know your facts! Watch the documentary film *Blood Diamonds* or the feature film *Blood Diamond* to further your understanding of slavery.

81. Host an information session at home, school, your house of worship, or your workplace and invite a local anti-trafficking organization to come speak to you and your friends about what they do and how you can help.

82. Learn about those who are most often targeted by traffickers. Visit https://humantraffickinghotline.org/what-human-trafficking/human-trafficking/victims.

83. Write an old-fashioned letter of encouragement once a day for a month and send them to thirty different organizations combating human trafficking to encourage the leadership.

84. Get informed and know your facts so you can be a better abolitionist! Watch the documentary film *Born into Brothels* to further your understanding of slavery.

85. Pray for an end to modern slavery in all of its forms.

86. Get informed and know your facts! Read the book *The Locust Effect: Why the End of Poverty Requires the End of Violence* by Gary Haugen to further your understanding of slavery.

87. Ask local businesses if they have vocational programs for survivors. If they do not, encourage them to learn more about how they can help survivors get back on their feet and help them return to a more normal life by training and hiring them as part of the staff.

88. Get informed and know your facts so you can be a better abolitionist! Watch the documentary film *Amazing Grace* to further your understanding of slavery.

89. Find a project that inspires you to help. Visit https://www.freedomunited.org and learn more about or support projects that need your assistance immediately and raise money and awareness with their peer-to-peer platform.

90. Mentor someone. Friendship and care are an integral part of everyone's process.

91. Talk to those who see those most vulnerable on a daily basis in your community. Talk to social services, nonprofits, and law enforcement.

92. Learn about child and forced labor. Visit https://www.dol.gov/agencies/ilab/our-work/child-forced-labor-trafficking.

93. Get informed and know your facts! Watch the documentary film by Justin Dillon, *CALL + RESPONSE*, to further your understanding of slavery.

94. Be a digital defender! Apply for a fellowship at the Thorn Innovation Lab and help put a stop to online trafficking and sex slavery. For more information, visit wearethorn.org/thorn-innovation-lab.

95. Get informed and know your facts! Subscribe to the journal *The Journal of Human Trafficking: A Powerful New Journal Addressing a Global Human Rights Crisis* to further your understanding of slavery.

96. Find opportunities for survivors to tell their stories. Host a survivor at your school, workplace, house of worship, or home and help them have their story and message be heard.

97. Learn about the leadership in this fight. Visit EndSlaveryNow. org and look under the "Connect" tab to read about a new organization each day for a month.

98. Get informed and know your facts so you can be a better abolitionist! Read the book *The Slave Next Door: Human Trafficking and Slavery in America Today* by Kevin Bales and Ron Soodalter to further your understanding of slavery.

99. Slavery touches every corner of the earth—no man, woman, or child, no state, city, or town is immune from this societal plague. Take the time to visit with victim centers, anti-trafficking nonprofits and NGOs, or law enforcement wherever you travel and learn about how different communities around the world struggle with and combat slavery.

100. Remember that as you love those most vulnerable, you are investing in the world in which you want to live.

NOTES

Introduction

1. This claim appears to be the common assumption. However, according to several sources there is no way to actually verify the claim. See the following for more information: Mary Ann Badavi, "The Super Bowl Myth," *The Polaris Project*, February 5, 2016, https://polarisproject.org/blog/2016/02/05/super-bowl-myth.

2. See the Global Slavery Index at www.globalslaveryindex.org.

3. "Human Trafficking Frequently Asked Questions," United Nations Office on Drugs and Crime, accessed March 21, 2018, http://www.unodc.org/unodc/en/human-trafficking/faqs.html#Which_countries_are_affected_by_human_trafficking.

4. "The Facts," *The Polaris Project*, accessed March 21, 2018, https://polarisproject.org/facts.

5. Thank you, Brooke Axtell, for giving me this definition.

6. Author got the wording "vulnerability hangover" from Brene Brown.

Section One: When Vulnerability Is Exploited

1. "The Victims," The National Human Trafficking Hotline, accessed March 21, 2018, https://humantraffickinghotline.org/what-human-trafficking/human-trafficking/victims.

Chapter 1

1. The following story has been adapted from a story that I wrote for *The Baptist Press* entitled "When Dying Is Gain," http://www.pbnews.net/41318/first-person-when-dying-is-gain.

2. As Christians, we should really explore whether we hold to a theology of glory or a theology of the cross. To learn more, check out this article from my good friends at *Mockingbird*. Sean Norris, "Theologians of

Glory vs. Theologians of the Cross: An Intro and Definition," *Mockingbird*, June 18, 2009, accessed March 21, 2018, http://www.mbird.com/2009/06/theologian-of-glory-vs-theologian-of/.

3. Michael Wittmer, *The Last Enemy* (Grand Rapids: Discovery House Publishers, 2012), chapter 1, Kindle Edition. Quote was also taken from an article the author wrote which can be found at http://www.bpnews.net/41310/firstperson-when-dying-is-gain.

4. William Cowper, "God Moves in a Mysterious Way," Hymn #514 in *The Lutheran Hymnal*, 1731–1800, accessed March 21, 2018, http://www.lutheran-hymnal.com/lyrics/tlh514.htm.

5. Though Davin did not ever fulfill his dream of planting or pastoring a church, his ministry has impacted people around the world. The way that he lived his life especially at the end is a challenge for all of us.

Chapter 2

1. Not that this is wrong, but our advocacy need not stop here.

2. "Movies and Myths about Human Trafficking" by Jonathan Todres in *The Conversation*, http://theconversation.com/movies-and-myths-about-human-trafficking-51300.

3. Mellissa Withers, "Untangling Myths about Human Trafficking," *Psychology Today*, July 26, 2017, accessed March 21, 2018, https://www.psychologytoday.com/blog/modern-day-slavery/201707/untangling-myths-about-human-trafficking.

4. Ibid.

5. Kathryn Westcott, "What Is Stockholm Syndrome?" *BBC News*, August 22, 2013, accessed March 21, 2018, http://www.bbc.com/news/magazine-22447726. Also look at Chris Lim, *The Heart of a Healer* (Meadville, PA: Christian Faith Publishing, 2000), 50–51. Lim's book is a helpful resource for understanding the role of trauma in human trafficking.

6. "Myths and Misconceptions," *The National Human Trafficking Hotline*, accessed March 21, 2018, https://humantraffickinghotline.org/what-human-trafficking/myths-misconceptions.

7. We often miss vulnerable people in need of help because we have already labeled them as perpetrators. More about this in Section Three.

8. Eric Denton, "Anatomy of Offending: Human Trafficking in the United States," *Journal of Human Trafficking*, volume 2(1): 32–62. 2006, http://www.tandfonline.com/doi/full/10.1080/23322705.2016.1136540. This study and other pertinent studies cited in this chapter can also be found in World Without Exploitation's report: *Prevalence of Sex Trafficking, Prostitution, and Sexual Exploitation in the U.S. February 2017*. This report can be downloaded at https://www.worldwithoutexploitation.org/stats.

9. Jessica Ashley and Jody Raphael, "Domestic Sex Trafficking of Chicago Women and Girls," *Illinois Criminal Justice Information Authority*, page 6; a report from the Schiller DuCanto & Fleck Family Law Center, DePaul University College of Law, and the Illinois Criminal Justice

Information Authority, https://traffickingresourcecenter.org/sites/default/files/Domstic%20Sex%20Trafficking%20Chicago%20-%20ICJIA.pdf.

10. Celia Williamson and Tasha Perdue, "Domestic Sex Trafficking in Ohio," *The Ohio Human Trafficking Commission*, page 11, August 8, 2012, accessed March 21, 2018, http://www.ohioattorneygeneral.gov/getattachment/1bc0e815-71b6-43f5-ba45-c667840d4a93/2012-Domestic-Sex-Trafficking-in-Ohio-Report.aspx.

11. Sebastien Malo, "Is the Super Bowl Really the U.S.'s Biggest Sex Trafficking Magnet?" *Reuters*, February 1, 2018, accessed March 21, 2018, https://www.reuters.com/article/us-football-nfl-superbowl-trafficking-an/is-the-super-bowl-really-the-u-s-s-biggest-sex-trafficking-magnet-idUSKBN1FL6A1.

12. "ILO says forced labour generates annual profits of US $150 billion," *The International Labor Organization*, accessed March 30, 2018, http://www.ilo.org/global/about-the-ilo/newsroom/news/WCMS_243201/lang--en/index.htm.

13. Tori Utley, "The Trauma Economy: The Demand for Sex Trafficking and the Fight to End It," *Forbes*, January 27, 2016, accessed March 30, 2018, https://www.forbes.com/sites/toriutley/2016/01/27/the-trauma-economy-the-demand-for-sex-trafficking-and-the-fight-to-end-it/#43d83d5676af.

14. Mary Ann Badavi, "The Super Bowl Myth," *The Polaris Project*, February 5, 2016, accessed March 30, 2018, https://polarisproject.org/blog/2016/02/05/super-bowl-myth.

15. "365: How the Focus on the Super Bowl Hurts Trafficking Victims," Girls Educational and Mentoring Services (GEMS), accessed March 30, 2018, http://www.gems-girls.org/shifting-perspective/365-how-the-focus-on-the-super-bowl-hurts-trafficking-victims.

16. Tom W. Smith, *The General Social Survey*, GSS Project Report No. 32, 1972–2010. Data can be accessed at http://gss.norc.org. For more statistics on commercial sexual exploitation, see https://www.worldwithoutexploitation.org.

17. Traffickers and sex buyers are often well-versed in technology. For example, up until recently backpage.com was a website where commercially sexually exploited youth were trafficked. Though it has been shut down, we need to be aware that traffickers have and will continue to use technology. For more on this reality, you can watch "Sex Trafficking Survivor Melanie Thompson on Why FOSTA-SESTA Is So Important," https://nowthisnews.com/videos/her/sex-trafficking-survivor-melanie-thompson-on-fosta-sesta.

18. I would argue that the operation was a success because they listened to a survivor. Survivors should be a major part of the process. When we refuse to consult survivors, we will find ourselves missing the point.

19. Christine Hauser, "Two Tennessee Ministers Are Among 30 Arrested in Prostitution Sting," *New York Times*, May 27, 2016, accessed March 30, 2018, https://www.nytimes.com/2016/05/27/us/two-ministers-are-among-30-arrested-in-tennessee-prostitution-sting.html.

20. This has been the case with the Trafficking Victims Protection Act of 2000 (TVPA). One must prove force, fraud, and coercion in a federal court of law. The 2015 Justice for Victims of Trafficking Act amends the definition of the

TVPA 2000, defining sex trafficking as the recruitment, harboring, transportation, provision, obtaining, patronizing, or soliciting of a person for the purpose of a commercial sex act, in which the person induced to perform such act has not obtained eighteen years of age.

21. Even in this moment, there is someone who is reading this that is thinking, *Was she eighteen?* This mind-set can allow for the trafficking of a minor.

22. According to the International Labor Organization, 71 percent of those who are forcibly trafficked for sex or labor are women and girls. "Global Estimates of Modern Slavery," 8.7 Alliance and International Labor Organization, 2017, accessed March 30, 2018, http://www.ilo.org/wcmsp5/groups/public/---dgreports/---dcomm/documents/publication/wcms_575479.pdf.

23. "The Global Estimates of Modern Slavery: Forced Labour and Forced Marriage," *International Labor Organization and the Walk Free Foundation*, 2017, 5, https://www.ilo.org/global/topics/forced-labour/publications/WCMS_586127/lang--en/index.htm.

24. "FACT SHEET: Sex Trafficking," *U.S. Department of Health and Human Services*, August 2, 2012, accessed March 30, 2018, https://www.acf.hhs.gov/otip/resource/fact-sheet-sex-trafficking-english.

25. Norma Hotaling, Kristie Miller, Elizabeth Trudeau, "The Commercial Sexual Exploitation of Women and Girls: A Survivor Service Provider's Perspective," *Yale Journal of Law and Feminism* volume 18, no. 1 (2006): 182.

26. "New ILO Global Estimate of Forced Labor: 20.9 million victims," *The International Labor Organization*, June 1, 2012, accessed March 30, 2018, http://www.ilo.org/global/about-the-ilo/newsroom/news/WCMS_182109/lang--en/index.htm.

27. Learn more at polarisproject.org.

28. For more information, read the U.S. Department of Labor's 2018 List of Goods Produced by Child or Forced Labor, https://www.dol.gov/sites/default/files/documents/ilab/ListofGoods.pdf.

29. "Sweatshops Under the American Flag," *New York Times,* May 10, 2002, accessed March 30, 2018, https://www.nytimes.com/2002/05/10/opinion/sweatshops-under-the-american-flag.html.

30. Debt bondage can occur in both sex and labor trafficking.

31. "The Global Estimates of Modern Slavery: Forced Labour and Forced Marriage," *International Labor Organization and the Walk Free Foundation*, 2017, 5, https://www.ilo.org/global/topics/forced-labour/publications/WCMS_586127/lang--en/index.htm.

32. Debt bondage is a key means of exploiting people through both sex and labor trafficking. Basically, if you know the person owing you money, they will be compelled to stay.

33. "Federal Labor Trafficking/Forced Labor Cases in the United States," *The Polaris Project,* 2010, accessed March 30, 2018, https://www.casa17th.org/filelibrary/Labor%20Trafficking%20&%20Forced%20Labor%20Cases.pdf.

34. *United States v. Flores*, 289 U.S. 137 (1933).

35. "Slavery in the Fields and the Food We Eat," *Coalition of Immokalee Workers*, accessed March 30, 2018, http://ciw-online.org/slavery/.

36. Lisa Cohen, "How America's 'Ground-Zero' for Modern Slavery Was Cleaned Up by Workers' Group," CNN, March 14, 2018, accessed March 30, 2018, https://www.cnn.com/2017/05/30/world/ciw-fair-food-program-freedom-project/index.html.

37. "Miguel Flores and Associate Sentenced to 15 Years for Enslaving Migrant Workers," *United States Department of Justice*, November 14, 1997, accessed March 30, 2018, https://www.justice.gov/archive/opa/pr/1997/November97/482cr.htm. html.

38. "Protocol to Prevent, Suppress and Punish Trafficking in Persons Especially Women and Children, supplementing the United Nations Convention against Transnational Organized Crime," *The United Nations*, ratified November 2000, accessed March 30, 2018, http://www.ohchr.org/EN/ProfessionalInterest/Pages/ProtocolTraffickingInPersons.aspx.

39. "Mexican National Sentenced to 15 Years for Participating in a Brutal Family-Run Sex Trafficking Organization," *United States Department of Justice*, January 26, 2015, accessed March 30, 2018, https://www.justice.gov/opa/pr/mexican-national-sentenced-15-years-participating-brutal-family-run-sex-trafficking.

40. "The Global Estimates of Modern Slavery: Forced Labour and Forced Marriage," *International Labor Organization and the Walk Free Foundation*, 2017, 5, https://www.ilo.org/global/topics/forced-labour/publications/WCMS_586127/lang--en/index.htm.

41. "Hidden Slaves: Force Labor in the United States," *Free the Slaves*, September 2004, accessed March 30, 2018, http://www.freetheslaves.net/wp-content/uploads/2015/03/Hidden-Slaves.pdf.

42. "Mexican National Sentenced to 15 Years for Participating in a Brutal Family-Run Sex Trafficking Organization," *United States Department of Justice*, January 26, 2015, accessed March 30, 2018, https://www.justice.gov/opa/pr/mexican-national-sentenced-15-years-participating-brutal-family-run-sex-trafficking.

43. Withers, "Untangling Myths about Human Trafficking."

Chapter 3

1. It's the home of the "Big Wick," a ten-pound pizza. Regardless of whether you like NY Pizza, Chicago Style, or Pizza Rolls, you owe it to yourself to try this modern marvel.

2. "Why He Matters: Luis C. deBaca," *Washington Post,* accessed March 30, 2018, https://www.washingtonpost.com/politics/luis-c-de-baca/gIQAMGF-GAP_print.html.

3. E. Benjamin Skinner, "Obama's Abolitionist," *Huffington Post,* May 25, 2011, accessed March 30, 2018, https://www.huffingtonpost.com/ben-skinner/obamas-abolitionist_b_178781.html.

4. Anthony DePalma, "In Mexico, Deaf Finds the Future Lies North," *New York Times,* July 26, 1997, accessed March 30, 2018, http://www.nytimes.com/1997/07/26/nyregion/in-mexico-deaf-find-the-future-lies-north.html.

5. "Luis C. deBaca,"*Washington Post*, accessed March 30, 2018, https://www.washingtonpost.com/politics/luis-c-de-baca/gIQAMGFGAP_print.html.

6. Deborah Sontag, "Dozens of Deaf Immigrants Discovered in Forced Labor," *Washington Post,* July 20, 1997, accessed March 30, 2018, http://www.nytimes.com/1997/07/20/nyregion/dozens-of-deaf-immigrants-discovered-in-forced-labor.html.

7. Gene Edward Veith, "Glory Versus the Cross," *Tabletalk Magazine,* March 1, 2008, accessed March 30, 2018, https://www.ligonier.org/learn/articles/glory-versus-cross/.

8. DeBaca continues, "That was just because Cadena was in the spring of '98, so March 11 of 1998 is when the executive order—the 'Three P's'—basically gets announced on March 11 at the International Women's Day event at the White House. That's when the official tasking of the Attorney General to come up with solutions happens."

9. https://fightslaverynow.org/why-fight-there-are-27-million-reasons/the-law-and-trafficking/trafficking-victims-protection-act/trafficking-victims-protection-act/.

10. "Federal Law," *National Human Trafficking Hotline,* accessed March 30, 2018, https://humantraffickinghotline.org/what-human-trafficking/federal-law.

11. https://fightslaverynow.org/why-fight-there-are-27-million-reasons/the-law-and-trafficking/trafficking-victims-protection-act/trafficking-victims-protection-act/.

12. Thanks to Chris Lim for helping me see this.

13. "Sex Trafficking: Power and Control Wheel," *Polaris Project,* 2010, accessed March 30, 2018, http://project-intersect.org/wp-content/uploads/2015/06/Power-and-Control-Wheel.pdf.

Section Two: Recognizing Vulnerability in Scripture

1. Francis A. Schaeffer, *Francis Schaeffer Trilogy: The God Who Is There, Escape from Reason, He Is There and He Is Not Silent* (Wheaton: Crossway Books, 1990).

Chapter 4

1. David Paul Kuhn, "The Gospel According to Jim Wallis," *Washington Post*, November 26, 2006, accessed March 30, 2018, http://www.washingtonpost.com/wp-dyn/content/article/2006/11/21/AR2006112101801.html.

2. Tim Keller, *Ministries of Mercy: The Call of the Jericho Road* (Philipsburg: P&R Publishing, 2015), 176.

3. For more on systemic injustice, see Corey Fields, "Bridging the Gap Between the Heart and Systemic Injustice," *Baptist News Global,* May 11, 2016, accessed March 30, 2018, https://baptistnews.com/article/bridging-the-gap-between-the-heart-and-systemic-injustice/#.WsAFn2aZPOQ.

See also: Bryan Stevenson and Rev. Tim Keller, *Grace, Justice, and Mercy: An Evening with Bryan Stevenson and Tim Keller*, video, directed/produced by Center for Faith and Work (2016), Vimeo.

4. Bethany Hoang, *Deepening the Soul for Justice* (Downers Grove: InterVarsity Press, 2012), 7.

5. The Hebrew word *mishpat* is found more than four hundred times in the Old Testament.

6. Tim Keller, "What Is Biblical Justice?" *Relevant Magazine*, August 23, 2012, accessed March 30, 2018, http://www.relevantmagazine.com/god/practical-faith/what-biblical-justice.

7. Thayer's Greek Lexicon definition, accessed March 30, 2018, https://www.blueletterbible.org/lang/lexicon/lexicon.cfm?t=kjv&strongs=g1343.

8. For a quick explanation on the different types of justice, see "Four Types of Justice," ChangingMinds.org, http://changingminds.org/explanations/trust/four_justice.htm.

9. Nicholas Wolterstorff, *Justice: Rights and Wrongs* (Princeton: Princeton University Press, 2008).

10. Tim Keller, *Generous Justice* (New York: Riverhead Books, 2012), 2.

11. For more on this defining aspect of justice, see Gary Haugen, *Good News about Injustice* (Downers Grove: InterVarsity Press, 2009).

12. Tim Keller, "What Is Biblical Justice?" *Relevant Magazine*, August 23, 2012, http://www.relevantmagazine.com/god/practical-faith/what-biblical-justice.

13. Polly House, "Blackaby's 'Experiencing God': 15 Years of Seeing God Work," *Baptist Press*, accessed March 31, 2018, www.blackaby.net/exp god/2010/12/02/blackabys-'experiencing-god'-15-years-of-seeing-god-work/.

14. Throughout the Old Testament, the word *mishpat* is oftentimes used alongside several groups of vulnerable people—the widow, the orphan, the sojourner, and the poor. These groups serve to summarize all who lack status and the financial, social, and family protection needed to survive. With this population in mind, God would define the rights of the Israelites, and follow with a command to remember the rights of the vulnerable among them (Exod. 22:21–24; Lev. 23:22; Deut. 24:19; 26:12). When Moses gives the law in Exodus 22, the Israelites are strictly commanded to "not wrong a sojourner or oppress him," because they were once sojourners in Egypt (v. 21). God reminds them that as they remember their own sojourning and subsequent redemption, they should love other sojourners. The point from these texts is that their love of neighbor is grounded in their own redemption, just as our love of our vulnerable neighbor is grounded in our redemption.

15. Gary Haugen, *Terrify No More: Young Girls Held Captive and the Daring Undercover Operation to Win Their Freedom* (Nashville: W Publishing Group, 2005), 241.

Chapter 5

1. We find this theme repeatedly mentioned in Jesus' teaching, specifically in the parables.

2. This table was created by my former research assistant Hannah Grundmann.

3. Mae Elise Cannon, *Social Justice Handbook: Small Steps to a Better World* (Downers Grove: InterVarsity Press, 2009), 34.

4. Ken Wytsma, *Pursuing Justice: The Call to Live and Die for Bigger Things* (Nashville: Thomas Nelson, Inc., 2013), 292.

5. Tim Chester, *Good News to the Poor: Social Involvement and the Gospel* (Wheaton: Crossway Publishing, 2013), Kindle Locations 1501–1505. Kindle Edition.

6. The name has been changed.

7. Joy Farrington, *Broken by Beauty* (Crown Hill: Authentic Media, 2013), Kindle locations 436–471. Kindle Edition.

8. "Wounded Healer," *Wikipedia: The Free Encyclopedia,* accessed online March 30, 2018, https://en.wikipedia.org/wiki/Wounded_healer.

9. Wesley Hill, "Henri Nouwen's Weakness Was His Strength," *Christianity Today Online,* January 31, 2017, accessed March 30, 2018, https://www.christianitytoday.com/ct/2017/january-web-only/henri-nouwens-weakness-was-his-strength.html.

10. This is an ancient Near Eastern depiction of betrayal.

Section Three: Recognizing the Vulnerability Around Us

1. "What Should I Do If . . ." *The Coalition for the Homeless,* accessed March 30, 2018, http://www.coalitionforthehomeless.org/take-action/what-should-i-do-if/.

Chapter 6

1. "Live X Rachelle Starr," Reach Records, March 19, 2015, accessed March 30, 2018, http://reachrecords.com/116-life-x-rachelle-starr-2/.

2. In the context of *Crazy Love*, the author is not encouraging readers to stop praying and do something. Rather, he is encouraging readers to stop talking at God and start pondering. Nonetheless, in this story, Rachelle got the first two words and felt God clearly leading her to stop wondering about what she should do and simply get going.

3. "Live X Rachelle Starr," *Reach Records,* March 19, 2015.

4. Raleigh Sadler, "When Human Trafficking Victims Are Among Your Church Congregation," *Huffington Post,* January 12, 2016, accessed March 30, 2018, https://www.huffingtonpost.com/raleigh-sadler/when-human-trafficking-happens-in-church_b_8958050.html.

5. To learn more about Let My People Go, go to lmpgnetwork.org.

6. This idea will be further fleshed out in Section Three: Recognizing the Vulnerability Around Us.

7. Kate Taylor, "New York City Asks Clergy to Calm Ire over Homeless Shelters," *New York Times,* August 1, 2014, accessed March 30, 2018, https://www.nytimes.com/2014/08/02/nyregion/new-york-officials-facing-outcry-on-homeless-shelters-ask-church-leaders-for-support.html.

8. Tim Keller, *Ministries of Mercy: The Call of the Jericho Road* (Philipsburg: P&R Publishing, 2015), Kindle Locations 116–352. Kindle Edition. Table was created by my former research assistant Hannah Grundmann.

9. Yes, feel free to write in your book. It's okay. I mean, you paid for it—unless it's a library book. If it's a book that you have checked out, then I rescind the invitation. Don't write in library books. Ever. Please don't be that person.

10. I want to be clear that those listed here are in no way deficient nor do they need us to be their savior. They are just in life situations that make it more difficult to thrive and flourish.

11. Brené Brown, "America's Crisis of Disconnection Runs Deeper Than Politics," *Fast Company,* September 12, 2017, accessed March 30, 2018, https://www.fastcompany.com/40465644/brene-brown-americas-crisis-of-disconnection-runs-deeper-than-politics.

12. This list is based on the list available at the Polaris Project. For more information, see: "Recognize the Signs," *Polaris Project,* accessed March 30, 2018, http://polarisproject.org/human-trafficking/recognize-signs

13. This is taken from the LMPG "Vulnerability Response Plan" document. See https://static1.squarespace.com/static/57bbb6482994ca8e30d59067/t/5a2081 73e2c483d7912f13d9/1512079793823/Vulnerability+Response+Plan*.pdf.

14. John Nolland, "The New International Greek Testament Commentary: The Gospel of Matthew," *Biblia Online,* accessed March 30, 2018, https://ref.ly/o/nigtcmt/2093504?length=982.

15. https://www.thegospelcoalition.org/article/5-ways-to-help-the-least-of -these-in-the-church/.

Chapter 7

1. To learn more about GRACE, go to their website: http://www.netgrace.org.

2. "NetGRACE: Board of Directors," accessed March 30, 2018, http://www.netgrace.org/board-of-directors/.

Section 4

1. C. S. Lewis, *The Four Loves* (Harvest Books, 1971).

Chapter 9

1. Brené Brown, *Daring Greatly: How the Courage to Be Vulnerable Transforms the Way that We Live, Love, Parent, and Lead* (New York: Penguin Random House, 2012), 34.

2. Jürgen Moltmann, "Liberate Yourselves by Accepting One Another," Human Disability and the Service of God (Nashville: Abingdon Press, 1998), 110.

3. To learn practical ways that you contribute to modern-day slavery, see "How Do You Contribute to Modern-Day Slavery of Human Trafficking?" *The Christian Science Monitor,* September 9, 2012, accessed March 30, 2018, https://www.csmonitor.com/World/Global-Issues/2012/0909/How-do-you -contribute-to-modern-day-slavery-of-human-trafficking.

4. Tony Sagami, "The Consumer-Driven Economy Has Hit a Brick Wall," *Forbes,* June 13, 2016, accessed March 30, 2018, https://www.forbes.com/sites/

tonysagami/2016/06/13/the-us-consumer-driven-economy-has-hit-a-brick-wall/#50acc0b81b57.

5. "Supply Chain," *Wikipedia: The Free Encyclopedia,* accessed online March 30, 2018, https://en.wikipedia.org/wiki/Supply_chain.

6. "2017 Global Estimates," *Alliance 87,* accessed March 30, 2018, https://www.alliance87.org/2017ge/modernslavery#!section=0.

7. Jonathan Walton gave me this idea years ago.

8. I am quoting Justin Dillon from a panel discussion on human trafficking and demand that he and I were both on in New York City.

9. Stephanie Keller, "Straight Talk on Fairtrade vs. Direct Trade According to Brazilian Coffee Farmers," *Huffington Post,* December 6, 2017, accessed March 30, 2018, https://www.huffingtonpost.com/stephanie-keller/straight-talk-on-fairtrad_b_8305090.html.

10. For more information, check out fairtradeusa.org and https://madein afreeworld.com.

11. This is a phrase that Ben Skinner, the founder of transparentem.com, uses quite frequently. In our conversations, I have adopted it. But I aim to give credit where credit is due. To learn more about what is being done to address exploitative supply chains, check out this website.

12. "Pornography by the Numbers; A Significant Threat to Society," *WebRoot,* accessed March 30, 2018, https://www.webroot.com/us/en/home/resources/tips/digital-family-life/internet-pornography-by-the-numbers.

13. "Know the Facts," *ProvenMen,* accessed March 30, 2018, https://www.provenmen.org/pornography-survey-statistics-2014/.

14. Victor Malarek, *The Johns: Sex for Sale and the Men Who Buy It* (Toronto: Key Porter, 2009), 196.

15. "Pornography," *Merriam-Webster Online Dictionary,* accessed March 30, 2018, https://www.merriam-webster.com/dictionary/pornography.

16. Maggie Jones, "What Teenagers Are Learning from Online Porn," *New York Times,* February 7, 2018, accessed March 30, 2018, https://www.nytimes.com/2018/02/07/magazine/teenagers-learning-online-porn-literacy-sex-education.html.

17. "Stop the Demand: The Role of Porn in Sex Trafficking," *Covenant Eyes,* last updated 2014. Accessed March 30, 2018, http://www.covenanteyes.com/stop-demand/?_ga=2.251744329.1995133877.1539900895-351557755.1539900895.

Chapter 10

1. Tomas Chamorro-Premuzic, "Strengths-Based Coaching Can Actually Weaken You," *Harvard Business Review,* January 4, 2016, accessed March 30, 2018, https://hbr.org/2016/01/strengths-based-coaching-can-actually-weaken-you.

2. Ibid.

3. This sermon and approach has helped shape my understanding of this concept. John MacArthur, "Strength Perfected in Weakness" cited below.

4. This sermon and approach have helped shaped my understanding of this concept: John MacArthur, "Strength Perfected in Weakness," March 6, 2016,

accessed March 30, 2018, https://www.gty.org/library/sermons-library/90-483/strength-perfected-in-weakness.

5. Included in article author wrote for The Gospel Coalition, https://www.thegospelcoalition.org/article/finding-hope-in-the-fight-against-human-trafficking/.

6. Bill Mounce, "Is God's Discipline Teaching or Chastisement?" *Bill Mounce: For an Informed Love of God,* December 21, 2008, accessed March 30, 2018, https://www.billmounce.com/monday-with-mounce/god's-discipline-teaching-or-chastisement-hebrews-12-3-11.

7. The idea of a "Vulnerability Time Line" came from my mentor and friend Lewie Clark. When he first took me under his wing, he challenged me to not run from my weaknesses, but to look for God's presence in them. In his book, *Imitating Jesus* (West Bow Press), Lewie gives a great example of how you can create your own suffering time line.

Chapter 11

1. "Fact Sheet #9: Vicarious Trauma," *The American Counseling Association,* October 2011, accessed March 30, 2018, https://www.counseling.org/docs/trauma-disaster/fact-sheet-9---vicarious-trauma.pdf.

2. "Vision: The Rest Initiative," *The Rest Initiative,* accessed March 30, 2018, http://therestinitiative.org/the-initiative/the-vision/.

3. "About Diane Langberg," *Diane Langberg, PhD,* accessed March 30, 2018, http://www.dianelangberg.com/speaking-schedule/experience/.

Section Five

1. Jean Vanter, *Community and Growth,* 2nd rev. ed. (Paulist Press, 1989).

Chapter 12

1. Emily Marie Waters, "From Victim to Healer: How Surviving Sex Trafficking Informs Therapeutic Practice," *Dignity: A Journal on Sexual Exploitation and Violence,* 1, no. 9 (2016), http://digitalcommons.uri.edu/dignity/vol1/iss1/9. This article has been used in its entirety with permission from the author. In one section, it does differ from the original article, however the words used are taken from an interview that I had with Emily in March 2018.

2. This paragraph is taken from my interview with Emily from March 2018.

Chapter 13

1. Nicole Wingfield, "Mother Teresa: 'Saint of the Gutters' Canonized at Vatican," *The Morning Journal,* September 4, 2016, accessed March 30, 2018, http://www.morningjournal.com/article/MJ/20160904/NEWS/160909808.

2. David Van Biema, "Mother Teresa's Crisis of Faith," *Time,* August 23, 2007, accessed March 30, 2018, http://time.com/4126238/mother-teresas-crisis-of-faith/.

3. Read more at: "Mother Teresa Quotes," *Brainy Quote,* accessed March 30, 2018, https://www.brainyquote.com/quotes/mother_teresa_142106.

Section Six

1. Martin Luther King Jr. quote. Original source not known.

Chapter 15

1. For the original version of this story, see Raleigh Sadler, "The One Who Showed Mercy," *The Gospel Coalition,* March 9, 2015, accessed March 30, 2018, https://www.thegospelcoalition.org/article/the-one-who-showed-mercy/.

2. Timothy Keller, *Generous Justice* (New York: Penguin Books, 2012).

3. Erin Blakemore, "Why Are There So Many Urban Legends about Mr. Rogers?" *History Channel,* February 16, 2018, accessed March 30, 2018, https://www.history.com/news/urban-legends-mr-rogers.

4. Amy Hollingsworth, *The Simple Faith of Mister Rogers: Spiritual Insights from the World's Most Beloved Neighbor* (Brentwood, TN: Integrity Publishers, 2005), 102. Kindle Edition.

5. Ibid., 104.

6. Kate Reilly, "10 of Mother Teresa's Most Powerful Quotes," *Time,* September 3, 2016, accessed March 30, 2018, http://time.com/4478287/mother-teresa-saint-quotes/.

7. Chris Huber, "Q&A with Brian Fikkert, author of 'When Helping Hurts,'" *World Vision,* September 17, 2013, accessed March 30, 2018, https://www.worldvision.org/charitable-giving-news-stories/when-helping-hurts-brian-fikkert.

8. Robert D. Lupton, *Toxic Charity: How Churches and Charities Hurt Those They Help (And How to Reverse It)* (New York: HarperCollins, 2011), 3.

9. Maggie Becker, "Charity vs. Empowerment," *Mission: Saint Louis,* June 26, 2017, accessed March 30, 2018, http://www.missionstl.org/blog/2017/6/23/charity-vs-empowerment.

10. I have my friend Josiah Haken to thank for teaching me this concept.

11. Grace Thornton, "Sex Trafficking: One Click Led NYC Church to Action," *The Baptist Press,* January 31, 2017, accessed March 30, 2018, http://www.bpnews.net/48258/sex-trafficking-one-click-led-nyc-church-to-action.

Chapter 16

1. This has been adapted from an article that I wrote for Christ Hold Fast, http://www.christholdfast.org/blog/dont-share-the-gospel-with-me-luther-forde-and-a-seminarian.

2. Gerhard O. Forde, *Justification by Faith: A Matter of Death and Life* (Eugene: Wipf and Stock Publishers, 1990), 22.

3. Ibid., 23–24.

4. My friend Josh Shank reminded me of a great example of this principle recently that comes from the days of the original Nintendo entertainment system. If you were like me, you probably logged countless hours playing Contra. This game in particular featured two heroes who essentially went to war fighting all sorts of "bad guys" with advanced weaponry. Given the difficulty of the game, I played conservatively because I didn't want my player to die. Then came the

advent of the "Konami Code." Grabbing your controller, you could press "up, up, down, down, left, right, left, right, B, A, Start." Now, when you played you had unlimited lives. There was nothing that you wouldn't attempt because you had nothing to lose. You go farther and score more points, because you aren't afraid to die. With the gospel compelling us, we are freed to love like we have never loved before, because Christ tasted death for us, and in him, we live.

5. "About Us: Where Did We Come From?" *The White Horse Inn,* accessed March 30, 2018, https://www.whitehorseinn.org/about-us/.

Appendix

1. This has been adapted with permission from the Nexus Global Youth Summit's 2014 "100 Acts of Abolition," accessed March 30, 2018. Find the original version at https://drive.google.com/file/d/0B3KaLcP6Bz6gYW9jWTJYTlpPU1E/view.

YOU'VE READ THE BOOK, NOW BRING IT TO YOUR CHURCH

LET MY PEOPLE GO IS DEDICATED TO BUILDING A NETWORK OF WELL-EQUIPPED CHURCHES CAPABLE OF LOVING THOSE MOST VULNERABLE IN THEIR CHURCHES AND COMMUNITIES. PRACTICALLY, THIS "LOVE" IS EVIDENCED THROUGHOUT THE CONGREGATION AS THE CHURCH IDENTIFIES, EMPOWERS, PROTECTS, AND INCLUDES THOSE WHO TRAFFICKERS WOULD NORMALLY TARGET.

LEARN MORE AT

LMPGNETWORK.ORG